I WROTE THIS *for* ATTENTION

LUKAS GAGE

SIMON & SCHUSTER
New York   Amsterdam/Antwerp   London
Toronto   Sydney/Melbourne   New Delhi

Names have been changed, personalities embellished, and events remembered to the best of my abilities—because that's how stories work.

Simon & Schuster
1230 Avenue of the Americas
New York, NY 10020

For more than 100 years, Simon & Schuster has championed authors and the stories they create. By respecting the copyright of an author's intellectual property, you enable Simon & Schuster and the author to continue publishing exceptional books for years to come. We thank you for supporting the author's copyright by purchasing an authorized edition of this book.

No amount of this book may be reproduced or stored in any format, nor may it be uploaded to any website, database, language-learning model, or other repository, retrieval, or artificial intelligence system without express permission. All rights reserved. Inquiries may be directed to Simon & Schuster, 1230 Avenue of the Americas, New York, NY 10020 or permissions@simonandschuster.com.

Copyright © 2025 by Hypoplastic Business, LLC

All rights reserved, including the right to reproduce this book or portions thereof in any form whatsoever. For information, address Simon & Schuster Subsidiary Rights Department, 1230 Avenue of the Americas, New York, NY 10020.

First Simon & Schuster hardcover edition October 2025

SIMON & SCHUSTER and colophon are registered trademarks of Simon & Schuster, LLC

Simon & Schuster strongly believes in freedom of expression and stands against censorship in all its forms. For more information, visit BooksBelong.com.

For information about special discounts for bulk purchases, please contact Simon & Schuster Special Sales at 1-866-506-1949 or business@simonandschuster.com.

The Simon & Schuster Speakers Bureau can bring authors to your live event. For more information or to book an event, contact the Simon & Schuster Speakers Bureau at 1-866-248-3049 or visit our website at www.simonspeakers.com.

Interior design by Carly Loman

Manufactured in the United States of America

1 3 5 7 9 10 8 6 4 2

Library of Congress Cataloging-in-Publication Data is available.

ISBN 978-1-6680-8007-8
ISBN 978-1-6680-8009-2 (ebook)

*To Phoebe, thank you for teaching me what tenses are,
even when things got tense.*

*To Sam, thank you for teaching me where a comma goes—it's just
when you take a breath.*

*To Hana and Haley, thank you for taking a chance on this book,
even when no one was asking for it.*

*To Travis, thank you for telling me to write a book;
I guess one person wanted it.*

*To Cole, thanks for being a bro, and a Brody.
There were just too many C names in the book.
It's not personal, I would never try to protect your identity.*

*To Mom, thank you for giving me life; this book wouldn't exist
without you, because I wouldn't exist without you. I love you.*

Contents

	Introduction: I Killed a Kid	1
1.	Lies I Told My Journal	5
2.	LadiesManLukas	19
3.	Red, White, and Feeling Blue	27
4.	Till Camp Do Us Part	39
5.	Poppers	53
6.	Little San Diego Bitch	73
7.	Gas, Grass, or Ass	95
8.	TRUST NO BITCH$	107
9.	Where the Rubber Meets the Road	121
10.	Good Things Come to Hoes Who Wait	137
11.	The Last Bite	157
12.	Leaving Las Laughlin	175
13.	The Shitty Committee	185
14.	The D in Apartment 23	199
15.	The 14 Percent	221
16.	Don't Put Me in a (Four-by-Four) Box	239
17.	Big-Penis Disorder	255
18.	u dont know my alphabet	281
	Conclusion: With a *c* not a *k*	291
	Acknowledgments	301

It matters not what you've done but what you do with what you've done for others.

—NOAH CENTINEO

INTRODUCTION

I Killed a Kid

At the end of sixth grade, I killed a kid.

I'd gone to school with him my whole life and had never been particularly fond of him. He was meek, and when he did speak, it was with the soft, nasally voice of what my friends and I would call a "milk drinker." His only real value was that he could make people laugh. He'd go up in front of the class and act out little stories he'd written, and it would be like the circus had come to town. Everyone would laugh and applaud, and he would stand there, soaking it all in. You could tell that every shred of his self-worth was wrapped up in those brief moments of adulation, standing at the front of Mrs. Smith's classroom. . . .

It made my skin crawl.

The way he'd dance when they said dance, a faint glimmer of hope in his eyes, like maybe this time would be the last time he'd have to dance for them. With every laugh (usually at his expense), you could tell he'd be thinking this would finally get him invited to all the sleepovers or to trade Pokémon cards or whatever else the other kids did after school. You could tell that he really thought that this would be the time when he had finally won them over for good. The whole thing reeked of desperation.

But sure enough, eventually, he wore them down. They anointed him. He started playing football and dressing like an athlete to fully embrace his new identity. He walked around with the popular crew, struggling to keep up at the back of the pack, but he was there nonetheless. He even managed to land "the third hottest girl in school."

A few months into middle school, just when it looked like everything was finally falling into place, a rumor surfaced. Word was he had stolen his brother's Lucky Strike cigarettes, and forced some of his new, popular friends to smoke with him. His attempt to reinvent himself had blown up in his face, because no matter what, he would always be that little milk drinker. They had sensed his desperation, just like I had predicted they would, and it all came crumbling down around him. Now all those popular kids, the ones who he had performed for and catered to, were going around school telling everyone to watch out—that there was something wrong with this kid. All of a sudden, he was back to where he started. Actually, he was worse off. Before, he was invisible. Now, he was a target.

So, of course, there were more rumors. There was a rumor about him being gay and trying to kiss one of the football players while he was passed out at a team sleepover. There was another (oddly specific one) about him having really long pubes that he would groom into a pompadour.

This went on for most of the year, with the attacks growing more ruthless and more creative, until one day after school, as the kid was walking home all by his lonesome, they descended upon him with airsoft guns. The kid was surrounded, and he started whimpering like a little bitch. Which, of course, the popular kids loved. When he tried to make a break for it, they shot his ass up. Thud after thud, the pellets had rained down on him.

The kid was never seen again.

Some people said he ran away from home. Others thought maybe he went to juvie for forcing kids to smoke those Lucky Strikes. But I know the truth.

The truth is, that night, while he was sitting at home watching *Jerry Springer* with his mom, she discovered the welts all over his body and resolved to not let him go back for the rest of the year. In the fall, she would transfer him to a new school, fifteen minutes south. The truth is, sitting on that itchy living room sofa, I decided to kill him.

And let me tell you, Lucas died slowly. Fucker was more resilient than expected. That version of myself had to be suffocated, snuffed out, day after day, month after month. Throughout that spring and into the summer, I took him apart piece by piece, and by the time August rolled around, he was dead.

I actually started to take pleasure in it. I played with the body. I wasn't heartless, though. I knew it would be cruel to leave his mom without her youngest son. So I replaced him with someone new, someone edgier, someone with sharp teeth who wasn't going to take shit from anyone. I dyed his hair black and dressed him up like a Hot Topic mannequin. I propped his lifeless corpse up in front of the mirror and imagined a whole new personality for him, one that would make him worth keeping around this time. One that people would pay attention to.

Because really, that's what I've always wanted. Attention. Only the way I'd been going about it was all wrong. That was the version of Lucas that needed to go. The one that danced too hard for everybody else. The one that was desperate, *embarrassing*.

That was the little boy I had been forced to kill. The one I had been since I was old enough to remember, the one no one ever paid attention to no matter how hard he—*I*—tried. The only thing I didn't change was his name. That felt like a bridge too far. I mean, his mom had named him after her favorite movie, the one with Corey Haim and Winona Ryder, where Corey played an awkward teenager who was bullied by the cool kids. She loved a "standing up to the bullies" type of movie.

Lucas. Except she swapped the *c* for a *k*. Just to set him apart.

1.

Lies I Told My Journal

"Your son is naked."

I was, in fact, not naked—I was wearing lingerie and Playboy Bunny ears. Unfortunately for me, my family was too simpleminded to see my vision.

Earlier that day, my father sat me down and informed me that I needed to look and act nice for the summer barbecue he was throwing later that night—a tall order for a four-year-old, but I've always been eager to please. Believing I understood the assignment, I immediately thought of the most provocative person I could imagine, which to four-year-old me just so happened to be my mom. Specifically the time she dressed up as a Playboy Bunny for Halloween while my dad went as Hugh Hefner. I dug through her closet, looped her bra around my spindly shoulders, wrapped a T-shirt around my waist, and polished off the look with some leftover bunny ears from some Easters ago.

Downstairs, the party was in full swing as I emerged onto the patio by the pool, standing on my tiptoes to mimic walking in high heels, puffing up my chest—ready to bask in the adulation of the crowd. I felt the energy of the party shift as everyone turned their attention to little old me, smiling and laughing. Everyone except my father, whose face was turning a shade of red I hadn't seen before.

"Why is he naked? What is he doing? Stop him from doing that," my father hissed to my mom, quietly enough not to disrupt the party but loud enough to pierce right through me.

"He's not hurting anybody," my mom responded, waving off my dad and returning to the guests.

"He's embarrassing me," he repeated again, now attracting onlookers.

That's my first memory: *He's embarrassing me.*

I couldn't understand how I was embarrassing him. I thought I looked fucking hot. My dad begged to differ. He always got a little mean under pressure, and that night he was under a lot of it. The contempt in his eyes set me ablaze. Something ignited in me.

Couldn't he see that I was being *entertaining*?

"For God's sake, get him down from there. He's making me crazy."

I'm not sure how most children would have behaved in this situation. My three older brothers—Jesse, Cory, and Travis—probably would have been embarrassed. They might have slunk away, unhooked their bra straps, and locked themselves in their rooms for the rest of the night. But not me. I kept dancing.

While the classic rock ballads blared from the surround sound, I proceeded to gyrate for hours, discovering new and exciting dance moves that still have not been replicated to this day. I don't know how long I danced for exactly, but people were worried that this little four-year-old freak might never stop swaying his hips.

Eventually, the crowd's joy turned into genuine concern. What had started as a cute, funny thing had devolved into something uncomfortable and weird. Nevertheless, I persisted, determined to see it through to the bitter end. As the adults my dad so deeply wanted to impress milled about the backyard, I soldiered on. I had hired myself to be the entertainment for the night's festivities and goddammit—I was going to fulfill my obligations. People *would* be entertained. They were going to love it whether they liked it or not.

Unfortunately, they did not.

Nor would they for many years to come. But I did know that someday somebody was going to appreciate me and that I would not stop until they did.

As the party was wrapping up, I decided my shift as the dancing Playboy Bunny had come to an end. Exhausted, I collapsed into the pool, stretching my limbs wide before I hit the water. When I reached the surface, I heard it: the sound of my parents—*both* my parents—laughing. Not at me, but together in delight. I had made my dad laugh. Mission accomplished.

That barbecue was the last time I remember my parents together. Within a few months, they were divorced. And I would spend the rest of my childhood wondering if I was part of the reason why. No wonder I had wanted to kill that kid.

WE MOVED OUT of our house in the rain; water pelting the windshield as my mom drove me and my brothers away from the only world I had known up to that point, to a different life, a different house. Two houses, actually; neither of which had a pool. And as a seven-year-old living in sunny California, this was honestly more upsetting to me than my parents' divorce. So instead of swimming around the backyard while my brothers practiced their kickflips on their skateboards, I ended up spending my afternoons immersed in . . . bathwater.

I can probably chalk this up to some subconscious desire for me to go back to being an amorphous blob of cells floating in the abyss of my mother's womb (didn't Freud say every boy wants to kill his father and float in his mother's uterine fluids?), but regardless, while most boys were playing outside, I spent the majority of my free time in the tub, writing.

The cover of my journal came with the word *DIARY* in gold letters, but I'd crossed that out and scribbled *JOURNAL* in black ink. Little gay boys who love taking baths wrote in diaries. Men recorded their observations in a journal. Or a podcast. Or a premature celebrity memoir. But since I didn't know what those things were yet, I settled for a journal.

I had an elaborate ritual. I would come home from school, lower the lights, and put on my favorite music. Sometimes, I'd even bring my "son" along with me: a pet rabbit named Silver that was a gift from my Uncle Mike (who was not an uncle, just some guy named Mike who my mom was sleeping with and whom she had told us to call Uncle Mike). With or without Silver, I would sink into a warm bath, crack my knuckles, open my journal, and lie my fucking ass off.

Everyone is born with one special gift. For some people, it's athletic ability. For others, it's being good at math or whatever engineers do. But me?

I was born a liar.

So when I sat down to write, I'd end up with something that could only be classified as "fiction with benefits."

Still can't do a bakhand spring, and my Coach can't teach me any longer cuz he burned in a fire, I lamented in one entry. *I'm on American Idol this season! Simon said I was his faverit and Randy even called me his dog. Also, SARS is going around, and I have it. I touched a dead seagull on a dare with my brothers and have been coffing ever since. I have to hide from evryone so I don't get them sick*, went another. You know, the usual musings of a child.

Look, I was hell-bent on living a life worth writing about, even if that life was a collection of falsehoods and fantasies. Even if the life I was describing wasn't actually, *you know* . . . mine. Because in reality, every day of my life was pretty much the same. Mom would pick up Cory, Travis, and me in her Nissan Quest. Then we'd stop for fast food, and she'd drop us off at home so she could hurry back to work. Not exactly the makings of a riveting journal entry.

So instead, I would sprint to the bathtub to reinvent my day for my journal, as my CD player blasted Britney Spears's "Lucky" on repeat.

Oh, who was I kidding? It was a fucking diary.

I dont even go to highscool yet but they just crouned me prom king, now the only thing I have to do is fined a dait. I'm thinking of askin Hayden Panettiere, I began my entry one afternoon, but the opening chorus of "Lucky" had just started over again . . . and I couldn't resist.

"'She's so lucky. She's a star! But she cry, cry, cries,'" I began to belt, beautifully I might add, until—

"Holy shit, dude, he's singing like a little bitch in there."

The voice behind the door belonged to Jace, one of my brother Cory's bandmates, who always wore a top hat and was vegan before it was trendy. The rest of my brother's bandmates behind the door were less memorable, but that didn't lessen how mortified I felt as they all burst out laughing at my expense.

Cory's voice floated up from beneath the bathwater, warped but still clear enough. "Dude, he does this all day."

Cory was six years older than me—and was technically my half brother—but in my eyes he was more than a sibling. He was my idol. A literal rock star. A leather-clad force of nature who I would do anything to impress. I attended every single one of his band's shows, despite never being able to pronounce their name—I was pretty sure it had something to do with the war in Afghanistan or 9/11. Everything kind of did at that time.

So, when Cory wanted to do a prank in some lo-fi skate video he was filming, I was always the first to volunteer.

Running into the Vons on El Camino Real, I'd call out to unsuspecting shoppers exiting the store, grocery bags in hand: "Um, excuse me, miss?"

"Yes?"

"Your labia . . . it's stuck in your zipper."

And every time, without fail, they would look down and check.

When Cory and his friends laughed at my stunts, I felt like I was levitating, as if there were a beam of light shooting out of my chest. But now, as they laughed outside the bathroom door, I realized that Cory's feelings about me were more akin to how a child feels about a firefly—exciting at first, but then, eventually, it's just another thing buzzing around. You can either let it be free . . . or torture it and let it die in a jar.

"Can you hear him still?" one of Cory's friends asked.

I stayed mute and motionless in the tub, quietly withering while I waited for them to get tired of teasing me. But they kept going. Torture and death in a jar it was.

After what felt like hours but was probably five minutes or so, I finally heard them in the backyard crushing beer cans and shouting over the Dead Kennedys blasting out of the stereo. I figured they were distracted enough that I could sneak outside to go get my emotional support animal from his cage.

"I loved your vocals, Lucky!" Jace called out from behind the trampoline. They were all gathered back there, throwing errant items from the house—cardboard boxes, newspapers, anything flammable, really—into a giant hole they'd dug up in the lawn.

Momentarily forgetting about Silver and their previous torment, I crawled up on the trampoline to get closer to Cory. He immediately pushed me back.

"Hey, come on, you can't stay down here with us. We're doing stuff," Cory said.

I started to whine, but he cut me off.

"If you go to your room, I'll teach you a new chord on the guitar tomorrow."

I pleaded with him, trying to think up some elaborate stunt that would convince him to let me stay. I would happily degrade myself and let them film it just to get back in their good graces. Cory shook his head. He knew all my tricks, and he wasn't falling for any of them.

I shrugged off the rejection, trying to seem nonchalant as I headed back inside, my eyes welling up with tears. I was almost in the clear when suddenly I whipped around and blurted, "Fuck you guys! I wasn't even singing, that was the radio!" then ran upstairs, their laughter echoing behind me.

I tried spying on them from the kitchen window for a little while before I retreated to the room I shared with Travis. When I entered, he was just sitting there, playing video games. He had been there for hours, perfectly and completely content with being alone. We were very different, Travis and I. He was four years older than me and with my eldest brother, Jesse, having already moved out of the house, Travis became the textbook middle child: He was highly allergic to the spotlight, and his moral compass was intrinsically pure. That last part really pissed me off because I wanted that needle to point in the opposite direction at least some of the time.

"Do you even know what they're doing out there?" I asked him, secretly hoping he would rat on them to Mom, allowing me to get revenge while keeping my hands clean.

"I dunno, same thing as they always do?" Travis shrugged.

He was right, but it still pissed me off.

"Just forget it." I sighed, flinging myself on the bed, shielding my eyes with my forearm dramatically.

"I just want Mom to come home."

Travis paused his game to turn back and look at me. "Why are you obsessed with her? It's kinda gay."

"I'm not gay; you're gay! Look at what you're doing!" I pointed at the screen, paused on two sweaty, shirtless men engaged in *Mortal Kombat*.

He punched me in the arm until I curled into a ball, squealing, "Wait until Mom gets home! You're finished in this town!"

But my brother was right. I was—and still very much am—a certified mama's boy. I ride hard for that bitch. Always have, always will.

When I wasn't bathing or lying to my journal, I spent most evenings after school counting down the minutes until I could climb all over my mom again, as if her body were a tree, and I, her feral emotionally complicated squirrel.

Before the divorce, Mom did nails at the beauty salon downtown. She'd sneak little bottles home that smelled like formaldehyde and indulge me as I pretended to be what I thought was a wide variety of characters—using different accents and body language—but, in reality, were all just versions of "vaguely fancy old woman" getting her nails done.

"How are the kids, Barbara?" she'd ask me, and I'd snap my imaginary chewing gum.

"Oh, they're good. Little Saulie just got into the Jehovah's Witness program at school, and Mindy's pregnant. Again!"

No matter what I came up with, she'd rub the oil into my cuticles, massage my palms, and encourage me on with *Oh, you* all afternoon long until I was ready to go back to being Lukas.

But after the divorce, she switched jobs and started selling real estate, and the bottles of nail polish were replaced by stacks of folders. There was a new edge to her, and she was always in a constant state of stress. I would sidle up next to her as she pored over those goddamned folders, putting on an affectation and flicking my wrist, pointing to a flyer of a modern Spanish revival for sale.

"My cat, Minerva, would just about waste one of her nine lives to get her litter box into that little number!" I'd say, trying to get our game going again.

"Sorry, honey. Not now," she'd respond, snatching her folders away and moving to the other side of the table.

It was jarring because when my mom was happy, she was fucking *giddy*, like she were projecting her happiness from a Broadway stage and the people in the back row could feel it. But when she was stressed, her sigh was loud enough to reach that very same back row.

So when my mom would come home at night and cook dinner while reviewing real estate contracts, I would try desperately to get that giddy version of her back.

"Mom, is the house in escargot?" I'd ask, feigning enthusiasm for her new job.

"It's *escrow*, you dumb bitch," Cory would correct me, laughing.

"That's what I said, asshole," I'd snap back.

"Lukas, language," Mom would warn me, pretending to give a shit. Every so often, she felt the need to pretend that kind of language wouldn't be tolerated in our household.

So when I heard "Where the fuck is your brother? Why isn't he watching you?" fly out of my mother's mouth when she came home later that afternoon only to find Travis and I still hitting each other and fighting over who was gayer, I knew that something was seriously wrong.

Come to think of it, the air had started to smell funny . . . like burnt toast, but this was no stroke. I had the sinking suspicion it had something to do with the flaming pit of garbage Cory and his friends had assembled in the backyard.

"Where is Cory, Lukas? I know you know. I see it in those eyes, you know I know when you're lying," my mom said.

I looked from Travis to my mother and shrugged, feigning innocence.

If Cory taught me anything, it was that if I wanted to be like him, I couldn't be a snitch. *Snitches get stitches, and little snitch bitches with stitches get their ass beat.*

"Goddammit," she said under her breath, shaking her head.

"Cory!" she yelled again. "Stay in your room, guys."

We did as we were told . . . for about twenty seconds. As we crept out behind her, camping out at the top of the stairs, I wrapped my arms around my body and curled into a little ball. The spaces between the banister bars provided a view of the downstairs as if it were the balcony of a theater.

"Why does it smell like smoke?" she shouted.

Cory appeared through the sliding glass doors, and the interrogation began.

"What's burning? Why did you leave your brothers alone? Why does it smell like burnt toast?" she asked, looking past him into the backyard.

But he wouldn't look at her, let alone respond. When he tried, his words were too slurred to comprehend. So he just stood there, staring at his feet, until finally Mom noticed something out of the corner of her eye.

"Oh my God—Silver!" Mom screamed as she darted toward the smoke-filled hutch at the edge of our yard.

"Get the fuck out. Go home, all of you. *Now!*"

She was angrier than I'd ever seen her. Even when she was livid she just sounded exhausted. This time was different.

Cory and his friends scattered, exchanging looks like my mom had lost her mind.

I ran right past them, following the sound of her wailing over to the cage, only to find my pet rabbit lying belly up. My two-year-old son, dead from asphyxiation. Silver, we hardly knew ye.

"You murdered your brother's rabbit?!" my mother howled.

"I didn't do anything! I was just making a fire," Cory said, his glassy eyes now widening in shock. "We didn't see his rabbit was back there; we were just trying to make . . . s'mores."

My mom tried grabbing his shoulders, but he wriggled away.

"What's gotten into you?" she asked, her tone laced with disappointment and exasperation. Whatever she was feeling in that moment, it was too much for Cory to bear. He began shouting angrily, fighting fire with fire. "I can't be around all of this! I don't want to live here anymore!"

I felt my body stiffen. I'd barely had a moment to process Silver's death, and now my real worst fear was coming to pass. *Cory's leaving me.* This was my Red Wedding.

"Then go! I give up. I don't know how to help you anymore," my mom shrieked back.

Cory didn't say anything. If my superpower was lying, his was saying nothing when he was angry. I wish I had inherited that skill. Mom waited for him to give in, to submit, to at least say something. But Cory had the power to destroy in silence: He didn't slam the door. He didn't even speak. He just left.

That night, I crawled back into my castle-shaped bunk bed, hugging my journal to my chest. Maybe I could rewrite this, too.

Silver had to go. He was too clingy, so my mom got me a new son. A gurgeus Palumino ponie named Lucky. They both eat carrets. Cory's going to teach me how to ride him when he comes back from vecation.

Mom came in and sat down at the foot of the bed. The bonfire smoke had seeped into her pores, while the frown lines on her brows seemed more pronounced than usual.

"Your brother left. I put Silver in the freezer. We can bury him tomorrow," she said plainly, letting out one of her epic sighs. "What are you writing about?"

"Nothing," I lied.

Cory had run away. Silver was dead. Mom was a shell of herself. Dad might as well have been gone, because even when he *was* there, he wasn't really. And I was a sad, scared little bitch who lied to his own *diary*.

Silver had the most beautiful funeral, people are saying it was pretier then Princess Diana's. Everyone who is everyone came, and I would be more sad if it wasn't preity.

"Lulu," she said, taking the pen out of my hand and wrapping her arms around me. "You can cry. It's okay."

While Freud might've been a perv and a raging cokehead, he was also right about a lot of things. Burrowed into my mother's chest—the closest I could possibly get to being back in her womb—I finally felt safe enough to cry.

"It's all going to be okay," she continued.

But as much as I wanted to believe her, I knew it was just another story she was telling me. That she was rewriting the future in real time. She was lying, but it worked. I felt better. Lying, I had discovered, was a good thing.

2.

LadiesManLukas

My parents stared at me.

"Hug each other!" I pleaded.

They stared at each other.

"Pleeeeeeeease hug!" Travis and I cheered in unison.

I beamed as my parents grimaced through a tepid hug. I stood, looking between the two of them. If they were Barbies, I would smash them together. I didn't understand that they didn't want to hug each other. How could two people who used to be married—who used to share a bed, share a life—now not even want to touch each other? It didn't make sense to me.

My mom pulled away first.

Then she left to catch the next train back to San Diego, and it was just the three of us, standing there, with nothing to say to one another.

Dad was designated for the weekends. Mom on the weekdays. My mom's house was maximalist and cluttered. Her kitchen was done over in a pastel wallpaper, faux wood cabinets, and laminate countertops that made it feel like the set of an NBC sitcom. The living room even housed a teal sectional that was perfect for hanging out.

Dad's house was the opposite. Minimalist would be putting it kindly. It felt empty—a sparse, nineties suburban attempt at modernity. The appliances were unboxed and forgotten. The house was completely empty except for an IKEA sofa and a fridge packed to the brim with nothing but strawberry SlimFasts.

In short, it was a child's worst nightmare: hollow and quiet. But there was one thing my dad's house had that my mom's house didn't: *The Sims*.

My dad's house was my house, but my Sims house? That was my *home*.

My babysitter had introduced me to the game when I first moved to Long Beach, and from then on I was hooked. My pride and joy was my Moroccan-inspired mansion, and I would spend hours tweaking it until it was just right. I'd sit in my dad's computer room, gazing out the window at the pump jacks lining the hills, dreaming of the day I could live as extravagantly as my wealthiest Sims. I turned my nose up at the "low rent" Sims families who worked for their money, while I used Rosebud;! and control + shift + control to make my way to the top with a motherlode of riches. For those of you who have never played *The Sims Online*—that was a cheat code in the game. I was a cheater. But God, was I rich.

The only thing I loved more than the architectural aspects of the game was its WooHoo feature. You see, while San Diego was for surfing, and Long Beach was for oil refineries, Sim Nation was strictly for fucking.

In real life, I was your average eight-year-old with a bowl cut and oversize Billabong hand-me-downs I'd inherited from my older brothers. But in the Sims world, I was a goateed stud with blond tips who looked straight out of Sugar Ray. Or, sometimes, if I was feeling a little risqué, I was a busty redheaded seductress in a cowboy hat, like Lindsay Lohan in *Georgia Rule*. No matter who I was, I loved *The Sims* because I could be anyone—and do anyone—I wanted.

I wasn't quite sure what those pixelated freaks were doing between the sheets when they WooHoo'ed; all I knew is that I was desperate to partake. Because deep down, I was just a horny little kid desperate for any kind of attention, even if it happened to be from strangers online.

Everything I said to these digital strangers was stitched together from fragments of dialogue I'd borrowed from my other "Dad's house hobby"—soaking in all the Skinemax soft-core porn I could get my hands on. With my thumb hovering over the power button on the remote in case anyone walked in, and the volume turned down as low as it could possibly go, I would listen intently. The story and the character development was more important to me than the actual sex. I liked the sex, but what really did it for me was the tension, the human connection, the way the actors gazed into each other's eyes as they faked one orgasm after another. That shit was my bread and butter.

For a time, at least.

"Did you do this, or did Travis do this, or do I have to fire someone?"

My dad had sat me down one day, grilling me to get to the bottom of the dozens of cable charges for something called *The Sex Files* on the cable bill (not to be confused with *The X Files*, which is famously pretty sexless). I tipped my chin defiantly.

"It's Travis. And I don't know what you're talking about."

We all knew it was me.

"You shouldn't be watching that stuff. You're too young; it'll warp your development," my dad said, reading me for filth.

"It's not me!"

"It's pornography, Lukas. You can't watch pornography."

"Well . . . then you have to stop listening to Howard."

This gave him pause.

My dad was Howard Stern's number one fan. His late-night show echoed through the halls of our empty house, and his radio show was the soundtrack to our many car rides. He listened every single day without fail. Sometimes on repeat. It was all Howard, all the time. Stern was as much a part of our family as Travis or my mom. He was—I was sure of it—making me into a man. A *real* man. Everything I thought I knew about sex, about life, I learned as an eight-year-old from Howard Stern.

I didn't understand everything Howard said, but I liked the sound of his voice, and I liked how he made my dad laugh. Howard was irreverent in a way that felt like he didn't belong in Hollywood, or at least that's what my dad would tell me. Howard taught me that being cheeky or crass could get you all the way to the top. The more outrageously he behaved, the more entertained his fans were. Once he even called his mother and asked her if she'd ever done anal. She hadn't—but it still became one of his most famous bits. My dad loved it. What was painfully obvious was that my dad wanted to *be* Howard, which meant I did, too.

"Oh, Howard, you didn't! You devil, you," Dad would say, shaking his head in laughter as Howard's voice boomed through the car speakers.

"I want Subway—" Travis started.

"Shh, Howard's on." Dad grinned, cranking the volume up higher.

"What does *anal* mean?" I asked my dad.

"Uh . . ." He cleared his throat, then trailed off without giving me an answer, trying to hide his smile. I realized much later that despite his protestations, my dad was secretly pleased that I could reference Howard, that I understood the appeal of off-limits conversations, that I was like him.

Because what I discovered about my dad, after my parents' divorce, is that there was nothing he loved more than tits and, to my delight, talking to *me* about tits.

The tits on the cashier at the grocery store.

The tits on the neighbor.

And the unlimited, all-you-can-eat tits at his favorite restaurant: Hooters.

GOING FROM OUR neutral Scandinavian-style prison of a house to Hooters was like walking into a titty-themed circus, an adult Chuck E. Cheese where men could run wild and free. For me, it was sensory overload. The air was thick with the smell of hot wings and spilled beer; herds of men shouted at their favorite teams and pounded their tables in unison. Everywhere I looked, towering women in skintight orange shorts were weaving through the chaos.

On any given Saturday night, Dad, Travis, and I would settle into our favorite corner. My feet dangled awkwardly from the barstools—always just a little too high for my legs. A busty waitress would glide up to the table with a lascivious grin, and we'd all fold our menus. We didn't need to look. We knew our order already.

"Buffalo wings and a pitcher of Coke," Dad would say to our waitress.

I was transfixed by these women and how their snug outfits revealed everything to me. My eyes scanned every bump and lump. Dad, however, would barely glance in their direction. But as soon as the server would walk away, Dad's face would light up.

"Wow, did you see her?" he'd ask, his voice filled with the same awe usually reserved for natural wonders—like when he took us to the Grand Canyon or Old Faithful.

"Yeah, wow," Travis and I would say, trying to match his enthusiasm.

I liked what I saw, too, but I saw these meals mostly as an opportunity to bond with my dad. Beyond that, it was also a place where I could practice my flirting in real life, far beyond the realm of a computer screen.

"I like your necklace," I said when our server came back with the pitcher of Coke.

"Thanks, sweetheart," she said, clutching the lucky horseshoe that hung around her décolletage.

I looked over at my dad, who was eyeing me approvingly, wearing an expression that said, *That's my boy.* His pride only emboldened me further.

"Can I give you a hug?" I asked. This was my most impressive move, the one my dad and brother loved most, a technique that worked only because of my age.

The waitress smiled. "Sure, honey."

I stood up and wrapped my arms around her, nestling my head on her breasts and looking up at my dad. He grinned. There was something in his eyes that went beyond pride. It was like he'd come alive.

It was something I'd seen before, only when he listened to Howard Stern. He woke up. If I talked about tits, he woke up. I filed these moments away on a secret list of every little thing that sparked this reaction from him. I chased that spark.

As he watched me chat up those Hooters girls, his face would fill with joy. The truth is that what my dad really wanted was a friend, not a son. So I decided that that's what I would be to him. I'd be his friend. I'd be whatever he wanted me to be.

Maybe one day I'd finally get to touch someone and WooHoo them in person, like I did online. It would be exciting and irreverent like Howard but sensual and loving like the Skinemax couples I watched. I would be my father's son.

What I really wanted was for someone to see me for who I really was—and to want me, all of me—but if being at Hooters with my dad, with my face mashed between a pair of heavy naturals, was the closest I could get, who was I to turn away?

3.

Red, White, and Feeling Blue

Back in San Diego, my mom's house had acquired two new permanent squatters: her new boyfriend, Sean, and Cory's first girlfriend, Tessa. While I took to Tessa almost immediately, Sean was a bit harder for me to warm up to. Maybe it was his Cadillac hearse with the spiked chrome license plate that read "HEVY MTL." Or maybe it was the way he and his band of fortysomething metalheads converted our garage into a recording studio where they proceeded to play the most off-key Iron Maiden covers I'd ever heard for hours on end. What bothered me most wasn't his car or his shitty taste in music—it was that his constant presence meant my mom had less time for me than ever. Because even when I was with her, he was still more of an attention whore than I was.

When it came to Tessa, I was the one monopolizing all of her attention. She and Cory had met at the continuation program they were sent to after they were both kicked out of their high school for doing drugs—though, at the time, I didn't know the exact reason for their expulsion. I understood that Tessa was "like Cory"—she was fourteen but seemed older, she drank and smoked clove cigarettes, and lived and breathed punk music. She didn't look nearly as troubled as Cory. There was a lightness to her, a natural sweetness. Any darkness she may have possessed was disguised behind her crooked smirk, strawberry-blond hair, and a willowy frame, a combination that made her look like a marionette doll whose strings had been cut.

Even with Tessa in the picture, it didn't stop Cory from disappearing at a dependable rhythm. He'd run away every few weeks, only to return a day later as if nothing had happened. But Tessa stuck around, and after a while, it felt like she wasn't just there for him anymore.

"Does Cory tell you stuff he doesn't tell me?" I asked her during one of those punishing nights when Cory was nowhere to be found.

"Of course, we're in love," she said.

"I want to be in love," I murmured.

"You will be," Tessa said confidently.

"I talk to people in chat rooms . . ." I offered, as if this were even remotely the same thing as dating—but hey, I was a child of the early 2000s, so to me, it kinda was.

"Yeah? What kind of talking?" she asked.

I grinned. She smiled back. It was like we were sharing a secret without having to say a word.

"Are your *friends*. . . boys or girls?" she asked me, point-blank.

"Both . . ." I whispered, my voice barely audible.

"Well, the girls, they like a slow burn, but with boys, they usually wanna get right into it," she responded, not missing a beat.

"It?"

"You know, the dirty shit . . ." she suggested, watching me try to mask my confusion.

"Fucking, sucking, choking. All that stuff," she clarified.

"Oh," I said.

Though Tessa was, first and foremost, Cory's girlfriend—she quickly became someone unique and special to both me and my mom. To me, she was the sister I'd always wanted. To my mom, she was a best friend. And while I treasured our unique bond, I wanted to be the third in her and Mom's relationship, too. Some nights when Cory was missing, Tessa would show up and run straight to my mom's room. Her thick black eyeliner streaked across her lower lids, mascara spilling down her cheeks. As soon as I'd hear the lock twist shut, I'd creep over to the door, listening to them murmur late into the night.

"I've been there. Trust me, Cory's dad almost killed me," my mom said.

"I love him so much. He's my everything," Tessa cried.

"I know, sweetheart. Love's a bitch sometimes, but it's going to be okay, I promise," she said.

"I'm scared I'm going to get that call," Tessa whispered.

"We won't," my mom snapped, like she was trying to banish the thought.

Sometimes, when their conversation would begin to wane, I'd bang on the door and beg to be let in. But the response was always the same: "Nothing's wrong" or "You wouldn't understand."

I couldn't help but feel a little insulted. How could I be old enough to witness Cory's constant breakdowns, my mom's emotional spirals, and Tessa's lovesick sobs, but somehow not old enough to understand why the fuck everyone was acting this way? What secret about Cory could a fourteen-year-old grasp that I couldn't? A part of me couldn't help but wonder if Cory's restlessness was somehow my fault. I'd idolized him for as long as I could remember. It wasn't his attention I was after when I followed him everywhere—it was *him*. Despite his erratic behavior scaring the shit out of me, he was also still somehow my safety net.

"You okay?" Tessa asked me, sneaking into my room one night after I'd been excluded again from my mom's room.

"No, I'm not," I huffed from atop my castle bunk bed. "I'm only four and a half years younger than you; it's not fair. Why won't anyone tell me what's going on?"

"Cory's just going through a tough time," she said, changing the subject.

"But what does that mean? Why does my mom feel comfortable talking to you about it but not me?"

"I'm not sure, but I'm here. I'm not going anywhere," she said.

A few months later, Tessa formally moved in with us. She'd basically been a fixture at our house since she first started dating Cory six months prior, but now, she was making it official, like she wanted me to know that her promise to stay was true. And as the summer stretched on, Tessa never wavered. She was as reliable as Cory's next disappearance—spending quality time with me, helping with the dishes, and becoming something akin to a surrogate sister or a second mom.

Romantic love wasn't something I'd personally witnessed before Tessa came into our lives. I was too young to remember a time when my parents could stand being in the same room as each other. And though it didn't take long after my mom and Sean met for them to fall into a relationship, they felt more like two friendly roommates than two people madly in love. But Tessa and Cory? That was *real* love.

Their love story followed a predictable pattern. They'd fight, he'd storm out, she'd track him down, he'd apologize, they'd hook up, then fight again—and through it all, their feelings for each other remained solid as ever. From watching the two of them, I learned to view love as something that was predicated on high stakes, big emotions, and never-ending uncertainty. I had no idea that Tessa's devotion to Cory, while noble, contained more than a touch of codependence.

Just in time for their six-month anniversary, Cory left again. This time, though, he wasn't back within twenty-four hours. There was no phone call. No front door slamming open, letting us know it was okay to exhale. My mom tried her best to convince us that this was just Cory being Cory, and we did our best to go along with her charade. Travis and I were the emcees, cracking jokes and distracting everyone with flips on the trampoline. But our performances were no match for Cory's disappearing act.

When Fourth of July rolled around and he still hadn't surfaced, the terror my mom had tried bottling up in those closed-door conversations with Tessa began to pervade every inch of our home like a cloud of toxic gas.

"That's it, we're getting out of this house," Sean declared after we'd spent the majority of the holiday sulking inside.

"Do not—" my mom began to interject.

"Just let him figure it out on his own!"

"You didn't give *birth* to him; you don't fucking get it!"

LATER THAT AFTERNOON, we all headed off to the Del Mar Fairgrounds: a San Diego staple where you can see a pig race, an awful cover band, and your favorite contestant from *Flavor of Love* assisting in a hypnotist show, all in one place.

Walking along the dusty path leading up to the entrance, I

was hit with the sticky, burnt-sugar smell of caramel apples and the earthy scent of fresh hay. Lights pulsed from carnival games while the creaky Ferris wheel whirled against a pink sky. When we reached the ticket booth, families jostled past us, high on patriotism and funnel cake.

"How many tickets does fifty dollars get us?" Mom asked before whipping her head around to see my and Travis's reactions.

"Three hundred and fifty," the unenthused teenage girl behind the window responded.

"Perfect," Mom said, sliding her a crumpled wad of cash like it was a stack.

Tessa grabbed my hand, guiding me through the bannered gates. We passed a fried-avocado stand that reeked of fish-and-chip batter and a run-down petting zoo that consisted of a tub filled with horseshoe crabs that you could touch.

In spite of Cory's absence, I was happy to have Tessa all to myself for the night. Friendship was something other kids at school had. Now, for once, I could be the kid who not only had a best friend but a best friend who was older and cooler than anyone else's. I could have a family that knew how to celebrate national holidays like other people did. At first glance, we looked just the same as every other sun-damaged family in SoCal—except in our house, our Christmas wasn't stolen by the Grinch but by Cory, who pawned our gifts for his next fix.

Our first stop inside the fairground was the Tilt-A-Whirl. Tessa had promised to go on it with me, but once we were standing in line, she grew quiet and distracted. My mom was a few yards away, pacing around and talking on the phone, and Tessa's eyes tracked her movements, hawklike and shrewd.

"Let me just go see if it's about Cory," Tessa said.

"But, it's almost our turn . . ." I whined.

"It won't take long, I'll be back for our turn, I promise," she said, leaving me with Travis.

I knew Tessa was right. It had to be about Cory. But it wasn't like he was in some hostage situation—surely she had time for one ride before dealing with whatever mess he'd gotten himself into.

Cory always comes back, I thought to myself. *Why couldn't Tessa and my mom seem to remember that?*

"Wanna go just us two?" Travis asked me, forcing a smile.

"Sure," I said, forcing one back.

Travis and I piled into a cherry-red car that looked like a hollowed-out Christmas ornament. The platform beneath us started spinning, and the faster we went, the more everything melted together—colored cars swirling, lights flickering, arms flapping in the air as the ride picked up speed. At each turn, I craned my neck in the direction of my mom and Tessa. I could see from the brief flashes that they were too engrossed in their phones to notice me.

The kids in the other cars let out their *ooh*s and *ahh*s, performing for their parents who were watching and waving at them. I just sat there deflated and staring vacantly at Sean, who was watching from below and flipping me the bird. This move had become one of our only bits, and, usually, I'd crack up while throwing it back at him. This time, however, I couldn't feel anything except a looming sense that everything was about to go horribly wrong.

When the ride finally ended, I barreled out of the car before Travis could even finish unstrapping himself. But in my effort to reach my mom and Tessa as quickly as possible, I'd forgotten two cardinal rules about the Tilt-A-Whirl. The first is that the ride's structure is made of jagged, uneven metal. And the second is that when the ride is over, you have the balance of a drunk driver failing a sobriety test. Wobbling down the exit at full speed, I tripped and fell—skinning my knee on the metal cheese grater–esque ramp, drawing blood.

I stood up quickly, but when I looked back over at my mom and Tessa and saw their backs were still to me, that was the last straw. I was livid. Instead of standing up, I flopped back down, stretching my knee out in front of me and digging down into my skin, trying to turn my scrape into a gash.

"The ride broke down!" I proclaimed, limping up to them with a dramatic flair. When my mom turned to look, I stuck out my leg, now smeared with just a few drops of diluted blood.

"What?" she asked, then turned her attention back to whoever or whatever was happening between her, Tessa, and the phone.

"Do you not see that I'm *bleeding*? I need *help*!" I stomped my foot, pointing at my barely injured knee.

"Lukas, please—"

"I'm *wounded*! I could be permanently *disfigured*!"

"Not now, honey—"

"I might never *walk again* and you're saying *not now*?!"

When she took the phone back from Tessa and walked a few feet away, completely ignoring me, all the despair that had been hanging heavy over the fairgrounds felt like it finally collapsed on top of me. I fell to the ground and lay there convulsing and cradling my knee as though I were a Civil War amputee. Concerned bystanders gathered around me. One of them offered to call an ambulance. The only people who seemed unfazed were the people closest to me. This made me howl even louder. I didn't want an ambulance. I wanted my family's attention.

Unfortunately, they were wise to my games.

I had first started lashing out for attention when I was four years old, biting the kids in my preschool who didn't want to play with me. Then when cannibalism lost its charm, I leaned into biting remarks: I'd scream out for help and have massive outbursts in public. Sometimes I'd stand up in the middle of a shopping cart and announce to my family that I wanted them all to die. Some of this might seem extreme, but I was convinced that unless I was intense, loud, or dramatic, nobody would give a shit about me.

Cory, on the other hand, had a more refined, understated approach. He'd storm out of the house, slumped and silent. All Cory wanted was to be left alone. But the more he tried to isolate himself, to shut down, shut up, or shut himself away, the more everyone would fuss over him. I was in awe of his technique, but I was too needy to successfully emulate him. I wanted more—more attention, more comfort, more love. I was the kid with the loudest need. If I couldn't be the best, I could at least be the loudest.

"Lukas, you have to get up," my mom said, grabbing my hand.

"It hurts," I bawled, swatting her hands away.

"We have to get your brother. He's in trouble," she said.

The way she'd said *trouble* so bluntly, without sugarcoating, snapped me out of my tantrum. For once, I felt like Cory, slumped and silent as we drove away from the fairgrounds. From the window of my mom's minivan, I watched the neon lights disappear beneath the horizon, the joy I had felt earlier fading along with them.

"Cory's so broken up about his dad," my mom murmured, more to the air than to anyone. She massaged her jaw beneath her fingers as if she could knead the guilt away.

"But you make up for it. You're like his mom and his dad. You're incredible," Tessa replied from the back seat next to me.

"This is my fault. I should have never reconnected him with his father."

I had never met Cory's dad; by the time I was born, he was already out of the picture. When my mom first met him at a Halloween party, he'd been a successful lawyer in San Diego. Good on paper, just like my dad. It wasn't until I was older that I learned the truth: a drug-induced mental breakdown had unraveled the stable, family-man persona that my mom was initially drawn to. What replaced it was a deep-seated paranoia that had led him to build a doomsday bunker in Mexico where he could hide from the encroaching "nuclear winter."

We pulled into the district of San Ysidro, where the streets were lined with tattered tarps, piles of frayed blankets, and deflated tents. It was the last stretch of San Diego before you reached Tijuana, where Cory's dad was presumed to be living—just across the border.

"Lukas, you're going to stay back with Sean," my mom said, once we found a parking spot.

"Why? Cory's my family, too," I said.

"Jesus. Okay, just please don't cause a scene, and whatever you do, do not run off," she said, too tired to argue with me.

It was ten o'clock by the time we reached the encampment outside of Casa Familiar homeless shelter. That was where my mom had arranged to meet the man who called while we were at the fair, offering up Cory's location in exchange for fifty bucks and some Del Taco.

The encampment was tucked away in a barren riverbed and overrun with litter, dead shrubs, and makeshift clotheslines. Teenagers were lighting fireworks that exploded and fanned out over tents, while families huddled together, roasting hot dogs over campfires. We trudged single file through the community like disillusioned soldiers marching into battle. My mom's eyes were darting frantically all over the place. Tessa held her hand, looking younger and more troubled than I'd ever seen her look before, chewing on her lower lip ring, biting so hard that all the color drained from her mouth. Sean fell back with Travis and me, corralling us back in line every time we tried to pick up one of the discarded firecrackers.

My mother paid the informant, and we waited.

"That's gotta be him," my mom gasped, pointing in the direction of a gangly, hollowed-out teenager who vaguely resembled the Cory I had known.

Where Cory was, there were no hot dogs or firecrackers. He was slumped over with his arm hanging limply by his side, clearly broken. I could see every single bone in Cory's face. Where he once had pupils, there were now just microscopic pinpoints, which kept rolling to the back of his head.

"Oh. What are you guys doing here?" he slurred.

"You're coming home," my mom said as sternly as she possibly could, choking back tears. "We need to get you something to eat, and we're going to get you cleaned up."

"Why? I'm the happiest I've ever been," he said in a worn-out whisper.

Tessa dropped down next to him, touching Cory's cold, sharp cheekbone.

"Please, Cory. I love you so much. I don't want to be without you, come home with us," Tessa said, practically hyperventilating.

"You won't, and I will, just later . . ." he started, losing consciousness.

Cory had always seemed so massive to me. At sixteen, he was already clocking in at around six feet. His stature was only enhanced by the pedestal I put him on. Cory was the smartest person I knew. He had a mind that absorbed everything—he could learn the violin and cello after a day of teaching himself. Now I stood before him, all four feet and a half of me, towering over this diminished version of Cory, who could barely string a sentence together, he seemed so impossibly small and weak, almost corpse-like.

Sean and Mom started to hoist him up, and he whined like a child. I thought maybe it was because of his arm, but then I heard the tail end of his mumbling:

"I like it better here. I don't have to worry about anything."

I looked around, at the cold, dark encampment, and I wondered what the fuck he was talking about. There was our mom—our beautiful, warm-hearted mother—offering him food and love and attention, and he had the nerve to deny her? He had the *audacity* to turn her away, to refuse all the help she gave so willingly? I had never wanted to be less like my brother than in that moment.

On the drive home, Tessa and Cory huddled together beside me in the back seat. Cramped and still wired, I focused on the rhythmic roar of the passing cars, hoping they'd lull me to sleep. Instead, I kept catching hushed fragments of the conversation my mom and Sean were having in the front. Words bandied about like *sick* and *junkie*—and one particular sentence I can still hear if I close my eyes, "I failed him. My son's a drug addict."

I had no understanding of addiction then, what drugs Cory could have possibly been using, or what it was that he got out of them. But what made even less sense to me was how I was supposed to feel about Cory now, my big brother I had worshipped. What was I supposed to do with the love, anger, and fear that I harbored toward him—all in equal measure. What was I supposed to do with the inalienable truth: that my hero was a capital *D*, capital *A*, Drug Addict.

4.

Till Camp Do Us Part

In the absence of Cory's chaos at my dad's house, Travis and I found ways to create our own. My dad, like most doctors, worked long shifts at the hospital, leaving us with plenty of free time and a surplus of bad ideas. With no adult supervision, Travis and I had free rein to turn the house into our own personal playground. Whether it be flour-bombing the entire living room to simulate a snowy Christmas, prank-calling 911, or throwing kitchen knives at each other and calling it "target practice." Each weekend we pushed the boundaries further than we had before. The pinnacle of our brilliance came one Friday night when Travis, who, at fourteen, was convinced he "basically knew how to drive," dared me to steal Dad's car keys so we could hit up Jack in the Box for ninety-nine-cent tacos. It was a fairly seamless outing—and the whole thing went off without a hitch, until on our way back, our neighbor caught sight of two bobbing heads barely visible over the dashboard, and ratted us out to my dad.

Our punishment was that our grandma would now supervise our weekends with dad—a consequence that, to me, felt like a prize.

Nana would show up each Friday with a trunk full of groceries and an itinerary's worth of activities in a valiant attempt to pry me away from the computer and get me out of the house.

My grandma was nothing short of legendary. A single line of dialogue in *Evil Dead II* had earned her celebrity status in my book, as well as my favorite person to play make-believe with. Yet, none of our performances could keep me away from *The Sims* for too long.

"This again?" Nana said, switching off the monitor. "Is this really how you want to spend your whole summer?"

"Kind of." I shrugged. "My Sim family needs me. Ever since Jeffrey got promoted, he's been working crazy hours, which doesn't leave a lot of time for Diana to work on her skills. I mean, someone has to take care of all these kids, and Jeffrey just doesn't have what it takes to be a dad! And besides you, they're the only ones who really get me," I said matter-of-factly.

"Oh, for heaven's sake. That's not— Look, what if we found a way for you to do make-believe but in real life? You could make your own *Evil Dead*," she responded before handing me a brochure for a summer camp with an acting program in Lake Arrowhead called Mystic Pines.

Ever since I was little I'd been very vocal about how badly I wanted to become an actor. When the opportunity to finally pursue that dream arrived, the excitement made my brain short-circuit.

"'Campers will follow their dreams, have adventures, and gain lifelong friendships in a safe environment,'" Nana said, reading aloud from the brochure to my dad, later that night.

"What's wrong with the Boys and Girls Club?" my dad grumbled when he saw how much it cost. My grandma snatched the brochure back, insisting that it had to be this one—for Travis and me both. He finally gave a *What the hell?* shrug and handed his credit card to her. He already knew that when Nana wanted something, there was no stopping her.

A month later, I found myself kissing Nana goodbye and taking my rightful place in the back seat of my dad's Land Rover on the way to camp. Travis was listening to his iPod, and my dad wasn't keen on having conversation that early in the morning, so I played the game I'd often play when I felt I wasn't getting enough attention: I'd stare at the sun for as long as humanly possible, testing my limit, seeing how long it would take for me to go blind. When my eyesight returned, I could see the pine trees give way to a sprawling lake, zip lines, and an outdoor movie theater.

We pulled up to the campground and parked alongside a fleet of minivans, limousines, and charter buses, all unloading a stream of kids with wide smiles and oversize duffel bags. I couldn't believe my eyes. I was giddy with anticipation until it hit me. What if this ended up being just another place where I didn't quite fit in?

IT WAS HOT. It had been hot the whole summer, but that first day at camp orientation, my skin was burning and my lungs were filled with smoke. A stranger was burning to death. Right there on the big grass field next to the dining hall, he thrashed his arms and bellowed for help. My bunkmate, Simon, stood next to me, shaking so hard I thought he'd piss his pants.

For a few long seconds, no one moved—then finally, a counselor rushed toward the burning man with a fire extinguisher and sprayed it all over the burning body. A cloud of white smoke obscured my view. I was eleven years old and much too young to witness somebody die. I was just starting to get a handle on deodorant. Death still seemed like too heady a concept.

As the smoke cleared, I could make out a pair of crumpled limbs, hauntingly reminiscent of how Cory's looked when we had found him the previous summer.

But then he jumped up—extremely alive and undeniably pleased with himself. He ripped off his burnt clothing, revealing some sort of fireproof underlayer.

"And that is the kind of stunts I used to do working on big-time Hollywood studio movies," he said, high-fiving the counselor who'd doused him with the fire extinguisher.

"On the big screen, it should look so believable that you can't tell the difference."

All of us exhaled, our panic turning into awe. This guy was the real deal. I listened with rapt attention as he regaled us with tales of jumping out of helicopters and flipping cars in big-budget studio movies like *The Italian Job* and *Big Fat Liar*. He was fearless. Immortal.

Standing there, listening to this seemingly normal man talk about risking his life for a movie that starred Frankie Muniz and Paul Giamatti, something was awakened within me. I realized I didn't have to keep being the same me I had always been. I could transform myself. I could pick a new avatar. I could create my own Sim from scratch. I could be whatever the fuck I wanted—who I was born to be. I could be . . . a *star*.

That night in my cabin, I started crafting my new identity. I needed to become the type of person who'd be willing to set themselves on fire, or even fall flat out on their face in pursuit of admiration. Someone fearless enough to ask whatever questions were in their head without fearing the answers. The world needed an entirely new Lukas. *This won't be easy*, I thought to myself, making a list of character traits in my journal.

At the campfire that night, I marched right up to a group of kids who were all huddled on a log. There was room for exactly one more person on that jagged chunk of wood. I didn't hide or ask for permission. This Lukas didn't need to ask to be noticed. He *demanded* it.

"My friends call me Nova, as in Casanova," I said in my best Oz from *American Pie* voice.

The kids all turned to me, and, for a second, I froze. They were wearing plaid pajamas they'd bought at the camp store, with the sleeves rolled up in different ways, each putting their own customized touch to the look. Standing there, I braced for the worst, until finally one kid spoke.

"Oh my God, I fucking love *American Pie*," he said, and the rest of them cheered and laughed.

"Do it again! Come, sit down with us."

Do it again? Happy to.

Summer Camp Lukas was a lot like the Hooters waitress I admired with my dad: always cheerful, full of pep, and ready to serve. He hugged everyone. He kissed everyone. He got mono from grinding on everyone at one of the dances, that dirty little slut.

We were so enmeshed with one another that the same lice bounced between our heads all summer. When we washed our hair together with the medicated shampoo and fine-toothed combs, the other campers cried at the sight of the tiny insects flooding their scalp. I didn't care at all, but I forced my smile into a frown in solidarity; we were all in this together, for better or worse. Till camp do us part.

Camp was only ninety miles away from my dad's house, but it might as well have been an entirely different universe. Up was suddenly down, a counselor known as Johnny was now nicknamed

Spider, and another named Mary had transformed into Loco. And to survive in this new world I was taught new skills like how to hit campers over the head with glass bottles made of sugar candy that would shatter into a million safe little pieces. I'd even mastered the art of giving a massage. For reasons I still don't quite understand, the camp offered spa training. We gave each other facials and kneaded each other's baby fat with scented oils. I swear, it didn't seem weird at the time. We just all assumed every summer camp had spa lessons.

I found myself surrounded by kids from families that seemed larger than life, but none stood out quite like the boys I admired most—Marston and Cooper, the sons of Hugh Hefner. They carried with them an aura that was unmistakably their father's. I imagined they picked up their savoir faire from hanging by the Grotto with the Playboy Bunnies. They flirted with ease, making the female counselors blush with their smooth one-liners. I almost couldn't believe that they were just as entertained by my witty repartee as I was by theirs.

When I wrote a letter to my dad telling him "I'd made my first friends" and *who* they were, he was so excited that he finally came out of his stupor. It was the happiest I'd ever heard him.

"*The* Hugh Hefner? Oh, Lukas, you're living the dream. Put in a good word for me. What am I saying? Just keep them close, I'm begging you. I've always wanted to see the mansion up close," he'd say through the phone. It felt as though even my dad liked Summer Camp Lukas more.

For the first time, I didn't feel the frantic urge to constantly be by my mom's side, but I didn't want her to think I had forgotten about her, either. I sat in the gazebo overlooking a stretch of trees and upgraded from telling lies in my journal to telling lies in my letters back home. I rambled on and on about how I missed her so much that my heart literally ached and claimed that I had to go to the infirmary for my recurring chest pains.

In reality, I was gone the entire summer because she needed me out of the way while she attempted to rehabilitate Cory. She needed to know I was okay and that I wasn't angry at her for wanting me out of the house for eight weeks . . . but not *so* okay that she thought I could live without her.

But, the truth was, I never wanted to go home. I had no desire to leave behind the person I was becoming at camp. Summer Camp Lukas was the fucking man.

I was so taken with this new me that I somehow convinced myself that I was getting taller. (I was not.) But my voice was louder, and my body started taking up more space, arms flailing as I told animated stories, like one of those inflatable car wash balloons caught in the wind. Everyone there saw something in me, and it made me feel the thing I had always longed to be: special.

At lunch, Travis walked by, and I waved at him.

"Do you know that guy?" one of the theater kids asked.

"That's my brother," I said. *Wasn't it obvious?*

"That paintball kid is your brother?" he asked, and I nodded.

"Whoa. I didn't even know you had a brother."

I was no longer someone's kid brother. I wasn't my parents' overactive, needy little hell-son who caused them endless headaches. Finally, I was just Lukas, or whatever version of him I wanted him to be.

IT WAS OBVIOUS that all the counselors were hooking up with one another, but I couldn't figure out who was doing what with whom. Was Lasso with that Australian guy, the one with the testosterone-fueled muscles who pronounced *no* like *naur* and had helped me perfect my archery technique? (At the time, it didn't seem weird that we weren't allowed to know our counselors' real names. Lasso was just Lasso, Toucan was Toucan. We just accepted it, no questions asked.)

And what about Lasso and Hawk? She was always braiding his hair by the campfire, linking it to her own, the way the Na'vi fuck in *Avatar*.

Meanwhile, my body was out of control, overrun by curiosity and a strange new cocktail of hormones. Now that I was eleven, puberty had taken full charge, and with it came the notorious "nipple rocks"—which, if you aren't familiar, is the sensation during the first year of puberty that feels like a pebble is lodged in your nipple. And, as luck would have it, the camp's unofficial greeting ritual was a good old-fashioned titty twister.

I was consumed by urges I didn't quite understand but couldn't ignore—the most relentless of which was the burning desire to have my first kiss. Not a chaste peck on the cheek but a real honest-to-God kiss, with tongue and everything. Though I had regaled the Hefner boys with tall tales of hand jobs I'd been receiving since the third grade, the truth was, I was just hoping for someone—anyone—to let me put my tongue in their mouth before the summer ended.

One night, after a heated color war, my moment finally arrived. Still streaked with paint and flecked with shaving cream, my crush of the week and I stepped from the shore of the creek into the mosquito-infested lake. The water lapped at our legs as we nervously hesitated for a beat—and then our lips met, clumsy, but still charged with the thrill of firsts.

I WROTE THIS FOR ATTENTION

"I live in San Diego; it's not far. I'll visit you in the school year, I promise," I said while giving her my love beads. I greedily leaned in for one last kiss. No tongue this time, though. I had nothing more to prove.

When I came back from our outing, clothes still wet, I crawled into my bunk wide awake—exhilarated and restless. Camp was the horniest place on earth.

THAT SUMMER WAS a series of firsts: first friends, first kiss, first time nearly blacking out under the stage lights. On stage, I experienced a liberation like no other. I discovered a freedom I had never known before.

When I learned we would perform monologues for real Hollywood agents and managers, I was ecstatic. Nana was not fucking around when she picked this place—I knew I had to do something unforgettable.

After a few wild renditions of the *Erin Brockovich* "numbers" monologue, *The Notebook* "If you're a bird, I'm a bird" speech, and the Jesus song from *Sister Act* from the other campers, it was my turn to take the stage. My choice was easy: a monologue from one of my favorite movies, *10 Things I Hate About You*. But unlike Julia Stiles, I wasn't speaking to my crush. In my mind, I was pouring my heart out about how I felt about Cory, my dad, and how the kids back home saw me—the old me.

"'I hate the way you talk to me,'" I began, controlling my voice, as if the anger was tied up and couldn't move. Neither could my audience. I couldn't see them, but I could feel them watching me, and it gave me a high like I'd never experienced before. I was hooked.

The agents from the showcase gave the group some feedback, and a bullshit pep talk about the fact that just because you weren't picked, doesn't mean you're not amazing. Fuck that. I wanted to be picked. I needed to be picked. While they were giving this rundown, I locked eyes with a powerful-looking woman who was watching me intently from across the room. After the showcase, she approached me to talk one-on-one.

"We should have a meeting when you get home this summer," she told me in a raspy smoker's voice. She handed her card to me before heading out the door, just like in the movies.

My heart stopped. She turned around and smiled once more.

"Also, a gender swap. How very creative of you, young man."

It was easy for me to pick female characters, maybe because they made more sense to me, or maybe the roles had more emotional layers. Back home, when my child psychologist and I played the board game Guess Who?, I would always pick female characters. When he asked why, I answered simply: "They're prettier." I studied his face. "Is that wrong?"

He cleared his throat and said matter-of-factly, "No. But boys usually pick men."

Much like my tendency to choose women in games, my room became a shrine to the women I adored. My walls were now plastered with headshots of all my favorite crushes. I'd begged Nana to buy them for me at one of those weird little gift shops on Hollywood Boulevard that probably don't exist anymore. I was LadiesManLukas after all, and I was deeply in love with Jennifer Love Hewitt and Alison Lohman. My most prized possessions were their signed headshots. I was obsessed.

When I sat in the car with Nana after she picked me up from therapy, I needed answers.

"Is it wrong that I always pick the girl during the game?"

Nana simply smiled and said she didn't think so. It wasn't until camp that I actually believed her.

MY FINAL ELECTIVE of the summer was filmmaking. We had two weeks to create an original short film. I wrote and directed a zombie movie, wanting it to be both frightening but also philosophically meaningful. I wanted the creatures in my film to represent something deeper, too. The concept emerged gradually as I scribbled the premise in my journal. Each word felt profound, in the way only childhood revelations about the world can feel. *We've all been predators and prey, in one form or another. Just like the mammals on the Discovery Channel, we all play different roles*, I wrote.

I spent weeks shooting this "meaningful" zombie film, recruiting fellow campers to play the walking dead. I painted their eyelids gray, and filmed them staggering through the woods.

The night of the premiere, I couldn't bring myself to watch my own film. I was consumed by an overwhelming anxiety that I would fail. The confidence I felt onstage was nowhere to be found. So, instead, I focused on everyone's reactions. I surveyed the crowd, trying to read people's faces. Nina—the eleventh "love of my life" that summer, grabbed my hand.

"It's really good," Nina said.

"You really mean it?" I asked.

"Yes! You're amazing," she replied.

I smiled, feeling a momentary sense of relief. When the screening was over, she pulled me away from the campfire and led me to one of the teepees out in the woods. Nina bounced around, sharing with me her love of monster movies and anything that scared her.

Inside the tent, we sat down next to each other and listened to the crickets chirping and slicing right through the stillness of the night.

"You know, you can kiss me if you want," Nina said.

Feeling confident in my newfound kissing abilities, I moved in closer. But this time, it was different. Not only did the kiss not end, it started getting more intense. The amount of tongue action happening was at a level I didn't know was possible. I was totally out of my eleven-year-old depth, but she kept going, kissing me harder and harder. Even though we were the same age, I could tell she'd done this before. But I couldn't shake the feeling she was just going through the motions. Did she even like it? I couldn't tell. Did I?

We lay down on the ground and tangled our legs around each other. I wanted it to be romantic, but it felt awkward, like an MMA move gone wrong. Sensing my inexperience, she climbed on top of me, as my back scraped against the hard ground. It was as romantic as a rug burn could be.

Suddenly, the tent door unzipped, and we both froze.

A shadowy figure poked their face in. As the silhouette came closer, I realized it was the counselor who was always flirting with all the other counselors. The handsome Australian in his twenties: the one who exuded a raw, intoxicating masculinity and rugged charm that made him appear a decade older—the very man I longed to be.

We had all our clothes on, but we might as well have been naked. He looked us up and down, and I tried covering myself, even though nothing was exposed and there was nowhere for me to go.

"Aur naur, what are you two doing?" he asked.

My heart pounded in my ears, and Nina and I merely fixed our gazes forward. Taking this as an invitation, he stepped into the tent and zipped the canvas flap behind him.

"It's all right," he said, his tone suddenly nurturing. "I won't tell anyone what you're doing if you wanna keep going."

I hesitated as I tried to make sense of the options: I could either say no and maybe get in trouble, or I could give him what he wanted from me.

"Lemme help you. I'll tell you what to do," he whispered.

Something shifted in me. I wouldn't get in trouble. I could perform for him. He unzipped his pants as he started moving closer.

I knew it was wrong as it was happening. It was wrong of him. It was wrong that I was a little turned on, that I felt uncomfortable, that I felt nothing at all. It was wrong that I loved the thrill of doing something forbidden. My skin felt dirty, and my stomach tensed with fear. But I knew one thing for sure: I was good at putting on a show.

I wanted to compare bodies, but I also knew better than to look. The one thing I was curious about was the one thing that I had to ignore. I was shaking and scared, but like the consummate actor I was, I used it. I used the anxiety and tried turning it into excitement. My performance was so convincing that I frightened myself.

"Kiss her harder," the Aussie said.

Great. Now I was out of my depth with two people who were more experienced than I was. But I did what he said.

"Now take that off, and move your bodies on each other," he instructed.

I hesitated, then reluctantly began taking off my shirt.

Time began to speed up, and suddenly I wasn't as frightened anymore. I was no longer present for it. A whole new avatar had emerged. I was so disconnected from myself—watching, detached, as if I were on my computer screen controlling one of my Sims.

The counselor made a noise of relief and came on my sleeping bag. And then that was it. It was over.

That was kind of rude, I thought. *The bag was from REI and very expensive.*

When I came back into my body, I was now alone in the same sleeping bag, watching the sun begin to rise. *What the fuck happened last night?*

Nothing out of the ordinary, I tried telling myself. This stuff happens all the time, especially at camp. This is just what hooking up feels like. There's always someone with more power. One person's always a little uncomfortable. Questions swirled inside my head. Did he like it? Did I like it? Did Nina?

I never found out. The three of us spent the last days of summer camp sharing an unspoken agreement: *What happens in the tent stays in the tent.* I didn't mind, because pretending felt a lot safer than remembering. I'd spent so much of my life wanting to know the secrets of the adult world. Now I knew *way* too many of them.

When I got back home to San Diego, flashes from that night would sometimes creep back into my mind. But when they did, I would just remind myself that I'd always wanted an audience. I wanted to be special. And I got what I asked for.

5.

Poppers

I wasn't the only one in my house harboring secrets. My mom had mastered the art of living a double life, tucking hers away where no one could see it. She'd disappear to Harrah's casino, where the chime of the penny slots anesthetized her. Over time, her confidence grew and so did her bets. First the quarter slots, then the dollar machines. Her double life remained hidden until one day when she finally hit the $50,000 jackpot.

With her slot machine winnings, Mom came home with a life-size check, enough for a down payment on a new house—a place with more space, nestled in her favorite part of town, her own personal promised land: Encinitas.

Mom always said that Encinitas was different from the rest of San Diego. She wasn't wrong. In Encinitas, the sunlight would turn gold every afternoon at three. There were no seasons, it was summer forever: a laid-back paradise blooming with poinsettias and geraniums. Along Highway 101, beach houses sat stacked on a cliff, with tall, narrow staircases leading you down to the gritty sand where sunbathers basked all day long.

After I had been ruthlessly bullied by a pack of airsoft-wielding sixth graders, I buried the remains of my former self back at the school in the next town over. That other kid, the one from that other school—who, if you'll recall—had to be killed off.

I came to Encinitas as a new, more confident version of myself, ready to enter seventh grade that fall. All I needed was a best friend to make my transformation complete.

All day, I'd watch the surfers and skateboarders congregate by the lifeguard tower, moving with an ease that I both admired and tried to emulate. I'd sit and listen to the slap of the waves hitting the shore and the hiss of the water as it drew back in, daydreaming about finding a group I could belong to.

From my spot perched on top of Moonlight beach, I was convinced that the sky was bigger there. I'm still sure of it. Every moment at those cliff-lined beaches felt imbued with possibilities. The vastness, combined with the blazing sun, seemed to melt away all of my lingering anxieties.

Mom filled the new house with the same shit she'd hoarded over the years: me and Travis, her twenty different half-used Bath & Body Works lotions, plaques with swirly fonts that read "My dogs are my best friends," and endless tchotchkes. She had a propensity to hold on to every piece of paper she had ever touched. Things did not have to be valuable to be saved, such as expired Advils, ancient McDonald's ketchup packets, grocery receipts from the previous decade. It was like doomsday prepping, only with things that would probably never save our lives in the event of an apocalypse.

Sean made the move with us, too, which meant so did all of

his baggage—both literal and metaphorical. His collection of "vintage" cars transformed our driveway into something between a used-car lot and a junkyard.

"What is this?" my mom asked, holding up a package the size of her head.

Sean looked guilty but tried to brush it off, his burgeoning shopping addiction becoming harder to hide with every delivery.

"It's from QVC. Twenty percent off," he replied casually.

"I don't care how many percent off, where are we supposed to put all this?"

"With the rest of this shit, Paulina, I don't know!"

But as full as the house was, there were two essential pieces missing: Tessa and Cory. Tessa's parents sent her away to boarding school in Utah that restricted us from writing letters or visiting for holidays. And without Tessa around, Cory's disappearances became even more frequent. He'd turned eighteen and kept begging my mom to help him get his own place. Eventually, she secured him a trailer down the street, hoping that she'd at least know where he was even if she didn't know what he was up to. Plus, it was so close that my mom could sneak over to check on him, making sure he was still breathing, as if he were a giant newborn. Some nights, I'd wake up to the sound of her tiptoeing back into the house late at night.

"Where'd you go?" I'd ask quietly, standing in the darkness of the arched doorway.

She'd jump, startled, but would quickly recover.

"Nowhere, go back to sleep, sweetheart," she'd whisper.

Cory might have wanted to get away from her, but I still yearned to keep her close. No matter what color I dyed my hair, or the type of music I listened to, or the attitude I'd adopted in school—I couldn't shed the part of me that thought nobody would love me the way she could, no matter how hard I tried to outgrow it. After summer camp, I learned to contain it. I stopped following her from room to room like a shaky Chihuahua with separation anxiety, and instead I started letting the woman breathe.

Besides, we still had Sundays—our weekly date night at her favorite place on earth, Harrah's casino. It was only forty minutes from home, but it might as well have been Monte Carlo. After she won that $50,000 jackpot, it meant the hotel and buffet became free, too. Like all casinos, they knew how to keep you coming back for more, and my mom could never say no to free anything, especially all-you-can-eat crab legs.

Inside the casino it perpetually felt like it was four o'clock in the morning. It smelled like cigarettes and stale beer, which, for me, became the smell of comfort. That scent meant it was our time together. At every machine, dead-eyed gamblers mindlessly pulled levers, chasing the fleeting hope that came with each spin. I would stare at the carpet until the pattern started to dance, I couldn't stop making myself hallucinate, and Mom couldn't stay away from the slots.

At the casino, Mom was distracted, too busy counting her chips, slamming the machine for the hundredth time, or chatting with anyone who came within earshot. It was a different kind of distraction than she clung to at home. Not the midnight trips to Cory's trailer or the little white lies she fed us so Travis and I wouldn't worry. Here, Mom let her guard down.

"If you were sick, you'd tell me? Right?" I asked.

"'Course, sweetie," she said, before cursing the machine after another defeat.

"You son of a bitch!" she muttered, as she yanked on the lever again.

"I know, but . . ." I said as she pressed down on all the buttons, trying to crank out a win through sheer force.

"I told you, I took care of everything to make sure I'd never leave you guys."

The year before, Mom underwent a preventative hysterectomy and mastectomy and promised that what had happened to every woman in her family would not happen to her. Even as a little kid, I knew adults lied. Every other woman in her family had passed away too young, and I was frightened she would be next.

Death seemed to trail my mother everywhere. Shortly after her senior year, Mom found out she and her high school sweetheart, Gus, were going to have a baby. But four weeks before my eldest brother, Jesse, was born, Gus died in a motorcycle accident. Gus was the love of Mom's life, and whenever I asked her about him, she would sob uncontrollably. Though it had been decades, Mom's heartbreak never faded.

I think that was part of the reason she loved the slots so much. Life had taught her that nothing was promised, not even tomorrow. But Mom viewed this lesson through the lens of an eternal optimist: believing that victory was just as random and likely as failure and that high risk was always worth it for the high reward.

"Mom," I began again, hovering over the slot machine.

"What?" she muttered, her eyes glued to the screen as the reels spun.

I scooted down on the bench next to her. "I was wondering—"

"Stand up, I don't want security giving me a hard time," she said.

"Sorry. . . . Were you and Dad ever in love?"

All I'd known about my parents' split was that they hated each other when they were together and they hated each other apart.

However, the hopeless romantic in me couldn't accept that two people could just suddenly start despising each other. Didn't someone have to cheat or lie or run off with the neighbor? Our neighbors all hated us.

"So, then, what went wrong?" I continued.

"Growing apart is just the reality of life." She shrugged.

I knew better than to trust that understated answer from my mother. So the next week, when her spirits were high from a sixty-dollar win, I decided to try my luck again. Sitting at the buffet behind the craps table—our plates loaded up with free lobster tails, bok choy, and Flamin' Hot Cheeto sushi rolls—I pleaded with her.

"Come on, just tell me, please," I said.

"Your dad started to drift away." She shrugged. "It was like he stopped seeing me. He was just . . . gone."

The notion of my dad drifting away and becoming totally vacant felt all too familiar. With each visit to his house in Long Beach, I felt him retreating from me more and more. Maybe someone had half killed dad, like I'd half killed myself. If I asked him, he'd probably say that it was my mom who had done it.

"But . . ." she said, taking a big sip of her Coors Light, the only alcoholic drink she ever touched.

"But what?"

"I was getting . . . closer to your uncle Mike."

"Uncle" Mike had been in and out of our lives for years. I was never entirely sure how he was my mom's brother, but that was the story she always told us. Uncle Mike was the epitome of hypermasculinity: He rode a Harley-Davidson and had a big, shiny bald head. Though his gruff exterior didn't match what was inside. He was a gentle giant. He'd given me Silver simply because I'd told him I'd always wanted a rabbit. Something to call my own.

"What does Uncle Mike have to do with Dad?" I asked.

"Nothing," she said, chickening out. But her voice had slipped into a higher octave.

"You're lying," I said. "Were you fucking your brother or something?"

Her face went white.

"Lukas! Watch your mouth," she said.

"He's not my uncle, is he? Why do you call him Uncle Mike, then? That's so fucked-up—"

"Language, please," Mom said, looking over her shoulder. She put her hands on mine. "Okay, fine. He's not your uncle. I don't even know why I started calling him that. He was someone I was seeing. I cheated on your dad. And he found out, so we got a divorce."

I chewed my food, trying to process what she'd said. It was a shock and also the most understandable thing in the world. I knew who my dad was. She must have experienced exactly what I had: He could make you feel special one minute, and a split second later he'd recoil so harshly that you'd forget that he even knew your name.

"I'm sorry," she said, pulling away from me.

"It's okay," I told her as I grabbed her hand, hoping to make her understand she had nothing to apologize for. Now that camp had taught me what it was like to have a secret, I understood what a burden they were. Carrying them was punishment enough.

I wondered if Sean knew about Mike. Probably. Adults told each other the stuff they were hiding from kids. Or maybe she was hiding it from him, too. Mom's lies were never meant to hurt anyone. They just existed to preserve the narrative of her life that she'd pieced together, the abridged version that left out all the moments that were too painful to process.

Everyone was a pathological liar, not just me. Or, whoever the old version of me was. Doesn't matter, he was dead. I'd erased eleven whole years. Killed them all, of course.

I NEVER KNEW which version of Cory would show up. Sometimes, he was full of life, and we'd record music together for hours, improvising absurd lyrics, laughing, and singing along. Other times, a zombie would shamble in, his skin a dull, grayish hue, like a faded newspaper left on the porch for too long. That was the Cory I feared most—the one who reminded me that my brother was an addict.

Mom would find him catatonic on the couch, then she'd drag him into her room, shaking him and slapping at his face. He'd bat her away and groan, assuring her that he was just exhausted and that she was being neurotic. These episodes always seemed to end with Mom locking herself in her bedroom to call Sean for backup, while I resumed my usual spot just outside with my ear pressed against the door.

"I can't see him like this. I just can't," she'd cry.

"It doesn't matter that he's eighteen! He could be sixty and he'd still be my baby."

Silence would follow, then I'd hear something drop, like she stomped or hit something.

"I know he's a heroin addict! But what am I supposed to do, stop loving him?"

It wasn't until I googled heroin that everything came into focus. That's what had taken over Cory's body and brain. *That* was what had half killed my brother.

My sunny new town transformed into a somber place overnight. Our charming new home at the beach was now not so charming.

Neither was the new-and-improved version of myself. After a summer of observing the sun-bleached surfers—the future faces of my new school—I knew I had to change again. Although I still felt a kinship with the misfit allure of my favorite movie, *Donnie Darko*, I'd found a far more aspirational role model in Ryan Atwood. While I hoped this new identity would be the thing to help me fit in at school, what I wanted more than anything was for it to help me find that epic, Shakespearean kind of love that Ryan and Marissa had on *The O.C.* I craved that forbidden-sex teenage dream. I wanted that fucked-up kind of love. The kind of love that makes you want to die.

But first I needed the leather jacket with the gray hoodie that Ryan wore constantly. This was going to be my new trademark look. I could be Ryan. I could take my Marissa to Mexico, but I'd protect my girlfriend better than Ryan did. I would never let my girl get roofied in Tijuana. I'd be Ryan 2.0.

ON THE FIRST day of seventh grade, I sat waiting for Mom in her minivan, staring at the sun again until I went blind. I opened my eyes to us pulling out of our new cul-de-sac. When my vision came back, I saw Sean taking out the trash in his boxers. I flipped him the bird through the rearview mirror. He shot me one back and gave a wink like, *You got this.* A small grin cracked across my face, with the knot of anxiety in my stomach releasing.

When I walked into my new school, my leather jacket was my shield, protecting me from any potential problems. At summer camp, I'd felt invincible, with the illusion that I could reinvent myself into someone else. Except that confidence didn't make the trip back to Encinitas.

My middle school was like a time capsule from the 1970s, with all-beige buildings and vintage cars in the parking lot adorned with bumper stickers urging everyone to "Keep Encinitas Funky." The whole place oozed with pure Southern California nostalgia. Every Friday, the piano chords of "Don't Stop Believing" by Journey filled the quad at the center of the school. It was tradition, a weird one, but it seemed like everyone accepted it. Mrs. Pugh, our grizzly principal, stood near the flagpole, holding the microphone and belting out the lyrics with unshakable confidence: "'Just a small-town girl, livin' in a lonely world . . .'"

"Holy shit," the lanky kid next to me laughed. "It's so off-key."

He winced; I looked over, nodding in agreement.

I watched on as my new principal sang to Steve Perry, while I continued to scan the crowd for a potential girlfriend.

"You sure you're not gonna dance?" The kid smiled; his braces were laced with rubber bands and spit. "You're new. Everyone will be watching."

Part of me wanted to, but even with my leather jacket, I still wasn't ready to let loose in front of a crowd. Not quite yet.

"Nah. Not my thing."

"Aw, come on," he teased, nudging me with his elbow.

A disappointing realization set in: being the new kid didn't make me the most desirable bachelor at school.

I shot the redheaded kid a look.

"Don't fuck with me," I muttered under my breath. Didn't he know I'd killed a kid?

At home that night, I figured I'd have better luck with some of my old summer camp prospects. I'd been talking on AIM with Briana, a girl I had made out with at camp (and who maybe gave me mono), and I was starting to think that she could be the one. We had the same antibodies, so maybe I could make her feel safe. Maybe we could be happy together.

> @ladiesmanlukas: i just want to take care of you and do anything you want

> @runpelicanrun: r u saying u want to be my boyfriend?

> @ladiesmanlukas: ya. Can I take you on a date? U deserve 2 be pampered.

She lived just north of Long Beach, in South Bay, and one weekend, we convinced our parents to drop us off at a Chili's for a date. My dad wasn't thrilled about the idea of driving me up the coast, but he gave in. We spent the ride sitting in traffic, and mostly in silence. After a while, my dad turned on Fox News. He loved it as much as he loved Howard. Maybe more. Had this been a few years earlier, he would have asked me crass questions about someone's tits, and we would have laughed and he would have been proud that I'd scored a date. But now it seemed like he just wanted to get back to bed or get back to work. When we got to Chili's, though, he dropped me off and promptly dozed off in the parking lot, lulled to sleep by the soothing sounds of Sean Hannity.

Over a plate of jalapeño poppers, Briana and I held hands across the table. She went on and on about her school, her parents, and her siblings.

"What about your brother?" she asked in between bites.

I paused, hesitating. "Uh, yeah, he's great."

I wanted to be honest with her about my family, but the truth was a bit of a buzzkill. What I needed was not a therapy session; what I needed was a girlfriend to fall in love with and to fuck. I wasn't getting any younger, I was twelve after all, and surely everyone had left their virginities behind in elementary school. Having sex with this girl and falling in love, in whichever order it happened, was my new life plan.

Briana leaned back in the plush red booth, chewing rhythmically on her Orbit gum. "You know," she said, her voice casual but loaded, "we could have sex."

I blinked, unsure if I'd heard her right. "Wait, what?"

"We could have sex?" she repeated while blowing a small bubble that popped softly before she resumed chewing. Her tone was so casual, like she was asking me what my star sign was.

"But we haven't even finished the jalapeño poppers," I stammered. She tilted her head, the gum clicking between her teeth.

"And?"

Screw the poppers. My destiny was waiting for me in the least seductive place in the universe: the Chili's bathroom.

No one was in there, so we smashed our bodies into one of the stalls and started making out. It was easy at first.

I can handle this, I thought.

But then she took off her pink underwear and leaned into me, pushing me back toward the urine-splashed toilet. The air was thick with the unsexy scent of an antiseptic chain-restaurant bathroom, and though I tried to channel my counselor's unchecked confidence, I couldn't muster it, and suddenly it felt like I was choking.

Where was the romance? I wanted to lay her down on a four-poster bed with candles lit and rose petals strewn about. I wanted to play my iTunes hookup playlist packed with Imogen Heap songs that I had carefully crafted in Ryan and Marissa's image, not the Muzak that was rippling out of the bathroom speakers. This was supposed to be the perfect moment. Where was the buildup? The anticipation? The moment when love and lust finally intertwined? But the reality was far from that. Instead, we were just two awkward bodies, pretzeled around a Chili's bathroom stall.

My heart started racing. I was not man enough for this. I had to find a way out that wouldn't make me seem like a pussy. An out with dignity.

"Maybe let's just do a . . . hand job," I said.

She looked at me, confused, her face illuminated not by candlelight but by the buzzing fluorescents.

"I wanna be respectful."

"Lame." She shrugged.

Despite the Muzak and the stall and the fact that I wasn't actually in love with this person, the hand job worked out well enough. She washed her hands, and then we went back to our poppers and honey chicken crispers in silence before going home and removing each other from our buddy lists on AIM.

BACK IN ENCINITAS the next week, I told myself that solitude was better than embarrassment. Nobody would have to know that I had bitched out with Briana. Instead, I could skulk around school trying to look aloof and mysterious rather than lonely. But I *was* lonely, though I wasn't sure if I missed people or just the idea of them. So when some girl called out my name in the pickup line, I was sure she meant some other Lukas, probably one spelled with a *c*.

When I looked up, though, there was the redheaded, skinny kid from the quad, now accompanied by the female version of him.

"My brother said you freaked him out last week," the girl hollered.

"No, I didn't," the boy interjected.

"I'm Bunny. And this is my twin brother, Brody."

Bunny and Brody. The alliteration reminded me of something you would name a pair of malnourished golden retrievers. Along with their golden-red hair, they had hazel-colored eyes and freckled skin. I couldn't help but notice their clavicle bones jutting out through their shirts.

"You guys are so . . ."

"Skinny? It's because we were preemies," Bunny said with a practiced nonchalance.

"Yeah, but I used to beat your ass in the womb for nutrients, which is why I'm taller," Brody retorted. Brody was taller; and apparently had the quick wit of a stand-up comedian. Only he had too much crippling anxiety to ever perform.

Bunny gave him a dead arm, and I wondered if it felt like they were hitting themselves, like that thing that they say about twins, when one gets hurt, the other one feels their pain.

"So what's your deal?" they asked me in unison, a slurred San Diego version of *The Shining* twins.

"I got transferred here because they wouldn't let me back at my old school after I fucked some kid up really bad."

"Yeah, right," Bunny countered, her tone dripping with the kind of pseudo-intellectual confidence designed to make her seem like a bohemian "cool girl."

"I almost killed a kid."

They nodded, believing the lie—one that, I realized, wasn't entirely untrue. I straightened, letting the words settle in the air between us. The two of them exchanged a glance, wide-eyed, twin owls, blinking in silent bewilderment.

"Respect," Brody said, holding out a fist.

I bumped it back.

"Wanna come hang with us at Dinosaur Hill?" Bunny asked.

I had no idea what they were talking about, but I'd never been more excited in my entire life.

I soon learned that Dinosaur Hill was actually the grounds surrounding a mansion that had a sculpture with a life-size metal T. rex. I also discovered that this was where Bunny and Brody went to take cough medicine.

"You ever try Triple C?" Bunny asked, crouched under the thick foliage of succulents, rummaging through her handwoven Peruvian backpack.

"Like for your car?" I asked, genuinely confused.

"You're funny. No, it's cold medicine," she said, lifting up the label of the high-blood-pressure cough-and-cold medicine.

"Oh, I'm not sick," I said. "My voice just kind of sounds like this—"

"No shit," Brody laughed. "This gets you high or something. I saw 'em do it on *Degrassi*. Oh whoa, you kind of look like Paige."

"Thanks?"

Bunny and Brody swigged back a few pills at the same time, almost simultaneously.

"Here, take four at least," Bunny said, popping the tablets into my hand.

As I looked down into my palm, they looked practically microscopic, as if they couldn't possibly matter. I was aware of all the risks and side effects that they had shoved down our throats in D.A.R.E. classes—like lack of judgment and impaired memory—but I was okay with my brain cells eroding. I was good with not remembering some things from the past. I shrugged and threw back the little red tablets with a big gulp of Diet Dr Pepper.

"Now what?" I asked.

"I don't know. . . . Should we take more?" Bunny asked.

"Down the hatch," Brody said, and like a little drug fairy, he plopped the rest into each of our mouths.

Drugs were everywhere in my town: schools, gas stations, parking lots, steakhouses, the beach. While there was part of me that was afraid I'd turn out like Cory, for some inexplicable reason, that made me want to try them even more. The idea that I could get in trouble or fuck up my life was so terrifying that it also felt exhilarating.

Once the effects of the drugs kicked in, and my vision was like a scratched DVD skipping between frames, Brody grabbed a boogie board he'd stolen from the neighbors' yard, hoisting it up before dragging it toward us. His grin was wild, eyes gleaming with reckless excitement.

"All right, get on," he said, nodding toward the steepest part of the hill.

"I think—" The words barely left my mouth before the twins shoved me forward, sending my stomach plummeting.

"This is insane!" I screamed as we slid down the giant sand dune, the world spinning around me.

"Let's do it again," I said after we crashed at the bottom.

"Obviously!" one of the twins shouted back.

We ran to the top, throwing ourselves off the massive hill, until eventually we'd make ourselves sick and barf up pink slime and burst out laughing.

As the days passed, we kept hanging out, mostly just us three. I finally felt like I had a best friend, two, like we were triplets in another life. We exchanged new ways of getting high, things I'd learn from spying on Cory and things Brody had looked up online. I started off slow, popping more and more tablets of Coricidin.

After a while, the Coricidin buzz stopped hitting like it used to. The thrill was gone, and we were left hungry for something else to give us that rush. Brody suggested we go dig around their parents' house. It was my first time going to their house, so I had no idea just how much ground there would be to cover.

Taking in their eight-bedroom, six-bathroom mansion, I started to second-guess they could ever truly consider me their third. Then Brody took me to his room and showed me the entire closet reserved for his wig collection. That was the moment I realized they may have been rich, but being a freak doesn't discriminate.

Out in the garden, we howled with laughter, transformed by our new looks: me in a lavender bob, Brody in a platinum beehive, and Bunny rocking an Ellen DeGeneres–inspired cut. We soared across the garden's paths on roller skates, weaving among perfectly trimmed topiaries, wind chimes, and hydrangeas.

"Your house is incredible," I said, still in awe.

"My mom's a garden ho. Our house was in *Martha Stewart Living*," Brody replied.

Once we'd had our fill, I threw out a new challenge—raiding the spotless bathrooms for anything to up the ante. As I pressed open the mirrored medicine cabinet in the master bath, I found the usual stuff: toothpaste, tweezers, Advil. And then I saw the medicine bottle, with *Vicodin* on the label. Brody and Bunny watched me, a little awed, as I reached for it.

"Oh, I think those were from my dad's root canal," Brody said.

"It's gotta be heavy duty, then."

I lifted it up and examined the bottle. *Don't operate heavy machinery.* Perfect. I wasn't planning on operating a forklift that night. I was good to go.

"May I?" I said, shaking the pill bottle like a maraca.

The twins nodded in unison.

I shook two pills into my hand. I didn't need to get greedy and take them all. I looked at Brody and Bunny. They shrugged. I took a restrained amount. Respectable even. Instead, I put them in my pocket, saving them for the right moment.

I was still buzzing from the Coricidin when I got home. I darted into my bedroom, flung open the closet, and grabbed the red LEGO box I'd had since I was a kid. It usually held my journals, my stash of quarters, and postcards from around the globe. And now, the box would house the stolen medication meant for minor surgeries.

As I put the pills in between postcards, I stared at the white capsules. How could something so small wield so much power? If I really wanted to kill that kid I'd once been, this seemed like my best shot. It was what Cory had chosen. *They turn off the noise,* he'd tell me. I could use the quiet, too.

I briefly thought of Mom and how much it would destroy her to know her youngest son was starting down a path similar to my brother's. But maybe feelings were overrated. The kid Cory had been, the kid I was—we had sadness, shame, anger, despair, excitement, and hope, sometimes all at once. I realized, the only way to stop was to not feel anything at all. So I decided I would keep those pills. I would keep them, and I would take them. Not that night, or even the next, but I was going to take them sometime soon. Curiosity may have killed the cat, but I was no pussy.

6.

Little San Diego Bitch

I found myself avoiding trips to my dad's house as much as possible, because whenever I did go, I would wake up to total quiet. Nana had recently moved out after she met a new boyfriend on a Jewish dating site. I was happy for her, but I missed her presence. Her living with us was what had made the house feel like a home.

Although my dad took pride in his work, it also seemed like he was trying to keep himself busy to stave off his mounting paranoia. His anxieties were unfamiliar to me: Sure, he'd always been a little distant, but the parts of himself he shared with Travis and me were always steady and reliable. Now, we'd watch him shuffle around the house in his hospital scrubs, searching for his always-missing car keys, muttering to himself.

"Everything is so bad. The world's coming apart," he'd say under his breath.

"Why?" I asked.

"What do you mean why? Because I'm going to get sued. I'm

going to get my license revoked, and I'm never going to work again. I'm going to lose everything."

He'd start doing his nervous tick where he put his hand to his mouth, which I took as my cue to get the fuck out of there. Because I was thirteen, I didn't see these as signs of his unraveling depression. All I thought was that he was tired of playing the role of Dad, especially the part where he was supposed to be spending time with me.

So I'd grab my scooter and ride around the industrialized outskirts of Signal Hill with Travis until we'd get hungry for breakfast. We knew just where to go. One family nearby always let us in, always bought into my act, never realizing my hunger had less to do with food.

"I left the stove on in the house, and it filled up with gas," I said, projecting panic. "My dad left for work, and I'm just really freaked out that we'll get carbon monoxide poisoning or something. Can I come stay with you today?"

I didn't say, *I'm scared to go home because my dad ignores me.* Pretending to escape a carbon monoxide tragedy was more fun than my daddy issues.

"Oh, honey," she replied sympathetically, with a hand on her chest. "It's okay. Do you boys want to come in for breakfast?"

I let her hug me and take me inside for a full Sunday brunch: Belgian waffles and poached eggs and extra-crispy bacon. Their whole family sat around the table, holding hands for grace and listening as I spun my fabricated tales.

"I just got past the Hollywood round on *American Idol.*"

One of the kids gasped. Even the father, half distracted by the bacon on his plate, lifted his head.

"Yes, very intense. What else . . . Oh, I spent weeks in the UK, where my uncle . . . Uncle Mike, in fact, was a stand-in for Hagrid in *Harry Potter*. He took me to the set to see Aragog's lair in the dark forest."

The parents had either mastered their poker faces, or acting camp had really been worth my dad's money. Either way, they probably saw right through that lonely little liar. After all, no one leaves the gas on that often.

But telling lies to my neighbors was easy compared to facing the truth at home, or our home adjacent, Hooters. And that Father's Day, my dad, Travis, and I sat through forced small talk, pretending we were just another group of guys there for the wings and waitresses.

"So, how's work been? Any emergency room horror stories?" I asked, but he didn't bite.

"Fine," he started, too tired to fully finish his one-word sentence.

I looked over at Travis, who was too deep in his text conversation with his new girlfriend to contribute.

"Good talk," I said.

Every time I let my guard down with my dad, I was reminded why I put it up in the first place. The waitress stopped by to drop off a pitcher of Coke.

"Did you see her?" I asked, figuring that surely he would give a shit about a hot waitress.

Turns out I was wrong. He wasn't impressed by tiny orange shorts anymore, and thirteen was too old to nuzzle the waitress without it being creepy. Now that I was finally old enough to get his tit fascination, he all of a sudden lost interest. Maybe there was an end to a parent's love. At a certain point, they become exhausted, and the novelty of having a child wears off during the sullen teenage years. I wasn't a cute kid anymore; I was an awkward teen still trying to get his attention.

Sometime that spring, I had accepted that my dad was done with me, but in the weeks leading up to Father's Day, my mom kept trying to convince me otherwise.

"I would rather sit on a knife than be stuck with him," I begged her.

"You and me both, but this might be the last chance you have to fix things. You never know, maybe it'll be like . . . sitting on a butter knife," my mom said.

I relented despite having no faith that we were ever going to fix thirteen years of dysfunction and misunderstanding with a few hours of Buffalo wings and no eye contact. Nothing could make me into a good son and him into a good dad.

Still, there we were, slouched in the same booth under the glow of the TV screens, the smell of fried food thick in the air. A waitress brushed past our table, clearing the one beside us, as I nudged my dad to check her out.

He ignored me. When I nudged him again, he finally responded, "Are girls the only thing that interests you now? You used to be such a curious little boy, what happened?"

"You're going to die alone," I said. "Stick to the SlimFasts, you fat fuck."

I waited for the explosion—some glorious rage that I could push back against, leading us to finally talk. Then we'd bond and he'd apologize for all those distant months and years. Maybe we'd order another round of wings. Instead, he just blinked. Maybe dying alone sounded like a compliment to him. Maybe I should have said, "You'll die surrounded by love and attention." Maybe *that* would have set him off.

Still, he didn't say anything. We finished our meal and went home. Back at his house, I locked myself in my bedroom and did sit-ups and push-ups to burn off some of the discomfort in my body, in my mind. I looked in the mirror and flexed the muscles I was trying to build, my hair freshly box-dyed the same shade as Cory's. I studied my reflection and wondered what it was my father saw when he looked at me. I did more push-ups.

IT WAS PAST midnight when the pounding started at the front door. My eyes shot open. The pounding on the door wasn't just loud—it was unnatural, relentless, like something trying to break in rather than knock. My heart hammered so hard it felt like it might break free of my chest.

Downstairs, I heard my dad answer the door, followed by the rumble of unfamiliar voices. I crept down the hallway, my breath shallow, straining to see what was happening.

Two massive men stood in our doorway. I couldn't make out their faces, but I sensed them looking me up and down.

"Do you want to go the easy way or the hard way?" one faceless man asked.

My throat felt tight, like the words were stuck behind a wall.

"Either way, you're coming with us, Lukas," the other one said.

They knew my name? For one split second, hope rose in my chest. Maybe my dad would step in and stand up for me, protecting me from these kidnappers.

He didn't move a muscle. Didn't say a word.

I stood barefoot on the stairs, wearing an oversize band T-shirt and basketball shorts that felt too loose on my frame, as a realization began to slither down my spine, slow and sickening, causing my knees to shake.

"What's happening? What the fuck did you do?" I asked my dad.

He didn't respond. He wasn't going to stop this. He wanted this.

It had all been a trick. Father's Day weekend was a setup. They were there to take me.

"Dad, don't do this. Please don't do this," I begged, shaking.

My dad kept his eyes trained on the wall behind me, like I wasn't there. The men edged closer, boxing me in.

There was no way out. I glanced at my dad one last time, silently begging him to stop this. To look up at me and to tell these men to fuck off. His gaze never shifted from the wall.

"I'll go the easy way," I said.

They hauled me out the door. I caught one last look at my father, praying he'd snap out of this to see how scared I was. He could help me if he wanted to. This was his chance to make it right. He just stood there.

"You are actually dead to me," I said, trying one last time to hurt him, though I knew it wasn't going to work.

It was pitch-dark outside except for the harsh glow of the garage floodlights as they escorted me to the street. Even the pump jacks had turned off, as if they couldn't bear witness to this betrayal. The men pushed me into an ominous white van.

I'd seen vans like this before on TV. It was the kind of van that comes for every kid. There would be some perv inside with a name like John Bob Garret or Wayne Dacy Jones, waiting to get his hands on me.

Great, here we go again, I thought. *I hope he at least gives me a piece of candy instead of ruining a three-hundred-dollar sleeping bag.*

As the sliding door slammed shut, it marked a finality that made my stomach feel as if I were on a roller coaster, suspended in mid-air. This was it. There was no waking up from this. The engine roared, and we peeled out of the driveway, away from my dad's house, away from Long Beach, toward the dark unknown.

I stared out at the shadowed scenery, squinting as if I could force myself to wake up from this. For one, all I wanted was to be back in my barren bedroom, overlooking the endless pump jacks.

As my heart rate started to steady, it became clear these weren't kidnappers. I knew why they had come. I knew kids who'd been sent away. Tessa was still at her reform school in Utah, and while she was gone she missed everything from the opening of American Apparel to the launch of the iPhone and even that infamous Britney Spears crotch shot. What was I going to miss, too? I was terrified that whatever had happened to her was about to happen to me. But what had I done to warrant this? Cory had done every drug imaginable, and he still got to stay in Encinitas.

I wanted to scream, but nothing came out. Up front, the two men in black murmured to each other, their words drowned by freeway noise. I glanced around, ready to make a desperate move, ready to make a run for it, until I noticed there were no rear handles on the doors. My heart pounded. Even if I had the balls, there was no way out of this.

THE SUN BEGAN to rise.

"Where are you taking me?" I asked.

Silence.

"Hello? Where the fuck are you taking me?" I said, louder. They still didn't answer.

The van turned at an unfamiliar exit toward a camplike complex. It was clear that we weren't in Lake Arrowhead. Instead of lush, green grass and pine trees, it was dead ugly. Bone-dry. The trees were sparse, and instead of air-conditioned cabins, there were cement tables and mold.

They yanked me out of the van and shoved me toward a bathroom that reeked of piss and mildew. The air was sharp with cold. The floor felt metallic and unwelcoming. The men patted me down, their hands digging into my pockets.

"Clothes off," one of them said.

I didn't move.

"You deaf? Clothes off," he said, overenunciating every word.

I scanned around for a way out, but he was posted between me and the rusted door. I peeled off my clothes, cupping my dick with my hands, my last grab for dignity.

He began examining me, with clinical hands that felt as if I were livestock being examined before slaughter. They made me open my legs, my ass cheeks, my mouth—so they could check to see if I was smuggling anything in. I might as well have been Pablo Escobar, not some kid with exactly *two* Vicodin in his LEGO box and no idea what to do with them.

The grotesqueness of popping a squat barefoot in a public restroom barely even registered, because by then, I'd left my body. It didn't belong to me.

Outside, another man handed me a tent and a bag of plastic sticks.

"Build your tent!" he yelled. He threw a backpack as big as I was on the ground in front of me. I tried to put it over my shoulders, but it was awkward and weighed me down.

I didn't know how to build a tent. My dad never taught me.

I WROTE THIS FOR ATTENTION

The closest we came to camping were trips to faux dude ranches, where we'd lounge in cabins decorated with Southwestern motifs and pretend we were "roughing it."

Now I stood there, useless, staring at the crumpled mess of fabric and poles at my feet. Before I could attempt to figure it out, another automaton walked over, leading a ghost-white-haired victim with vacant eyes—a fellow casualty of this place.

"This is Wyatt. You're sharing. Build your tent together."

I'd seen kids like him, eyes empty but sinister, the type of kid you saw on *Dr. Phil* who poisoned their entire families and then laughed about it. Twitchy and full of darkness. And now we were supposed to build a tent together and sleep in it? *I had not had good luck with tents.*

We started fumbling our way through the pieces of the tent. I tried to not stare, but the way he moved was so childlike, as if he were ten years younger than me, even though he was twice my size. Each jittery motion turned my stomach, yet I pressed on, hoping we could finish before dark.

When we caught some momentum, I took a break and gave this kid a once-over; he was so pale he was practically translucent.

"What is this place? Did they kidnap you in the middle of the night, too?" I asked.

"Yeah. You got gooned," he said as he fumbled with the tent.

"What the fuck does that mean?" I asked. I knew words like *shanked* and *the yard* from watching *Prison Break*, but this was another level.

"It's when you get taken in the middle of the night and driven out into the middle of nowhere," Wyatt whispered. "I learned *gooned* when I went to this other wilderness program out in Idaho."

A "wilderness program." Wasn't that where they sent kids who got caught dealing meth or robbing a liquor store? I nodded along, hammering the stake into the ground, unsure of what to do next but too scared to ask.

"Why are you here?" I finally caved.

Maybe he did something stupid like me, and stole a Snickers bar.

"I strangled my brother with a telephone wire," he said, stopping to watch my reaction. "Parents freaked out. We were just playing around, but I guess it caused some damage." He shrugged.

I swallowed and went back to trying to build the tent. Wyatt was getting frustrated with figuring out where the pieces went. Besides the strangling thing, were we kind of the same? Two guys full of anger and with no place to put it. Just when I thought we might be kindred spirits of sorts, he started hitting himself in the head and face.

Nope, not the same. I wasn't into self-inflicted pain, and I was too afraid to ask my brothers to borrow their band T-shirts, let alone attempt to strangle them with a telephone wire.

A counselor was heading our way. I knew it was only about to get worse.

"You'll get to use the showers once a week," the counselor said as he handed me a packet of wet body wipes.

I smiled, figuring he was joking. I didn't expect hours in the bath with Britney, but once a week seemed extreme.

"Wipe that dumb smile off your face," he said.

"With the wipes?" I quipped.

He stared at me and then down at the sham of a tent in front of us.

"You think you're clever, smart-ass?" He leaned into me, and I stood there blankly. "You think you're above the rules, pretty boy? Get to work!"

I wanted to tell him that we'd been trying and that Wyatt had been freaking out and I couldn't build a tent because I was just a bitch from San Diego, but thank you for calling me pretty. I needed him to know that I wasn't insane like Wyatt, who was now in the midst of a full-blown exorcism. I was only flirting with being crazy.

Wyatt howled on the floor until the counselor/drill sergeant/whatever the fuck marched away, demanding that we build the tent "or else!"

"You need to chill," I said to him, "or they'll just keep messing with us."

Instead, he kept moaning and writhing around.

My dad's stern voice slipped out of me. "Wrap it up," I told him.

When I bent down to get back to work on the tent, my vision suddenly blurred. For a moment, I couldn't process what had just happened. Then the sharp, stinging pain registered. Wyatt had hit me across the back with a plank of wood. I turned and looked at him and saw the rage in his eyes. He didn't just want to hurt me. He wanted me dead. Instinct kicked in, I scrambled to my feet and punched him across his face. I'd only ever fought with my brothers like this, and even that had rules. This was feral. Wyatt and I fell to the dirt and kept swinging. After a few seconds, a mess of heavy arms hauled us apart, and the screaming started up again.

"I wouldn't recommend continuing this way. You will break, and we won't put you back together," he shouted, so close to my ear it made my head spin.

"You *will* break," he repeated, quieter this time.

Somehow, we managed to put the tent together. Inside, we made do with the little we had. A sleeping pad, a canteen, and a bug net were the contents of our new "home." But what was more unsettling, though, was how Wyatt could just switch back to normal, as if nothing had just happened.

Wyatt flopped down on his pad. "Not too shabby, huh?" he said, gesturing at our pathetic setup.

"Mhm," I said.

"Hey, fresh slate?" he said, offering his hand out.

I nodded, scared he might kill me in my sleep if I said no.

"How old are you? Why do you look both twelve and forty-two?" he asked.

"I'm thirteen."

"Nice, I'm fourteen, but I was held back, my friends in Boston say I got superpowers," he continued, running a hand through his white hair. "Type one albinism."

He paused, waiting for a reaction, propping himself on a pillow. "You ever been to Boston?"

"Nope," I muttered.

"Oh, well, Boston's a whole other world," Wyatt said. "Every neighborhood's this little microcosm of accents. Man, you'd think you'd stepped into five different countries just walking down the street."

"Sounds hectic," I said, hoping he would quit yammering in that marble-mouthed Boston accent.

"Oh no, it's a rippah, like, even the weather's got personality. Have you ever heard of microclimates?"

"Do you ever deal with macro stuff?" I asked, fucking with him.

"What?"

"Nothing." I waved him off.

I WROTE THIS FOR ATTENTION

THERE WAS NO writing letters to our family. There weren't any phone calls. There were no visiting days. It was as if we'd been erased, cut off from any world beyond camp.

I hated the cold, hated the dampness that clung to our tents in the early hours—those miserable mornings when the counselors stormed through camp banging on pots and pans, yelling "Meds!" like it was some kind of war cry.

Each morning started with a mood stabilizer and a repulsive capsule of valerian root: a sedative herb, with a stench so putrid it felt like a personal attack.

Eventually, I started to get to know the kids around me at "camp," even though we'd been told over and over again: "You're not here to make friends." The counselors repeated it like a mantra. All we were supposed to do were our chores, follow orders, and be the best-behaved versions of ourselves. Anything else was a distraction. They called it "compliance."

There was no ignoring Chase; he was the craziest of the bunch. His eyes were all pupil. He talked too high and too fast about conspiracies. Once, Chase got too close to my face, so I told him he smelled like he ate human shit. That was enough to set him off. He lunged at me, ready to fight. I braced myself, fists up, when Johnny from Jersey jumped in and grabbed Chase, locking his arms behind his back like he had done it a hundred times before.

Johnny was a wall-eyed guido who loved weight lifting, and apparently, doing blow. He liked to tell us he'd overdosed the previous year, when he was fourteen, died, and somehow came back to life. It was obviously a lie, but everyone there lied—and they were all terrible at it.

Every other day, we hiked eight miles through the summer heat. The trail was brutal on its own, but with the sedatives dulling my system, it became a special kind of hell. My legs shook, and my spine felt like it was folding in on itself. Once we were deep in the woods, far from anyone who might hear, it was time for SIC—"sharing is caring."

We'd sit in silence for thirty minutes, scribbling down whatever they assigned, and force us to read out loud. I knew the drill. Years of reading the room and trying to morph into what others expected of me had made me an expert at seeing through the bullshit. The whole point of SIC was to dissect whatever I said, twist it, break me down so they could rebuild me into whatever version of myself they deemed acceptable.

I played along. Told them I knew why I lashed out. "I'm angry because I'm understimulated." The more fucked-up reality was that I didn't know why I was like this. I didn't know why the anger was constantly spilling out of me. I didn't know why I was starting to lash out at my family—or why I couldn't stop.

But if I could give them something that sounded good, something that made them nod and move on, then no one would get hurt. I was good at that. I was a pro at giving people what they wanted. The previous summer, at the Del Mar Fairgrounds, I'd raised my hand at the hypnotist show so he'd pick me to be put under his "spell." After he went through his "magic" and cast his "spell," I felt nothing. Instead of ruining the illusion, I pretended to be in a trance and performed like I was his puppet. I dropped to the ground and milked my chair like it was a cow. I ran around on all fours like a chimpanzee, screeching in panic whenever he snapped his fingers. The crowd clapped and burst out in laughter. Compliance had earned me laughs at the fair. At boot camp, it earned me medication.

Eventually my lies ran dry, and glimpses of my true self began to emerge in SIC.

"I don't know. Guess I . . . lied a lot. Lied to my family. Lied to myself. I get angry, and sometimes I can't control my outbursts, I don't even know what it is that I'm so mad at," I said, surprising myself. It wasn't much of a confession, or a story, but this was the truth.

The others stared at me for a second before someone muttered, "Yeah, me too." None of these kids were the heist criminals they claimed to be. They weren't bad kids. They were just . . . lost. Trying to puff themselves up because it felt safer than feeling small.

The sergeant called out, "You're on dinner duty," he said, handing me plates and a ladle.

When I got up, Johnny slapped me on the back and whispered, "That was a nice share man. Simple's good."

Dinner was the same every night; we'd eat animal parts from a Kirkland bag. We'd cook them over the fire, as if cavemen had Costco. No seasoning, just a shoulder of a chicken thrown over the flames for every meal.

The counselors at this camp had real names, it turned out, and most of them had graduated from boot camps like this only to come back and put us all through the same hell they went through. It was like a pyramid scheme for delinquents. One of them, Ian, was the biggest narc of them all. Lanky and petty, he loved his power trips, standing over us as we scrubbed the toilets.

"You missed a spot," he'd say, with a sinister smirk.

The drill sergeants, however, all had the same name: "Sir."

We called them our keepers. The keepers would show up when the counselors couldn't keep us in line. They'd scream at us or call us pussies. They'd demand a hundred push-ups. That part I liked; I was the first to comply. At least it would help me lose more of my baby fat.

I refused to break. All I wanted was to sleep in my own bed. I wanted to go to the beach and be with the twins and eat a California burrito. Maybe I was just a little San Diego bitch, after all. But dammit, I wanted the creature comforts of Encinitas. I clung to those thoughts like a lifeline.

Not breaking was my ticket out.

Like a prisoner of war, I tallied the days I'd been there in the notebook they'd given me. Some days slipped through the cracks, and I'd lose count. I had no idea when I'd get to go home. We were around halfway through summer—maybe I had another half to go? Surely they wouldn't keep me until I was eighteen.

"Why can't you just tell us when we're going home?" I'd ask, trying my best to not sound weak.

They would roll their eyes, pissed they had to repeat themselves.

"If you start behaving, we'll tell you when you can go home."

My mind played a loop: *I'll never forgive my dad. Mom would lose her shit if she knew I was in a place like this.*

Every single second felt like I was a breath away from breaking. If I could just tell Mom what was going on, she'd come for me. She'd make this nightmare end, just like she'd done for Cory so many times before. She'd save me, too.

MAMIE, OUR WEEKLY life coach, had a sinister undercurrent. She said she was from the middle of California, but she had an affect to her voice that was unplaceable. She was a blank slate who could've been from anywhere.

"What goals do you have?" she asked, pacing in front of all six of us, hands clasped behind her back like some kind of motivational speaker.

I WROTE THIS FOR ATTENTION

"Let's reframe that. Where do you see yourself in five years?" she pressed on, blinking too often in between each question.

Wyatt raised his hand, cutting through the silence.

"Yes, thank you, good sir," she said, pointing at him in a sickly sweet tone.

"I'll be dead in two." Wyatt laughed maniacally.

"Let's hope not. Johnny, what about you, sir?"

"Join the circus. That shit sounds litty," Johnny said, fist-pumping Mike.

I started drowning everything out. I couldn't think about the future, beyond my dream of going home.

"Today we are going to make a vision board for our futures so we can see our path forward with a sharper focus," Mamie said as she handed out magazines, child-safe scissors, and glue sticks.

I started to cut out letters and paste them into *good person*, *wife and kids*, and other half-truths. As I pasted the letters into place, a plan for my immediate future came into sharp focus. I had an idea—my path to freedom, which Mamie had handed to me on a silver platter.

Help me. I'm here by accident. I copy and pasted together, searching the pages of *TIME* and *National Geographic* for every last digit of her phone number. *In danger. Please call my mom. 760-500-0150.*

It was the best I'd felt since I'd arrived, one singular moment where I felt like myself: scheming and trying to find a way out. I put the SOS notes in my pocket and pretended to listen to Mamie the life coach ramble for the rest of the activity.

That night, I waited for the camp to quiet down. Wyatt rustled next to me in the tent, and I strained to hear if everyone else had gone to sleep. The minutes dragged on. My eyes were wide open, and I itched to get moving, ready to run like hell.

When the place finally went quiet, I took off with a flashlight. It was wet and cold, but adrenaline carried me. I sprinted the whole way. I didn't have a destination. Just anywhere but where I was.

When I got to the campground, I saw a row of RVs. I took out the few SOS letters I had made and stuffed them in the slit inside the door of one of the trailers. In my scared-as-shit teenage mind, it was more logical than knocking and asking for help. I convinced myself that there was hope. I was going to get out of there. My mom was going to find out where I was and come save me.

THE NEXT MORNING felt different. The RV owners must have called my mom by then. She was probably on her way to get me. It was only a matter of time before I was free.

At breakfast, the sun's harsh light seared into my skin. I played the role of a hypernormal kid, and focused on my powdered eggs and oatmeal. I tightened my jaw, straining to not break into a giant grin. I had beat the system. I had won. I glanced around me with pity at all the boys who had to stay put. After a few weeks getting to know them I didn't understand why most of them were there. Wyatt and I locked eyes, he gave me a slight smile. I nodded back. Even Wyatt seemed like a good kid who was just overly medicated and not getting the help he needed.

The day started as usual with our morning lessons, some religious verse or a passage from a twelve-step manual. Our counselor Ian pulled out some papers to read to us. But when he unfolded the stack, it wasn't the usual handbooks.

No. No. No. No. No.

"Do you want to explain this?" he asked, holding my SOS note.

"Explain what? I don't know what that is." I shrugged, wishing

I WROTE THIS FOR ATTENTION

I could disappear. Some narc from the campground had narced on me to the head narc.

"That's your mom's phone number, right?"

The other kids all gave me looks or held back laughter that meant, *You're so fucked*, but I barely had time to register this before the drill sergeant appeared, already screaming. I hadn't even seen him coming.

He yelled in my ear.

"You think you're clever? You think these people don't all know why you're here? You think they don't know you're a fucking liar?"

I wouldn't break. I had worked so hard. Been strong for so long. My lip started to quiver and tears brimmed in my eyes. The last thing I wanted was for the instructors to know how weak I was, had always been. Now it was confirmed.

"Get your stuff," the drill sergeant said. Like the little San Diego bitch I was, I obeyed my orders, and I left the group. We hiked out into the wilderness, away from everything. For miles he didn't say a word. Just me and him until finally we were alone. He went back to his beratement, and I tried my best to tune it out.

"You're on your own now, no lies, no distractions," he droned on and on, until, finally, he was done and left me there alone.

I looked up at the sky. An eagle swooped down into the valley. It was empty, raw—almost peaceful. The serenity amid all the chaos. I heard the faint sounds of a far-away engine. I looked up at a plane overhead, a reminder of the world continuing on as it always had.

I took off my backpack and put the tent together. If getting kidnapped from my dad's house had taught me anything, it was how to build a tent. I collapsed onto my sleeping bag and tried not to lose it. My heart pounded in my ears. I focused on breathing.

My heart started to slow down. I was scared and weak, but I was finally alone.

For a moment, I was calm. And then it all came apart. *Why didn't my dad want me? Would anyone ever want me? Why can't I accept that my lot in life was to be alone?* I wondered to myself until the thoughts became too loud, too overwhelming, and I needed to numb out.

The only thing that made sense was to jerk off.

As I pleasured myself, I thought back to the tent from the previous summer. It was like I was right back there. I was in that teepee, just before the counselor told me and that girl exactly how he wanted us to touch each other. Before he joined in. My face heated with the shame of remembering that night, and I released. Humiliation had officially entered my teenage spank bank.

In the morning, the drill sergeant returned to collect me. I followed him back to the camp, knowing the only option was to comply. I did their lessons. I ate their bagged chicken. I went on their hikes. Whatever they told me to do, I did it and shut up.

MY LAST DAY finally arrived. We were told our families were on the way to pick us up. When I saw my mom's minivan pull down the dusty winding roads, a nostalgic calm settled deep in my chest. I was so glad it wasn't my dad. I was still so fucking pissed at him. I ran toward her and hugged her as tight as I could. I hadn't seen her or heard her voice in so long, I was worried I'd forgotten it. She looked exactly as I remembered. The same feeling washed over me as when I saw her after my first day of kindergarten—an overwhelming need for her embrace, the kind that made me crawl all over her like a rabid squirrel the moment we were reunited again.

I WROTE THIS FOR ATTENTION

I didn't say my goodbyes. I just got my notebook and got the fuck out of that place. On the drive home, everything outside of camp felt amplified, heightened. After months in a tiny tent, my mom's minivan seemed enormous—too big, too fast. The cracked sidewalks and rows of strip malls with flickering neon signs looked like they were warping in the heat, the world distorting around me. We stopped for powdered doughnuts at the gas station, and the sweetness of the packaged foods felt like a backhanded slap. Even the car radio was too loud. My mom put on P!NK's "U + Ur Hand," but it just sounded like more shouting.

In the car, I kept reaching for my mom's arm as I told her about the past two months. The screaming, the bags of chicken, the fights. How scared I was. How I tried to send her a message but it was intercepted. I needed her to know that I tried. She listened and kept her eyes focused on the road.

"I missed you so much, it broke my heart, I just can't have you going down the same path as your brother."

"What are you talking about?" I asked, my breath tightening.

"I found those pills in your room," she said, her voice starting to crack. "It killed me doing that to you, but I didn't know what else to do, I was so worried."

That fucking snake.

She'd been in on it. It hadn't just been my dad. She'd done this to me, too. The rage within me made me feel capable of doing anything. I started screaming.

"How could you fucking do this to me?"

She shook her head and pleaded with me to stop, then pulled the car over. She turned to face me, and her expression contorted into a look I'd never seen on anyone before.

"We're not going backward, Lukas."

Her lips snarled, but her eyes watered. The expression said it all: She couldn't handle another bad kid. That my brother was killing her. That boot camp was worth it if it would get me to comply. So I decided: We'd go home, and I'd be a good boy. I'd pretend that I'd changed and be the polite, curious, nice boy they wanted me to be. Whatever they'd tell me to do, I'd do it.

But deep down, I was already making plans. I was going to become their biggest fucking nightmare.

7.

Gas, Grass, or Ass

If you google *North County San Diego*, you'll find photo after photo of perfect California beaches stretching below steep, dramatic cliffs. Zoom in, and you'll see towering palm trees, surfers in the Pacific Ocean waves, and bonfires crackling in the sand. Zoom in just a little closer, and you'll see a bunch of bored fourteen-year-olds losing their fucking minds.

There's got to be something radioactive in the water, something that can take a bunch of otherwise normal kids and turn them into inebriated little demons. Or maybe it's not the water, maybe it's the heat; maybe it's because everything is the same color: tan. Whatever it is, there's an unmistakable shift that happens at fourteen, when San Diegan kids seem to transform overnight, that sends them all to the bottle.

My bottle started as cold and cough meds, but when I turned fifteen I graduated to Gatorade. Or rather, Gatorade-adjacent. Geographically, not metaphorically. The Gatorade in the Rite Aid at El Camino Real sat catty-corner to the bottles of Popov and

Captain Morgan lined up like little soldiers ready to do their duty and get me wasted for the cheapest amount possible. That's what I was after. But cheap wasn't good enough. I wanted free.

Stealing in North County was hard because everyone in North County stole. All the time. Everywhere. The stores all knew the game, the employees knew the tricks, and they watched like burnt-out hawks. To get what I wanted, I had to be crafty. Creative. Beyond reproach.

Clack. Clack, clack. Clack.

Clack. Clack.

Clack.

The sound of my cleats, from my one-month stint of soccer at the YMCA, echoed off the tiles as I made my way down aisle after aisle, fake sweat dripping from my curls and streaking down my jersey. An Adidas duffel bag and a disheveled, exhausted-from-an-intense-game haze in my eyes completed my look. I'd stalk the rows of employees stocking the shelves with Twizzlers and tampons, making a subtle show of just how terribly I needed to quench my thirst with a Glacier Freeze Gatorade.

I played my part perfectly—that of a jovial, healthy but parched kid devoted to a life of sports and clean competition. I played my part so well that even if someone rounded the corner as I shoved handles of alcohol into my soccer bag, they still wouldn't have pegged me for a thief. But I wasn't going to get too cocky. Because that is how you get caught. The whole operation had to go down quick, quick and dirty.

Before there was Uber, there was Eleanor. Eleanor was a taxi driver in town who resembled a shrunken Amish apple doll. She had a bird's nest for hair and lived out of her yellow cab and ran her business like a Greek fisherman, a true barter system. "Gas, grass, or ass, nobody rides for free" was not just a bumper sticker to Eleanor; it was gospel.

I'd pay for my Gatorade, regaling the clerk with tales of my grueling game. Occasionally, I'd even throw them a cheery wave goodbye, and the sensors would activate. My walkout turned into a run-out, cleats clacking, alarms blaring, as I bolted through the threshold. I jumped into the back of Eleanor's car, smacking the seat like it could rev the engine as I screamed, "Go, go, go!"

On the floor of the car, Brody and Bunny would lay waiting for me nervously. As soon as I got back from boot camp, we fell seamlessly into our old dynamic. All that mattered to us was making up for lost time by getting as fucked-up as often as possible.

"Do you think they're going to follow us?" Brody asked one afternoon while crouched in the bitch seat of Eleanor's taxi.

"Who cares? Look," I said as I opened the bag. His eyes lit up.

I had retrieved the goods.

When I unzipped that duffel bag, I was exhilarated. A thrill shot through me; the world had just shifted, and I was finally in the driver's seat—metaphorically speaking, of course, because physically, I was still sprawled across the floor of a yellow cab that smelled like incense and old perfume. But none of that mattered. I had purpose now.

Eleanor would step on it, tires screeching as we peeled out of the parking lot, the alarms still wailing behind us.

We exhaled in unison, cackling, and off to safety we'd go.

"Zip that shit up! I hate that damn sound!" Eleanor called back. She meant the glass bottles clinking against one another. I hurried to yank the zipper shut, fingers still vibrating with adrenaline.

As soon as we were far enough away, she'd pull over, and we'd give her a cut of our loot plus some weed for good measure.

Although Eleanor was well into her seventies, she had somehow become one of us. Beyond just being our getaway driver, she played an essential role in fostering the carefree lifestyle we were creating. She reminded us—constantly—to enjoy our youth while we still could, to savor the freedom before life sank its teeth in.

It was a magical time. I wasn't worried about my future or money. I had a few gigs besides my life as a thief—don't get me wrong, I wasn't *all* bad. Freshman year of high school also brought my first job at a Jewish retirement home, where my duties mostly consisted of playing referee between feuding war survivors over games of mah-jongg. And then, of course, there was my summer job of pushing kids around on a surfboard in the shallows and calling it *lessons*.

But I liked stealing the best. It felt like the only thing I was good at. Life was simple: I had my friends, and life was just getting high and hanging out at the beach until the sun went down.

When we finally needed a place to sleep after a day of aimlessly roaming the streets, I'd text Cory, asking him if we could crash at his place. He would write back incoherently, but whatever combination of letters and numbers, the message was clear: He was excited to see me.

That's how Eleanor dropped us at our last stop of the night: Cory's new place at the Lucky Clover. Inside the trailer, Brody and Bunny plopped themselves down on the carpet and started playing *Mario Kart*. We were barefoot, covered in sand, and feeling every bit of freedom that came with the last day of freshman year.

Next to us, Cory was on the sofa, skin and bones, intermittently nodding off. I hadn't seen him in weeks. He looked like he'd aged five years. I tried not to stare too long. My eyes strained to look at anything else.

"Hey . . . Oh, what's up, Luke . . . What are you doing here?" he asked.

"We were texting like ten minutes ago—"

I was interrupted by some loud shuffling coming from his bedroom.

"Who's here?" I asked.

"That's—" Cory said, snapping his fingers, trying to remember their name.

Cory sat blankly searching for his words on his burnt-sienna futon covered in burnt-sienna cigarette stains. I pretended to focus on *Mario Kart*, my thumbs mindlessly pressing buttons, but my eyes stayed on him in the periphery. A lit cigarette dangled from his lips, and the embers and ash kept falling on his lap. He was so out of it he didn't seem to notice or care. He mumbled half sentences and half names while he grabbed a plastic container in the shape of a coffin off the table. It was where he kept his stash.

I knew how much pain my brother's addiction brought my mom, but I still clung to that version I'd idolized. More than anything, I just needed him to know that I could hang, that I wasn't fazed by any of it. That no matter what the circumstances were, I could fit in. I could belong in his new life.

A voice called out from the back room, barely audible over the hum of the video games. With Tessa still away, he'd started seeing some new girl whose name barely stuck in anyone's mind, let alone his. She was a stand-in girlfriend with a tacky Mohawk who spoke in a muffled monotone. As soon as he opened the coffin, she stirred, crawling out of the back room like a dog who just heard the treat jar open.

Cory pulled out a little plastic baggie and a syringe while I pretended to be transfixed by my Luigi's attempts to win the race.

In the corner of my eye, I could see Cory take a burnt spoon and hold it up to a syringe from the table. He still looked like he had when we were kids, doing his science experiments and building his machines, carefully taking out one tool at a time.

As Cory took the torch and held it under the blackened spoon, the room filled with an unfamiliar scent but one I would, for the rest of my life, recognize. That same burnt, sweet smell of rotten cotton candy. I had seen heroin on TV on *Intervention*, but this was different. This was my older brother, and I was inches away from him. I'd never seen someone actually shoot heroin into their veins. Watching him, I saw the weight of his world drop off his shoulders the moment the needle punctured his thin, pale skin.

I was frightened but mesmerized. Brody, Bunny, and I sat there, posturing. Acting as if we didn't just witness something that would stick with us forever. His eyelids fluttered heavily like curtains, until they shut and he let out a sigh. He looked peaceful. It was like all of a sudden, everything he carried with him, all his heartbreak over Tessa and all his anguish over his dad, just floated away from his consciousness. I kept pretending to play the game even though it had been minutes since I lost the race.

When the Mohawked girlfriend eventually carried Cory to bed, I sat in silence with Brody and Bunny on the floor of the living room. We stared at one another. I hoped we could just close our eyes and erase the night by morning. Then, through the paper-thin walls, my brother and Mohawk lady started having belligerent sex. The slapping of flesh sounded like two fish flopping on a dock but somehow popped the heaviness that made the room feel so leaden. We broke into laughter, grateful for the white noise of my brother and his girlfriend's exaggerated sounds of sex.

"She sounds like a whiny Weimaraner," Brody whispered.

I started laughing maniacally, uncontrollably.

"Okay, it's not *that* funny," Bunny chimed in.

"My brother is literally fucking a dog," I said still laughing.

"It's not that funny," Brody lilted with his lilting drawl.

"She's a dog," Bunny and I said in unison.

"It's a double entendre, get it?" I said.

"No!" Brody laughed.

When we woke up, we were different. Bunny, Brody, and I had done our fair share of drugs since we started high school, but it wasn't about escaping or sinking into some deep sadness. We were in it for the laughter, for the wigs, for the weightlessness. When time was suspended and things didn't have to make sense. That was the point.

Whatever remaining innocence we had left died the night before. Getting high couldn't erase the reality of my dad retreating further into himself, or my mom's constant state of distress over everything. And it certainly couldn't dull how much I missed Tessa.

I had thought about Tessa every day since she was sent away almost two years prior, but that night in the trailer made the ache almost unbearable. Sometimes, I'd sit around and count the things I loved about her most to make sure I hadn't forgotten them. Like how crafty she was, sewing her clothes, painting in the backyard, or making gifts from scratch. I followed her everywhere, hoping her craftiness would rub off on me. I went with her whenever she got new piercings, though I'd spend most of the time with my eyes shut. She'd laugh as the needle went into whatever body part she was perforating that day and say she loved it. Just like she loved getting her blood drawn. She said it was comforting. It reminded her that she was alive.

My mom had become hyperfixated on Tessa, too. She was desperate to let Tessa know how dearly we missed her. For my mom, love was always best expressed through grand gestures. Cory and Mohawk had called it quits, so my mom hatched a plan to take a family road trip to Hurricane, Utah, to find Tessa. We weren't trying to undermine Tessa's recovery, we just had to let her know how much we loved her. We had to remind her that she wasn't alone, and, hopefully, seeing her again would remind Cory he wasn't as well.

"Let's just start driving and we'll figure it out," my mom said, pitching us all on the idea. "We can stop at Buffalo Bill's on the way and ride the roller coaster!"

My mom called the rehab facility, asking for a tour under the pretense of possibly checking in her own son. Without any other thought, my mom, Sean, Cory, Travis, and I all packed our bags and piled into her Nissan Quest. We were like a SoCal version of *Little Miss Sunshine*, but instead of a beauty pageant, our final destination was a Mormon rehab facility.

This was our grand adventure. Our family bonding time.

"Hey, Mom?" Travis asked, not looking up from his phone.

"Yes, honey," she answered, eyes on the road.

"Why are we going to Utah?" he asked, apparently having missed the memo.

"What do you mean, Trav? We're having fun," my mom said, smiling out the window.

Sean snorted from the seat beside her. My mom smacked him in the arm.

"We're gonna end up on the news," Travis mumbled.

"Would you shut up?" my mom snapped back at him.

"No, really, though . . . When we get to Utah, what are we going to do that's, like, fun?" Travis asked.

"We're breaking into a rehab," my mom said matter-of-factly.

My mom whipped her head back around to look at us. The only one unfazed was Cory, whose forehead was pooling with sweat. We were six hours into the drive, meaning it had been at least six hours since he last used.

"Oh," Travis replied, having finally looked up from texting his girlfriend. "For real?"

My mom sighed.

"Yeah, basically." She shrugged.

"Can we go snowboarding after?" Travis asked.

After a quick stop at Buffalo Bill's at the Nevada border, so Mom could play slots and Travis and I could get stoned and ride the roller coaster that cut through the casino, we eventually landed in Hurricane, Utah, nearly five hundred miles from North County.

As we pulled up, I could see cows grazing the dehydrated brown grass in front of the school's aged dorms, and the towering spiked gates around the campus came into focus. *This was so much worse than wilderness camp. This was a fucking prison for teens.*

Travis, Sean, and I waited in the van while Mom and Cory approached the admissions office. Inside, my mom gave her spiel about wanting a tour for her addict son—which wasn't really a lie—but when they led her through only the boys' side of the facility, she realized she had backed herself into a corner.

"You know," she told the employee leading the tour, "I *also* have a daughter . . . Ashley, who might need to come here, too. Can I see the girls' side, perhaps?"

"Sure, but your son's going to have to wait in the lobby."

Soon enough, Mom was being led around the women's side of the teenage penitentiary. After walking through a seemingly endless maze of rec rooms and classrooms, she bumped right into

Tessa, who looked nearly unrecognizable in her drab, shapeless uniform. Her big smile and lip ring were gone, and the bright red dye she'd loved so much had been washed out of her hair, leaving it dull and faded. Their eyes met, and in that instant, both hearts shattered simultaneously.

"Hi, sweetheart," my mom said, trying to contain herself.

"I love you. Please, please, get me out of here. Take me back home with you," Tessa said, breaking free from a pack of girls in the same uniform and with the same despondent look on their faces.

"Oh, sweetie. You're okay," my mom said, trying to signal to Tessa not to make a scene.

"I'm not! Nothing about this place is okay. Please, I'm begging you," Tessa continued between tears.

My mom's voice wavered as she tried to sound reassuring, but her words landed carefully. "I'm sure your family back home just wants you to know that they love you very much and miss you just as much, sweetie, I bet—"

Before my mom got a chance to finish, the staff pulled Tessa into a windowless room and locked the door. Another staffer grabbed Mom, tugging her along toward the office. The echo of Tessa's sobs ricocheted all the way down the hall.

They shoved Mom into a barren room with a loud click as the door latched behind them. Tessa's sobs vanished behind the door, leaving only a hollow silence.

"We know what you're doing."

"What am I doing? I'm simply touring a place to try to help my child."

"If you don't leave, we're calling the police."

"Go ahead. I'd love to see you try."

Before they could, my mom bolted out of the room and rushed toward the lobby. Cory, who had been sitting waiting, looked up at her, confused.

"Why are we running?" he asked, looking between her and the exit.

"Just move, Cory!" she snapped, before rushing out the doors and straight back toward us.

"Drive!" she screamed as she and Cory jumped into our open-doored van.

"Go! Go! Go!"

As the doors swung shut, Sean floored it, hauling ass out of town and onto the freeway. We slid through lane after lane as the sirens' echoes became closer, closer . . . and then almost as quickly as they came, they faded off in the distance.

After the adrenaline wore off, Sean pulled over. We sat by the side of the road, and Mom told us what had happened. She'd recorded the whole tour on a recorder she smuggled in her purse, and she played their conversation so we could hear Tessa tell us how much she loved and missed us.

After the recording ended, silence settled over us, thick and unspoken. We sat on the edge of the valley, staring out at the towering red rock and endless stretches of sandstone, each of us lost in thought. The view was stunning, almost unreal, but none of us could appreciate it.

As the sound of a distant siren blared again, we laughed, imagining the manhunt for a family of lunatics that tried to lie their way into a fundamentalist Mormon rehab.

"I never thought we'd be the kind of family that would break into a rehab," Sean mused aloud.

"She didn't really break in; she lied her way in," I added.

My mom shot me a sharp look. "Really? We didn't do anything wrong."

"Is that what you're gonna tell the cops?" Travis asked innocently. My mom's lip started to twitch, and I could see a laugh threatening to break through.

I looked at my mom, at Sean, at Travis and Cory. This dysfunctional little family hiding out from the cops in a canyon in the middle of Utah. They were far from perfect, but they were mine.

Eventually we got on the road and headed home, back to "paradise."

Cory went back to his trailer. Travis went back to his girlfriend. Sean went back to buying more shit. Mom went back to worrying.

I went back to getting high and searching for something else to fill the void.

8.

TRUST NO BITCH$

Months had passed since the heist mission at the Mormon rehab facility. Life settled into a new, uneasy rhythm. We spent what felt like an eternity waiting for Tessa to come back, unsure if it would ever happen. Then, on her eighteenth birthday, she showed up on our doorstep, luggage at her feet. My entire family felt the shift. Maybe, just maybe, things could be different this time.

Having Tessa living with us made us all better. It was like we were performing for God, as though if we all just did the right thing and played the role of "nice family," maybe we would get to keep her this time. Maybe we'd play the parts so convincingly that soon we'd become that nice family we were merely pretending to be.

Cory, in particular, was a brand-new man. That's actually what my mom and Sean started saying as they'd watch Cory cook family meals and clear the dishes: "It's like having a brand-new man around the house."

Both Cory and Tessa got clean and stayed clean. They got his-and-hers jobs, the cashier and line cook, respectively, at an In-N-

Out by the 405 freeway. Instead of living in Cory's trailer, they stayed with us. I'd come home from school to a full house, finding them laughing and dancing in the kitchen as they cooked dinner for the whole family.

"So, how was everyone's day?" Mom would ask a little too brightly, as we sat down for dinner.

"Busy day, work was a lot of cooking, and then came over here for . . . more cooking," Cory said.

"But we made it through; we're not borrowing anxiety from the future anymore, right?" Tessa would say, sounding as if she'd aged a decade in the two years she'd been gone.

"Right," Cory said. "How's it taste? Beer-can chicken—your favorite, right, Luke?"

"I've never had this in my life," I said. My mom lightly kicked me under the table. "Tastes amazing, though."

We'd pass the salt and ask each other about our days, about our lives, and it felt mundane in the best way possible. For almost twelve blissful months, our lives felt whole. We were suddenly a complete unit that did idyllic things like family ski trips, Fourth of July barbecues, and haunted hayrides on Halloween. It was perfect—so, of course, it couldn't last.

I was high sitting at the kitchen table, doing homework, when the call came.

"Hello, Paulina speaking," my mom said into the phone in her overly sweet real-estate-agent voice.

I was staring at a geometry problem, the sine, cosine, tangents swimming on the page in front of me, my eyes nearly crossed with concentration. I listened, waiting for the unusually elongated pause to end as she stood frozen.

Then, my mom screamed.

I WROTE THIS FOR ATTENTION

The phone fell to the floor, and she followed it down, crumbling into a sobbing heap on the linoleum floor. I had heard my mom do this before. Many times. We'd get this call when one of my aunts would get frail and sallow and bald. And every time, my mom ended up in the same place: on the kitchen floor, grief curling her into the same familiar heap.

The world tilted just slightly, flipping through the mental album of my mother's family: who had I not seen recently, who had I seen, who'd had the look. And then . . .

"Tessa. Not Tessa. Please, God, not Tessa," my mom cried out.

Tessa wasn't even sick. Whatever this call was about, it couldn't have been about our Tessa. She was just here. She was fine—

"Tessa's dead."

My brain short-circuited. Tessa wasn't using. She was healthier than ever. My mind raced, replaying the last time I said bye to her, how happy and together she looked. Not like the frail, fledgling young girl who showed up on her birthday, shell-shocked by the world. Or the pallid, withdrawn person she'd become in the months before she got sent away. She was just Tessa again, the sunshiny self she'd been when we all fell in love with her in the first place.

My mom wailed from the floor, raw and guttural. The words were there, but I couldn't make sense of them. My brain refused to process, stuck in the space between hearing and understanding. I just reacted, mirroring her grief.

I knelt beside her, rubbing her back, holding her tight as her sobs wracked through both of us. My mom choked out the details—*a car accident—a hit-and-run—dead on impact*. She was only nineteen years old.

My eyes started to sting, but it still didn't feel real. It felt like I was floating just outside myself, watching someone else's life fall apart.

Then the tears came.

And they didn't stop.

I cried and cried, not just mourning for Tessa but also mourning the version of my family that she took with her.

"I love you, Mom," I whispered into her ear. "I don't know how this is real—"

"How—how are we going to tell Cory?" she cut me off, shaking her head.

My stomach sank with dread, and I couldn't answer her. I just shook my head, letting my tears fall.

Lying on the floor, so many images of Tessa came back to me that they started to splinter. In one fragment, I saw her leading me through the aisles of Hot Topic, laughing as she threw the right band tee playfully at my head. Another memory of us, just weeks ago, playing *Guitar Hero* in the living room and singing along. The images started collapsing in on another as my fear that they'd wind up as memories of this family we once were began to encroach. The fear that we were going back to what we were when she was gone.

And I was right. We all changed back to who we were before, but maybe this time, even worse. Mom, a gambler; Cory, an addict; Travis, a recluse; Sean, the spendthrift; and me, an all-out liar.

Tessa's parents didn't want any version of us at the funeral. They held a private ceremony, leaving us to say our goodbyes at the roadside vigil that had been erected in her honor. In the days after Tessa's death, friends and onlookers had begun leaving prayer candles, lilies, and photographs in her memory. I left a bouquet of sunflowers I'd purchased from the Vons across the street. Mom couldn't contain her sadness. She stood, hugging herself, letting her tears fall down her face unabashedly. Cory could only stare, smoking his cigarette, trying his best to remain stoic. We exchanged quick words and prayers, but they all rang hollow. The one true emotion we felt that day was anger—from being excluded, sure, but the anger at having lost her.

A week later, Mom and Sean went back to work while I started ditching school and spending my days living out of my bedroom. It was a perfect existence. I sat there high, staring at the ceiling, existing in a strange, suspended state alternating between getting high and jerking off just so I could still feel anything at all.

Between my mom's hoarding and Sean's excessive spending on random shit, our house had never looked particularly organized. With Tessa gone, it crossed over to grimy. We'd all developed an aversion to going into the kitchen—even a glimpse of the pans she'd cook that beer-can chicken in was enough to draw tears. So we avoided it entirely, surviving on takeout, the empty boxes piling up in lopsided towers by the doorway.

Cory wasn't around much, but when he was, he was at war with the world, including himself. He spent his days using again. Nodding off, barely conscious, because at least then he didn't have to remember. Any hope I ever had that he could change, that we could all collectively change, was now long gone. The only person I could attempt to change was myself.

At this point, I had killed so many versions of myself that I was sure there was some sketchy, abandoned warehouse party somewhere where they were all hanging out, laughing at my lack of identity and drinking bottom shelf tequila and pouring one out in my honor. I continued to scrape away anything that reminded me of who I was, of who I was with Tessa. Anything creative, sensitive, or artistic, I discarded. I leaned into a heavy "hell yeah, brother" cadence and made my voice resonate deeper than ever before.

I smoked all day and all night and did whatever else I could find. Weed and mushrooms gave way to pills and powders. I swore I would never shoot up, and I kept my promise because I was too scared I'd end up like Cory. Everything else was fair game. I loved getting high. I loved the warm feeling in the center of my chest, filling the hole where the memory of Tessa otherwise burned hot. Everything seemed easier, and something felt comfortable about being a "bad kid." I had stooped so low at the bottom, and I quite liked it there. After all, at least when you got to the bottom, you knew where the bottom was.

Even as I embraced my new identity, I stayed close to my mom. Any resentment over boot camp disappeared after Tessa died—there were bigger things to be angry about. Besides, I knew it would break her if I ended up like Cory. Deep down, she knew I was acting out but would never go too far. So we'd fight, scream, and then, two minutes later, everything was fine, and we would sit together comfortably and rot the day away—our favorite pastime.

Some might call it wallowing, but we called it healing. On Sundays, when all my friends would still be hanging out, I'd come up with some excuse to bail. Without fail, I would shuffle into her room, cocooned in my white comforter where I'd find her waiting for me, curled up in bed with our dogs. I'd crawl in beside her, still coming down from a weekend of ecstasy and no sleep, and lie in her lap so she could scratch my scalp. The only light in the room emanated from the TV, playing the most important show to grace television screens this century: *Rock of Love with Bret Michaels*.

The contestants on the show looked like Sims characters who had somehow stumbled out of the digital world, their clothes a strange combination of neon, animal prints, and way too much hair gel. They were always so inebriated it seemed that they were all speaking in Simlish.

"I can't understand a single thing they're saying. It's just drunken gibberish," my mom said.

"I know. I love it."

"Me too." Mom nodded solemnly.

This show had us in a chokehold. There was something so therapeutic about watching these spray-tanned vixens pretend to be attracted to Bret and his toupee. The girl who ate Doritos, vomited, and then made out with Bret Michaels became my new obsession. I spoke like the contestants, working their catchphrases into my vocabulary. "Don't threaten me with a good time" became my life mantra.

I found myself wanting Sundays to last forever; I wanted to live in the world of the show. The more I watched, the more I became enamored by the idea of love. I wanted to experience love as quickly as possible. I was, and always will be, a love addict and a bit of a toxic romantic. I could find romance in anything, anyone— even in the absurd, destructive reality TV version of it. Where could I find my own Doritos girl?

Travis had a girlfriend, Cory had experienced true love, and even my dad had some mystery mistress who nobody talked about. I wanted more than anything to have someone to call mine, or to have multiple people to call mine, just to parade around like Bret Michaels did. Thus, the hunt for my rock of love was on.

LIKE ALL GREAT love stories, mine began in a 7-Eleven parking lot. When my friends and I weren't spooky suburban teens at parties or raves, we were getting fucked up in someone's car outside the 7-Eleven. And that night was no different, until I turned and saw *her*. Time stood still as I watched her glide across the parking lot, drinking a red Slurpee, wearing a bandanna as a shirt. The second I spotted her, I knew what all those reality TV shows were about. She was the most beautiful person I'd ever seen. She had a delicate, almost feline face, and the kind of eyes that pin you in place, like a needle in a voodoo doll. Forget *Rock of Love*. She was the star of her own reality show in my mind. She was my Doritos girl, my Lindsay Lohan–esque archetype of beauty with a lower back tattoo that read "TRUST NO BITCH$." She was a freshman, and I was a sophomore, but God was she ahead of her time. Her name was Kaylee, and I needed to be in her orbit.

She had moved to our school only recently. The whole school had heard rumors and tales of why PTA parents called Kaylee the "new bad girl." I watched, mouth hanging open, as she took out her pack of Marlboro No. 27s and shook one loose. I stood frozen as I watched her effortlessly rotate between a red Tootsie Pop, the cigarette, and the red Slurpee.

"Hey! Kaylee!" I called out, not fully processing what I'd just done.

"Who the fuck are you?"

"Um—" I backed up as she stepped forward, chin tilted defiantly.

"How the fuck do you know my name?"

"I'm Lukas."

"I didn't ask what your name is, dumb fuck, I asked how you knew *mine*."

"I'm sorry. I mean, I've heard about you . . ."

She stared at me for a long moment, studying my face. I swallowed, feeling my mouth dry up and the rest of my body break out into a cold sweat simultaneously.

"You're fucking weird, bro," she declared, her mouth still wrapped around her Tootsie Pop.

"Totally . . ." I agreed, nodding vigorously. Her catlike eyes narrowed and her lip twitched up into a half smile.

"I like it."

She put out her cigarette and opened her Hello Kitty purse, digging around for some unseen treasure. Finally, she pulled out two red Mercedes-pressed ecstasy pills.

"Wanna roll?"

When the ecstasy hit, I was running behind her, trying desperately to keep up as we rounded the corner outside my high school gym. When it felt like my heart was about to explode, she finally stopped running, and as I doubled over, catching my breath, she poked my shoulder.

"Lift me up," she demanded.

Before I could really process what she was doing, she was already hopping the fence of our school.

"Come on, pussy," she called back to me.

We tumbled onto the soft grass of our high school's field, just as the sprinklers sprang to life, drenching us. Our eyes locked, staring intently at each other as we both leaned in. We kissed frantically, as if we would never be allowed to kiss again. Neither one of us wanted to pull away. When she finally did, I opened my eyes. The lights of the track lit her from behind, her peroxide-bleached hair shimmering like a halo. She smiled at me, and I smiled back.

She told me about her dad, who she'd never known, and I told her about mine, who, at times, I wished I never knew. She told me her fears, including her worst one—that one day her sadness might be too big—that one day she was afraid she'll never care about anyone as much as she cares about getting high. She talked about her pain and struggles like they belonged to someone else, in the same way Cory would. When Kaylee felt like she revealed too much she took my hands, one in each of hers, and traced the lines of my palms. She looked up at me with big wet eyes. I wanted her to tune out the static of everything else, to just exist here with me, in this moment where nothing else mattered. Two sets of massive black pupils blinking back at each other, two lost San Diego souls swimming in a fish bowl.

"I'm in love with you," I said, looking up at her with my big saucer eyes.

The warmth pulsating throughout my body flooded to my face.

"What the fuck—" She paused.

I felt my hammering heart stop beating for a moment, then:

"I think . . . I'm in love with you, too."

And from that night on, we were in love.

It didn't make any sense, but we reasoned, neither did love.

Later that night, I finally lost my virginity. It was wild and reckless, exactly how I'd imagined it. She was feral and crazy, and so was I, so, naturally, our sex was also feral and crazy. Like we were two horny, rabid bunnies having epileptic episodes of copulation together. It was just like I'd been hoping having a girlfriend would be like. The only thing I hadn't quite fantasized about was that my girlfriend wouldn't be able to stay out of juvie.

Kaylee and I would be together, blissfully happy, fucking like maniacs—only for her to be ripped away to another stint behind bars. We would be mid-kiss, mid-dance, mid–deep talk, and a parole office would be knocking at the door, ready to drag her back to juvie for another violation of her probation. The volatility only added to the passion. Every day she was locked up, we feverishly exchanged letters.

Dear Kaylee,

I missed you more today than yesterday. I love you. I want you. I will write to you every day until you are back in my arms.

Love always,
Lukas

Lukas,

I wish you could visit me. I miss you more than air. The showers here smell like shit, and I think I have athlete's feet from them. Please send flip-flops for me.

Hopelessly devoted to you,
Kaylee

Our romance continued on like this—Kaylee finally, blessedly, returning home to me, then getting arrested again, leading us to break up only to get back together—on a never-ending loop.

Between jail stints, she would wear a heavy black ankle bracelet that monitored her location. The blinking light and quiet pulse constantly updated her keepers and ensured that she stayed within the parameters of her probation and inside by curfew. The anklet only felt like a challenge, daring us to rewrite the rules with every stolen second.

The restriction also fueled our lust. Ours was a forbidden love or, at least, a restricted one, because she wasn't allowed to leave the confines of her house unless granted permission by her parole officer. So, ankle bracelet intact, she would let me in after school and we would spend hours on end having sex wherever we could—in her room, in the driveway, in the backyard, while her mom cleaned the kitchen. It didn't matter. We were in love and ready to take on the world, as long as we stayed within the boundaries we were given.

We created our own kind of dates: a picnic on the driveway, a Yankee Candle flickering between us, and her favorite 7-Eleven red Slurpee sweating in the sun. But mostly, we'd fuck. With every thrust, the monitor would dig harder into her skin and clank against my ankle. The discomfort only made it hotter, and the threat of being found out only made me hornier.

Then, one day, the illusion of our passionate-to-the-point-of-insanity, wild love came crashing down, leaving nothing but the wreckage.

It was a mild Monday morning, just past six o'clock, when I was jolted awake an hour earlier than my Sublime-themed alarm intended, startled by an unexpected knock at the door.

I rubbed my eyes, trying to shake off sleep, and was overcome by an unease in my chest. I blearily peeked out of my window, unsure of what I would find.

What I found were SUVs and SWAT team Humvees stacked all around my cul-de-sac. A small army of men in tactical gear moved with purpose, their black vests bearing the unmistakable insignia of the FBI. They advanced to my front door. Each of them armed with assault rifles. I immediately assumed they were there for me.

"FBI, OPEN UP!"

I scrambled half-naked into the bathroom, my mind racing, heart pounding. I yanked open the bathroom sink cabinets, shoving my bongs and paraphernilia into the darkest corners I could find. I grabbed anything else incriminating, and rushed to the toilet, flushing anything left behind. Just as I thought I had covered all my bases, I heard my mom scream and rushed down the hall to protect her from the Feds.

When I rounded the corner, Sean was lying on the floor, hands behind his back, with two officers pinning him down into the shag carpet.

"Is this for illegally downloading movies on LimeWire? Because I'll never do it again! I promise!" he mumbled, chin pressed into the floor.

"You're being arrested for business fraud and wiring. You have the right to remain silent, anything you say or do—"

"*Cooperation* is my middle name!"

The officer pushed him harder, and he whined a little. My mom and I both grimaced.

"What are you doing to him? Stop! You're hurting him!" my mom shouted.

"Ma'am, you need to back up." The officer put his hand up, pushing her away.

"Don't you dare touch me!" my mom continued.

My mom reached out her hands for Sean's as they pulled him up, carting him away. She followed them out to the driveway, crying helplessly.

Suddenly, I had a horrible vision of Kaylee in the back of a cop car and imagined myself where my mom stood, sobbing. I pictured Tessa standing in the driveway of our old house, hoping that if she just waited out there long enough, Cory would round the corner of the cul-de-sac.

I realized how I had basically replicated the same relationships I saw day in and day out. Like Bonnie and Clyde, my mom was standing by her man, and it was then I realized I didn't want stupid love anymore. I didn't want the type of love that only led to a goodbye.

As the cops drove away with Sean, with the whole neighborhood standing outside tuning into this reality TV show that was my life, all I could see in life was endings bleeding into beginnings.

9.

Where the Rubber Meets the Road

There was nothing quite like a SWAT team raiding your house right before geometry class to calcify the belief that if I stayed in San Diego, there would be three outcomes: death, drugs, or jail.

The months that followed only reinforced it. Sean was stuck in limbo, caught between arrest and sentencing, railing against the system, convinced he should've been exonerated. Half a year had passed since Tessa's death, but her absence still hung heavy—so much so that Cory felt more like a memory than a brother. We were all trapped somewhere between who we were and what we'd lost.

If my life was going to crash and burn, I couldn't think of a better place than in a limo bus, and no better person to do it with than Kaylee. I couldn't quit her, no matter how much I tried. Despite swearing off stupid love, it only took a few days before I found myself coming back to her.

Limo buses in San Diego weren't just a mode of transportation, they were a part of the cultural ecosystem. The limo bus was not a vehicle, it was a statement. Naturally, they were used for every event—birthday? Limo bus. Football game? Limo bus. Homecoming? Limo bus. Funeral? Fuck it, why not a limo bus?

If you were lucky, if you planned in advance, you knew who and where to call to get the best bus available—the tricked-out ones with the lights and the poles and the slick, impossible-to-stain leather seats. Anyone who was anyone knew to call Susan, the head honcho of limo bus operations in North County. But Susan, being the head honcho, only dealt with the top dogs. And this year, that was me.

Well—not quite, but I needed to be a top dog. In years past, I had been one of the many left busless or with one of the stragglers on the night of a big event due to Susan's iron-fisted reign. But this was junior prom, and I was not going to be denied. No, this was my sweet sixteen; this was my year. I had my friends by my side, the love of a good woman, and now, God and Susan willing, a limo bus to take to junior prom. Surely whatever dry spell had befallen me the universe could afford me this one night's reprieve.

"Hi, is Susan available, please?"

I nodded at myself in the mirror, practicing under my breath as I dialed the limo bus place. I'd been trying to sweet-talk Susan for years now, and still she remained my most unimpressed audience.

"Hi, is—"

"CanIputyouonhold—"

"Oh—oh, sure. Sorry, I thought I . . . right, you're not even there. I'm talking to no one." I laughed to myself.

Defeated and Susanless, I was about ready to give up when—

"Hi, this is Susan. How can I help you?"

I straightened up—my moment was here; it had fallen into my lap. It was fate. I had Susan right where I wanted her.

"Yeah, hi. I'd like to book a limo bus for the night of the eighteenth . . ." I said, trying to sound as cocksure as the big dog I wanted her to think I was.

"Oh yeah, we've had lots of calls for junior prom." Susan then got quiet before whispering into the speaker, "I kept one deluxe on standby for you this year, you want it?"

"That'd be amazing. Thank you so much, Susan," I responded quickly, trying to mask my elation. I had won, but a winner doesn't need to gloat. Just to win.

So when the night finally came, there we were. Kaylee, still sporting her ankle bracelet (though now adorned with sunflowers), had managed to charm her parole officer into granting her permission to attend. That charm, plus her streak of good behavior, earned her the luxury of an extended 11:00 p.m. curfew. To us, it felt limitless. It felt as if the stars had aligned just enough for us to dance, laugh, and forget about the rest of the world, whose only aim seemed to be to keep us apart via the shackle clamped unceremoniously around her ankle.

Brody and Bunny had also opted to come on our limo bus but wanted it clear they weren't going as an incestuous date, rather my plus-twos. They were more like an extension of me, and at this point, Kaylee, effortlessly, as always, completed the picture.

Inside the bus, Pretty Ricky and Usher's smooth tones swam through the speakers. Our hormone-charged bodies moved in sweaty unison to the thud of the bass.

"Babe, tonight might be the night we mix things up and have a foursome, I thiiiiink . . ." Kaylee drawled.

Brody and Bunny exchanged slightly nervous glances, not sold that she was just kidding, because after all, this was Kaylee. I, myself, wouldn't have put it past her on the right (or wrong) kind of night—and this was junior prom night, anything was possible. For the next few hours, we would be invincible.

As Kaylee and I danced in the limo—and forced Brody and Bunny to bear witness to our frottage—the air was thick with Curious by Britney Spears, a scent Kaylee used too liberally but to me, was intoxicating. Maybe Kaylee wasn't just some stupid, fleeting love; maybe she was my soulmate. I couldn't believe how wrong I'd been about everything—I didn't need to change my life, my family, or myself. How had I not seen that I had everything I'd ever wanted right in front of me? My friends, the girl, good times. All I needed to do was to stop finding reasons to resist it.

Kaylee pulled out of my arms, looking me dead in the eye and whispered, "You ready, baby?"

Kaylee gave me a knowing look. I obediently stuck out my tongue where she placed a blue pill and a mint—ecstasy and acid. I'd done both before, just never together. She didn't blink—just loaded her tongue with the same pair. She swallowed hers dry, as I chased my down with Sprite. Brody and Bunny sat across from us, trying their best not to look entirely left out, though their glances gave them away. Kaylee smiled at me, having noticed, too. We really were so in sync.

"Start with half," she instructed the twins as she placed their treats into their jittering, eager hands. "You might even need a fourth, Brody. Bitch, I wish I was as emaciated as you!"

Brody narrowed his eyes at her, before defiantly taking the whole pill.

"Oh hell no. I am not dealing with your ass tonight; I'm a terrible babysitter." Kaylee laughed.

Bunny took an anxious inhale and followed Brody into oblivion. If he was going to be off this fucking planet, so was she. Soon enough, the drugs kicked in for the twins, and for a moment, we were all suspended there, experiencing what it felt like when the rush of doing something reckless still felt strangely pure.

Or maybe that was just the drugs. Because enough time had seemed to have passed, and suddenly, I was hyperaware of the vibrations emanating through the speakers again. I could now feel every inch of my body pressed against Kaylee's, and the endless strobe of color darting across my field of vision. Uneasiness started to creep in, and when I pulled back, Kaylee's gaze swept across the seats, taking in everyone's laughter. Her smile had faded, replaced by something quieter, almost solemn.

"You okay?" I asked, my voice barely audible over the music.

"You ever think about how nights like this mean so much to some people and nothing to others?"

I tilted my head closer to hear her, yelling back: "What do you mean?"

She locked eyes with me, her pupils wide: "Like this is the moment we'll look back on, years from now. Everyone talks about getting older and wiser, but I like the idea of us getting younger and hotter. Not boring, regular 'growing old together' shit."

"I kinda like the idea of us growing old together," I said, trying to hold her gaze, but her eyes were darting around the bus now, almost like she felt trapped, the strobe lights making her movements look fragmented.

"Right?" I prompted, trying to get her attention. "Kaylee—"

"Sorry to interrupt—is it normal to feel this tingly and warm?" Brody wiggled in between us, sweaty and loose-limbed. Brody's quick metabolism plus the regular portion of ecstasy had him peaking early. He grabbed me by the shoulders and stared at me, bug-eyed.

"Why the fuck have we waited our whole lives to do this? This is amazing, like . . . this is what I wanna do, like when I wake up in the morning for the rest of my life, I wanna go downstairs, make a cup of coffee, and then do this."

"I think that's, like, drug addiction," Bunny said, her head tilting to follow Brody as he ping-ponged around the bus.

"Not if I do it as, like, a job!" Brody giggled, swinging his way back toward her.

"There's no such job," Bunny mumbled.

"Then I'll invent one!" Brody declared.

"You're an idiot." Bunny laughed.

"I am not an idiot, but I am gay!"

Bunny's eyes widened, and so did mine and Kaylee's, as Brody's announcement started to sink in. We all stared at him as he collapsed in a fit of laughter.

"Holy shit, that feels good to say out loud."

Now, hearing him say it out loud wasn't a shock—it had been clear to us since we were twelve; Brody's "admission" that Nicole Scherzinger from The Pussycat Dolls was his only wet dream and his methodical passion for wigs since middle school had all led us to this conclusion—but seeing how free he felt, how unburdened he seemed now that he had said it out loud was a quietly beautiful moment (and not just because of the ecstasy and the acid).

"I love you," I said back, almost without blinking. I was full of feeling, and I didn't know what it was or how to express it into words. All I could think was, *If that were me, I'd want to hear "I love you" right now.*

Looking back, it doesn't take a rocket scientist to figure out it definitely had something to do with the fact that I, too, was trying to figure out my own sexuality. But the prevailing feeling I had in that moment was a swell of pure, unadulterated happiness for him. I could tell by the look on Bunny's face that she was feeling something similar. Kaylee, who had been drifting on the edges of her own bad trip, finally snapped back into focus.

"I'd suck your gay dick any day, Brody!" she screamed out, licking her lips, and with that, we all dog-piled on top of Brody, laughing until it hurt—all of us expressing our uninhibited affection for him in a little drug-filled, joyous pretzel.

I looked up at the ceiling, out of breath from laughter and exertion. Something started to shift and a creeping sense of dread, of impending doom, began overshadowing my euphoria.

If this was the peak, if this was as good as it could ever get, then what would the rest of my life look like? I felt a tightening in my gut, not my stomach, but something deeper. Kaylee looked at me, and the blacks of her pupils seemed to be melting like a candle, as her eyebrows tensed in concern.

"Why are you looking at me like that? Do I look like myself?" I asked, the panic bubbling inside my head had begun to leak out.

"Chill, kooky. You're good. I think you just need to hydrate," Kaylee said.

She scooped her hand into the ice bucket before plopping it in a red cup. The ice cracked and hissed. I stared into the cup, mesmerized. For a fleeting moment, I saw so many versions of myself inside it: the boy in the bunny ears, the fake soccer player stealing booze, the brooding goth at boot camp. All of me, swirling in that fizzy red cup.

The acid was hitting me so hard. Too hard.

I kept checking the time on my phone. It was 8:19 p.m. Around me, the swirling faces of my past selves appeared and disappeared: all in one fragmented jumble.

"I see so much of myself..."

"What the fuck is Lukas saying?" Brody whispered to Bunny next to me.

The floor beneath my feet seemed to swell and crash down the aisle of the limo. I turned to the window, needing something solid to anchor me in the moment, but the world outside felt even more hectic. The San Diego highways were a smear of liquid light, the street signs no longer made sense, letters dissolved into melted hieroglyphics. Kaylee grabbed onto my face and kissed me firmly.

"You're chill, papa, breathe."

I glanced down at my phone, half expecting the time to be hours later. But it was still somehow only 8:19 p.m. Time was slipping away from me, it felt like I was stuck in a loop, a loop that twisted back on itself again and again.

"Why does it feel like time isn't changing?" I asked Kaylee, checking my phone yet again.

"Look into my eyes," she commanded. The sound of her voice cut through, and I locked in on her. As I followed her direction, I felt myself sink into her blue eyes—and I know people use that expression all the time, but I swear, I felt myself literally sink into them. Every freckle, every speck of green or brown dappled beneath her sparkling wet cornea sent me down a long and winding road, wondering to myself... *How did it get there, this outlier of color? What is its purpose? What if my version of blue is different from her version of blue?*

Kaylee called my name—I was pulled back to her face—I don't know how long it had been, that I had been staring into her eyes, but it felt like I was very close to cracking the Da Vinci code.

"Do you trust me?" she asked, looking into my soul with her iridescent eyes. I nodded. It didn't matter if I trusted her—because at that moment, I wanted to. I wanted to do the opposite of her tattoo, I wanted to trust every bitch.

"Yeah for sure, I trust you, babe."

Her grin widened, but not into the mischievous quirk of her lips that I was used to. This smile was soft, almost tender. She grabbed my hands again, pulling them to her waist as we swayed to the music.

"You're safe here," she said, her voice quieter now. "With me."

I blinked, and then suddenly, I believed her. I was no longer trying to ignore the heat rushing to my face. I suddenly wasn't scared anymore, wrapped in her arms, even as the bus rattled and screeched to a jarring halt outside the Jack in the Box and Home Depot parking lot.

"Where are we?"

Apparently, even though my bad trip had finally begun to dissipate, Brody and Bunny had been persuading the driver to stop a few blocks away from the junior prom so Kaylee had worked to calm me down. It seemed the executive decision had been made—we, as a group, were way too high to enter the prom. We got off, and our limo bus went without us.

So there we sat in the parking lot, waiting for the drugs to wear off, sucking on binkies like deranged nightmare teens, giving each other back rubs, bear hugs, and light shows. It was during one of Kaylee's dizzying light performances that I wandered off to take a piss behind a bush. I was mid-stream, blissfully unaware, when out of the corner of my vision, I saw them. I blinked hard, then rubbed my eyes, convinced it was a mirage. The shapes didn't dissolve, though. They sharpened. I realized this was no hallucination. It was my principal, Mr. Stevens, and our vice principal, Ms. Harper, walking toward us down a steep hill.

They weren't just walking. They were charging. Storming, even. On a mission to find something . . . To find us.

I yanked up my pants—pee still dripping down my leg—and bolted toward Kaylee.

"Guys!" I hissed.

I ran toward Kaylee in a panic, trying to get her up and moving, but instead she crawled across the parking lot on all fours like a rabid animal, flopped down onto her stomach, and slithered underneath a car.

"What the fuck, Kaylee!" I shrieked, trying to get her to go where Brody and Bunny stood, frozen like two preemie deer in the headlights.

"Go! I can't get caught, dude. I'm sorry."

I tried to pull Kaylee out, but she refused, holding on to a tire, staying put underneath the car.

"What the fuck, you already took the drugs! Come on! They're gonna find you—" I said.

"I have Niacin for my pee test, and you're just mad 'cause you can't fit under here with me."

"Fuck you!" I said.

"Fuck you!"

"I love you."

"I love you, too."

Mr. Stevens and Ms. Harper were closing in. Brody and Bunny pulled away from me, and all three of us whipped our heads around. All was lost, until, in a moment of adrenaline-fueled genius, I grabbed Brody and Bunny and dove headfirst into the Jack in the Box dumpster. The stench hit immediately—a nauseating blend of rotten ninety-nine-cent tacos and sour milk. We crouched there pressed against greasy wrappers, whispering in frantic bursts as we tried to keep still.

"Kaylee's a cunt," Brody whispered.

"Dude, shut up," I whispered back. "Also, don't call my girlfriend a—"

"We know what you're up to, and we *will* find you in this parking lot!" Our vice principal's voice echoed through the night.

I peeked over the rim of the dumpster and saw Ms. Harper, standing over one of our backpacks. She crouched down to examine it, her expression grim.

"I found a Peruvian backpack—chockablock with alcohol, over," she murmured into her walkie-talkie, while the other hand rested on her hip.

From inside the dumpster, Brody let out a muffled snort. "Chalk block?" he whispered, biting down on the sleeve of his hoodie.

"Shut the fuck up," Bunny hissed, elbowing him.

We were surrounded. Ms. Harper had called for backup, and she was already rallying the troops outside of Home Depot. High school staff, security, and chaperones flooded the parking lot for a search and rescue, and within a few minutes, they found us. Our principals lined us up, single file, our pupils blown wide. The ecstasy had made everything sharper, and more defined.

"Who else are you with?" Ms. Harper asked.

"Just us. Everyone else is at the prom, madame, I mean ma'am," I replied, the English language slipping from my mind.

She narrowed in on my eyes, suspiciously, until finally opening her mouth.

"You want to tell me why you aren't at the prom?" Ms. Harper asked, her words turning to syrup.

I started to formulate my lie. "Brody is—"

"Gay," Brody interjected.

Ms. Harper stared at Brody. We all stared at Brody.

"Congratulations?" she muttered.

"Yes—" I jumped back in, before Brody could answer and derail us anymore. "But he was also carsick. And he loves Jack in the Box. Huge taco guy. So . . ." I managed to say in my drug-filled haze.

All the while, Ms. Harper's orange ringlet hair was transforming into wild flames. I locked eyes with Kaylee's ankle bracelet under the car, for a brief second, still hidden away under the shadow of the tire. I needed her to know that she would always be able to trust at least one bitch.

"We pulled over here. Just the three of us. Yes, that's our alcohol, and yes, we should be at the prom and not in a parking lot."

Mr. Stevens studied our eager faces.

"Fine. You want to call your parents or should I?" Ms. Harper asked, as Mr. Stevens studied us beside her.

I dialed, but after a few rings, my mom's voicemail kicked in—the one she'd had forever, with her asking her best friend how to hang up at the end of it.

"She's not picking up," I said.

Ms. Harper glanced at me, her expression unchanged. "What about your dad?"

"Trust me, he's not answering."

Brody exchanged a glance with Mr. Stevens and Ms. Harper, then sighed.

"I'd call our parents, but um, they're at a . . . symposium on desert plants," he explained.

"All right, Mr. Stevens is going to give you a ride home. I'll be sure to give them a call when they're back from the symposium."

Brody, Bunny, and I crammed into the back seat of Mr. Stevens's car. We all tried our hardest to act and be as normal as possible. The freeway lights flashing rhythmically through the windows didn't help much. Brody sat on one side of me, chewing on his lip like it was a piece of bubble gum, while Bunny sat on the other, staring straight ahead, fully dissociating. I, true to form, seemed to have no idea when to shut the fuck up.

"Hey, Mr. Stevens, I'm just curious, what do you want out of life?"

Mr. Stevens glanced at me in the rearview, his face unreadable. "Pardon?"

"I just . . ." I started, leaning forward. "Why this? Is it because you, like, *really* care about kids? Or what? Like, do you wake up and go, 'Yeah, this is it. This is the dream. I want to be a principal'?"

Mr. Stevens scoffed and shook his head.

"I'm not trying to be facetious. I know it doesn't seem like it, but I'm genuinely interested. Like did you know you wanted this, or did you ever have a different plan, and then life just found you here, principal-ing?"

Even though the reason I was asking was really that I was too high to handle the silences, there was also enough sincere curiosity behind the question that surprised us both.

"I don't know, Lukas. What do *you* want out of life?"

The car went quiet.

"I . . . I don't know," I said. "I've never really thought about it, you know? Like, no one's ever *asked* me that before."

The question scared the shit out of me, not because it was hard, but because I didn't have an answer—and I wasn't sure if I ever would. I stared down at my hands, I watched my hands grow bigger and smaller. Fuck. Not now. I closed my eyes tight to stop the visuals.

"I guess . . . I just want to figure it out," I said slowly, the words feeling small and unfinished on my tongue. "Like, I don't know. I want to figure out whatever the thing is, y'know, that makes it all make sense. I just don't want to be miserable and dead inside like most of the grown-ups I know. I also don't want to . . . I don't want to fuck it all up and end up—a failure . . ."

Bunny turned, giving me a look that screamed *Shut the fuck up*, her wide eyes darting toward Mr. Stevens, who nodded and then said, "That's not a bad place to start."

He started fiddling with the radio, which I took as my cue to actually shut the fuck up.

"To answer your question, I do, though. Wake up and think, *This is it*. I love what I do. So yeah. This is the dream, so all that stuff you were talking about, that's fine. But you might want to think about what it could be. It's probably not being a principal—"

"Definitely not."

"Think about it. Y'know? What's your version of the dream?"

Before I could answer, the acid's grip morphed into a chokehold. The versions of myself from the red cup had returned, now refracting off the back seat window. But they were different this time, happier. I was doing pranks with my brothers, as they cackled and cheered me on. Then there I was playing "nail salon" with my mom, her laughter filling the air. And finally performing Julia Stiles's *10 Things I Hate About You* monologue. That time at camp had been when I felt the most myself, the best version of myself, even. *Maybe little me had been onto something, maybe acting was my dream*, I thought to myself but was too much of a pussy to say out loud.

"I dunno yet," I said.

I stared out the window, the neon blur of the streetlights fading in and out. I wasn't ready to admit it. But I was already moving toward something, even if I couldn't see it clearly yet.

10.

Good Things Come to Hoes Who Wait

Though Kaylee was able to run from Mr. Stevens, she couldn't run from the law. She'd missed her extended prom curfew and failed the drug test her probation officer gave her the following day. Two strikes and there she was, back in juvenile detention for the sixth time that year.

I bided our time apart by Dear John–ing more letters, waiting for her release. (Why they don't allow conjugal visits in juvie, I'll never understand.) With nothing but free time, I turned my focus back to performing, steadily reclaiming the spotlight one small role at a time.

Without telling any of my friends or family, I found a local agent who worked out of her garage a few cities over from mine to represent me. And when she sent me the details of an "open cattle call for teenagers with blond hair in San Diego," I knew there was no teen blonder and no teen more San Diegan than me. I breezed through the audition—which, I learned when I arrived, was for a wart-removal medication commercial—and while I had to endure being called "General Warts" by the school for the rest of the year, booking that thirty-second spot was a monumental *breakthrough.*

It wasn't just the money—though I made more in that one day than I had in all my years of folding napkins at the retirement home. It was proof that I wasn't just another San Diego teen waiting for life to happen to them.

I had been chosen.

I was the face of warts.

If the ad proved anything, it was that I had a shot at something bigger. And with Dad having recently moved to LA, reconciling with him felt like the next step toward making that dream a reality.

Asking him for a favor also felt a lot easier than admitting the truth, which was that I really wanted a dad. Not the abrasive doomsdayer he'd morphed into over the past few years, but the source of stability and safety I'd seen so many of my friends' fathers provide for them. Now that I was genuinely trying to get my act together, I craved boundaries and structure more than ever. So I tapped into the role of reformed, ready-to-repent son and called him with my plan.

"Let's talk about it over dinner," he said, clearly dodging the question. He'd been so, so dodgy lately. And while he'd always been *aloof*, over the past few months he'd started leaving me on read, ghosting me, or making up strange, unbelievable lies.

"What does that mean?" I asked.

"It means we'll talk about it over dinner," he said before hanging up. His voice didn't change octaves like my mom's when he lied. Instead, he stayed monotone—a tell that something was up.

"Dick," I muttered into the phone.

A few days later, Travis and I met him in Costa Mesa—the halfway point between San Diego and Long Beach—for dinner.

Ever since boot camp, I opted out of weekend visits with him in exchange for a monthly meal.

Travis and I had driven up together in my beat-up little green Hyundai Elantra I'd purchased on Craigslist a few months prior for my sixteenth birthday. While driving, we kept passing a joint back and forth as the toxic waste-tinged air blew in through the windows from the San Onofre nuclear towers—the infamous "nuclear titties," named for their uncanny resemblance to a pair of double Ds. The towers loomed against the coastline, steadily leaking toxic waste into the ocean, but to locals, they just signaled you were leaving the San Diego county line.

"Why can't you just keep it green? Why do you have to do all that other shit?" Travis asked me.

"Because *just* weed makes you blow up like a whale, so you gotta balance it out with uppers," I said, coughing mid-hit. "It's basic chemistry."

Travis rolled his eyes.

"I'm fine. Don't worry about me—I'm not gonna ever—"

"You better not. I'll kill you before you get the chance."

"Aw, you love me," I said, putting my hand on his shoulder before Travis wriggled it away. "So, what do you think Dad's secret is? Think he's finally getting sued for accidentally amputating someone in surgery?"

"Who knows," Travis replied as he took the joint out of my hand.

No matter how I tried to lighten the mood, Travis still chewed his nails, a habit he'd had since he was a kid. Mom had tried to get him to break it when he was little by putting hot sauce under his nail beds every morning before school. When Travis was anxious, he looked unnervingly like my dad, his shoulders hunched up to his ears and his fingers tapping restlessly against the corner of his mouth.

I gently moved his fingers away from his mouth and put a comforting hand on his shoulder. He looked over at me with a slight smile. Travis and I had started relying more and more on each other. Everything felt more manageable with him in my corner. Together, we'd figure out what the hell was going on with our dad.

"So, uh, yeah. It's good you boys are here," my dad said once we sat down. He took a deep breath and heaved a sigh as he looked anywhere but at us.

"What is it? Just spit it out already," I asked.

"Well, I think you, maybe, probably know that I've been seeing this woman. . . ." His eyes stayed glued on the laminated menu, still never once making direct eye contact with us.

"Well, we got married . . . and she's pregnant . . . with twins." He delivered the news in that same flat, clinical tone he used at the hospital, the one I'd heard him use on patients when delivering the worst possible news. It was meant to soften the blow, but somehow, it always made things worse. If I ever wished my mom would have been less histrionic growing up, I regretted it now. I would've taken one hundred of her crying spells over this desensitized performance my dad was putting on.

Fuck it, I thought. *I'll be hysterical enough for the both of us.*

"What the fuck do you mean you got *married*? And didn't invite us?!" I yelled louder than I needed to be, making sure everyone in the restaurant heard me over the sports games on the TV.

"Keep it down!" he hissed, looking around nervously. "Look, she didn't think it was a good idea, okay? She didn't want to—"

"Didn't want to, what? Meet us? Ever?" I shot back.

"We wanted to wait for the right time," he said, his tone becoming more defensive.

"And you didn't think your *wedding day* might've been the right time?" I asked. (To this day, I still have never met her.)

"I wish it could've been different, but it's what she—"

"I don't give a fuck what she wants. She's a cunt and you're a pussy."

"LUKAS!" my dad yelled, finally matching my anger. "What the hell did you just say? What did you just call her?"

My fists curled into tight balls. This anger was a stronger high than any I'd experienced: just pure adrenaline. I felt like I could rip the table right off its studs and pummel him across the restaurant with it. Whatever that superhero phenomenon is where a mom can summon the strength to lift a car off her child to save them, this was its weird, demented cousin.

"Lukas. Just calm down," Travis said, placing his hands on my shoulders.

"Calm down?!" I spat back at him, laughing bitterly.

My dad looked on, dumbfounded. It wasn't that he was trying to be callous, he just genuinely couldn't fathom why I'd be so upset. He seemed almost embarrassed by my reaction, wincing the same way he did when I was a little boy throwing a tantrum. And there I was, a decade later, still screaming for him to see me, only to be met with the same pained exasperation.

"Oh, come on! Don't let him get away with this! Do you realize he is replacing us *with new kids*?!" I shouted.

"It's okay. We'll be okay," Travis said, forcing a smile, but I could see the tears forming in the corners of his eyes.

Deep down, I knew Travis was just as wrecked as I was, but he buried it, always playing the peacemaker. Between Cory, my mom, and me, there was never any space left for his own emotions.

"Go fuck yourself," I said, staring directly into my dad's eyes.

I stormed out, heading straight for the car. I didn't care if Travis made it out in time for a ride. Anyone even remotely defending my dad was the enemy, and the enemy sure as hell wasn't sitting shotgun in my Elantra. Travis came sprinting out after me, my dad trailing behind him.

"Lukas, wait, please!" Travis called out.

I charged toward them.

"Look at yourself. You're a coward. You can't stand up to your own wife. It's fucking pathetic," I screamed through the parking lot.

He stood there and just stared at me, blinking.

"SAY SOMETHING. FOR ONCE, FUCKING SAY SOMETHING!" I screamed.

"I'm lonely. I have been so lonely for so long. What am I supposed to do? Be alone forever?" my dad asked quietly and in all sincerity.

For a second, I felt myself soften toward him. My dad stood there looking submissive, and I saw him as a human. Fragile. A child. His shirt seemed too big for him; he looked small, as if all the years of loneliness had finally caught up to him. His phone rang in his pocket. He fumbled to pick it up and pressed Ignore.

"Tell me, what am I supposed to do?" he asked again.

"Be my father?" I asked, though it was more of a statement than a question.

"I . . ." He began to say something, but his phone started ringing again. He read the screen and looked down, contemplating if he should pick up.

"I should answer this, it could be an emergency. Let me just take this real quick."

He pressed Answer and walked a few feet away, covering the space between his mouth and the phone.

"Yes? No, I'm in the middle of it right now. Well . . ."

Before he could finish his thought, I lunged closer. My fists were still clenched, and all I wanted was to hit him so hard that he'd be forced to feel even one-tenth of the pain he'd caused me and Travis. Before I could get anywhere close to him, Travis pulled me back and shoved me into the car.

"Let it go. I'm driving," Travis said, reaching into my pocket and pulling out my keys.

I sank into the passenger seat, my breath shallow and uneven, my hands still vibrating.

It hit me all at once—the weight of what had just happened. Our dad got married. He was having kids. Twins. And not just kids. A whole other life where he could play the role of the doting, protective patriarch. A do-over. A life we weren't invited into. A life where we didn't exist to remind him of all the ways he'd fucked it up the first time and the fuckups we'd become.

From the window, I could see my dad, his recessed eyes devoid of emotion. It was a familiar scene: him just standing there, vacantly, while I tried to will him to become the father I needed him to be through sheer force. No matter how used to the disappointment I was, it still stung.

"Why didn't you have my back?" I shouted, shattering the thick silence between us. "Why are you so forgiving toward a man who couldn't care less about either of us?"

Travis tried to be the voice of reason: "We just have to make the best of what we've got—"

"We literally just got kicked out of our own family!" I screamed, trying to get him angry, too.

He tried to console me and make me feel better, promising me that things would work out. Fifteen minutes in, I was still screaming. My rage going nowhere. He lit up a joint, ignoring me in the hopes that I'd just tire myself out.

"He's your problem now," Travis said to my mom once we got back to her house.

"What do you mean? What happened?" she called after Travis, who was already halfway up the stairs to his room. "Lulu, you okay?"

"It's nothing. Just Dad being Dad," I said, and went off to my room. I wasn't ready to witness my mother's vigilante side come out just yet.

Later that night, I played back our afternoon. When my anger started to dissipate, it hit me that I was scared shitless. Scared that he'd stop paying my mom for child support, scared that if Sean actually went to prison and wasn't around to check Mom on her gambling addiction that we'd lose our house. But maybe I was the most scared of who I'd become if I couldn't get the fuck out of San Diego.

Instead of confronting my anxieties, I did what any frustrated, rejected son would do to get his revenge and his father's attention . . . I started buying a shit ton of sex toys on my dad's credit card.

I didn't know where the idea came from, or whether it was something I inherited from my dad—the man who started talking about tits before I was anywhere close to puberty.

Or maybe I thought if I surrounded myself with enough *stuff* to distract me, it would fill the space left by everything I couldn't face. Whatever it was, the next thing I knew, I was going to town on Amazon using the picture of my dad's credit card he'd sent me the year before to pay for my SAT prep. I don't know why I'd never thought to use it before, or why I didn't use it for more practical things, but I was a petty little bitch, and spending my dad's money on new and depraved ways to get off—from a silicone pocket pussy to a Tenga silky egg portable suction stroke—became top priority.

I'd watched my mom hoard things for so long—collecting clothes, tchotchkes, and expired foods—that I thought I was also being practical. She'd ingrained a scarcity mindset in us that convinced me I needed to stockpile as many things as I could before the well ran dry. (Sex toys included.) I was sensible, though, it wasn't just fleshlights and silicone eggs. I continued to fill up my Amazon cart with more random things I was convinced I needed: Stüssy and Supreme T-shirts, clothes that were in style, but always extra large and never fit; creatine for muscles I didn't have; and gauged earrings that were too big for the small holes I'd been stretching into my ears.

THREE MONTHS PASSED, and neither Travis nor I had heard from our dad since the big blowout, though our nana had continuously done her best to try to mediate things. She alternated between talking him down and promising me that he'd come to his senses. It only further reinforced the way I saw him—an overgrown child still depending on his mom to clean up his mess. So when he finally called a few months later, I thought Nana had gotten through to him. I was wrong.

From the second I answered, his tone was the most incensed I'd ever heard him. If I wasn't so pissed, I might've been impressed.

"Did you seriously think I wouldn't look at my credit card statements?" he squawked into the phone.

"What do you mean?" I asked.

"I saw all that freaky shit you've been buying online. This is a crime. This is theft. Have you lost your mind? I'm calling the cops—"

"No, no. Look, I'm sorry. I'll never do it again . . ." I said, now scared.

I treated our call like the audition of a lifetime. *Hi, I'm Lukas Gage: sixteen but can play eighteen, a little weathered from not enough sunscreen, five ten and a half, and I'll be reading for the part of the remorseful, humiliated, and apologetic son #2.*

I summoned the tears I'd been practicing ever since I used to lie my way into my neighbors' homes in Long Beach, and honestly? It might be my best work to date.

"Dad, I've been such an idiot. Don't you remember what it's like being a teenager? My frontal . . . what is it called?"

"Lobe?" my dad offered.

"Yes! MY FRONTAL LOBE IS MISSING! I'm so mixed-up!" I pleaded and cried.

My dad made one of his excruciatingly loud sighs.

"Okay, fine. But hear me clearly, if you so much as use my cards to buy a pack of Tic Tacs I'm calling the cops."

"Tic Tacs?" *Click.*

THAT SEMESTER, I distanced myself from the twins in favor of hanging with a new group of guys who did the kinds of drugs Travis continuously warned me about. To them, girls weren't soulmates, friendship wasn't about belonging, and drugs didn't carry any weight. Everything was about the chase and the score. The doing, not the meaning.

For the first time in my life, I loved how invisible I felt. In their company, I was just another posturing pothead; a burnt-out carbon copy like the rest of them. I both didn't quite belong and completely blended in at the same time.

The guy in the group I became closest with was a kid named Owen. He'd moved from Portland at the start of the school year, and his Pacific Northwest accent instantly set him apart from our vocal-fried drawls. He stood like a seahorse, the way he'd puff up his chest, making his lower half protrude in overcompensation. His confidence wasn't exactly palatable, but he fascinated me. I could tell that he was hiding something beneath all that bravado, because I too was hiding beneath the same thing.

There was also one other thing Owen seemed to have going for himself: dumb luck. Sometimes we would go on night walks, or, as he would call them, scavenger hunts.

We'd wander until we reached the palatial homes with terracotta roofs and ocean views. From there we'd break into the cars parked out front.

"I'm gonna get rich or die trying," Owen would mutter, checking each car door to see if it was unlocked.

"Isn't the alarm going to go off?" I nervously asked during our first "scavenger hunt."

Before I could say more, Owen found a car that opened easily and silently. Dumb luck.

"See? Rich people are stupid." He grinned at me with his crooked smile.

Lying right there on the console were pristine bottles of Xanax and Adderall. It was as if an orb of light refracted off the labels, beckoning us. We took off with the bottles until we got to Orpheus Park to see how much we had retrieved. I floated the idea of taking a little from both bottles to see what happened, but Owen had a more ambitious plan.

"Do you know how much we could make off this?" he asked.

"Yeah, but . . ." I hesitated.

"What's the worst that could happen? We can't get away with this shit when we turn eighteen, bro. We gotta take advantage of our youth."

The logic was sound enough for me. Plus, I had the perfect place to set up shop. I knew better than to deal at school or home. The retirement home that I worked at was the safest spot to do business. As long as I flirted with the old ladies, and snuck extra Manischewitz to the old men, I was free to do as many drive-by deals as I pleased.

Word quickly got out that I was the new plug, but demand started to outweigh supply. I did what any teenage clueless dealer in over his head would do. I went back to window-shopping: scoring more prescription pills from the rich neighbors' cars.

Now, I know I'm a self-proclaimed liar, but I promise none of this narration is unreliable. No matter how many bottles I stole, people just kept leaving them back in there for the taking. *I guess rich people really are stupid*, I thought to myself.

Owen, thrilled to finally have something to back up all that bravado, spread the word about our booming business. Eventually, the news made its way to Kaylee, who had been recently released from juvie and had brought along a new boyfriend, Javi, who was, unfortunately, much hotter and much cooler than me.

For the past few months, I was completely clean from Kaylee. No slip-ups, no love letters, no fantasizing about her lower back tattoo. She had a new boyfriend now, and I was not about to be treated like some second-rate second fiddle. I swore off dumb love for good.

But because I'm a prideful, jealous bastard, it was only a matter of time before temptation struck again. I found her one day—resting the curve of her lower back tattoo on my green Hyundai in the school parking lot. Her eyes still carried that juvie glow: clear, bright, but twinkling with trouble.

"Miss me?" she asked, dragging a finger along the hood of my car.

"Actually was enjoying the peace and quiet, but here you are."

"Really?" She laughed, not convinced.

"Yeah, you're like a mosquito always—"

"Sucking you dry?" Kaylee interrupted as I searched for my words.

She smirked.

"Well, I missed you . . . Javi was cool," she said, flicking her peroxide hair over her shoulder, "but you were a better ride."

My stomach dropped, the sweet taste of her validation pulling me in. I knew it was just a line, a cheap thrill, but for a moment, I let myself believe it.

"I'm seeing someone else," I lied.

"Who? Is it Haley?" she snapped. "I'll fight that brown-haired, extension-ass bitch and win," she said, and I knew she meant it.

"You have extensions."

"Yeah, but people who have brown hair are lame. That's not the point."

She took a deep breath, her voice softening as she tilted her head. "Look, kooky, I know you're pushing. I want in, and I want to do it with you, baby. I miss you."

She smiled, her eyes locked on mine. "Come on, we can be a power couple."

Her manipulation skills were even hotter than her ultra-low-rise jeans and bedazzled crop top that read "Good things come to hoes who wait." I didn't stand a chance.

"How do I know you're not going to fuck it up and get us rolled?" I asked, trying to sound nonchalant and not intrigued.

"Because being locked up gave me the serenity to accept the things I cannot change, the courage to change the things I can, and wisdom to know the difference."

"Huh? Isn't that from AA—?"

"Whatever! Give me another chance. If I fuck it up, I'm dead to you. Let me fix this. Let me fix *us*," she begged.

"Screw it." I shrugged.

I fell stupidly in love all over again.

"Oh, kooky Lukey baby. We're gonna be unstoppable together," she said before jumping into my arms and wrapping her legs around my waist.

Kaylee and I had broken up and fallen back together more times than I could count. Every time, I swore it would be the last—that I wouldn't repeat the same toxic cycle I'd watched Mom and Sean cling to for years. I told myself I'd focus on my future, on getting my life together. But all it ever took was Kaylee—her crooked charm, that knowing smirk—and just like that, my resolve crumbled.

To her credit, Kaylee helped transform my fledgling operation into a full-blown drug ring with Owen. Instead of burglarizing my neighbors, we decided to take a trip down south to the Tijuana pharmacies to stock up on Xanax and Adderall. While I'd dealt only to my circle of friends and a few peripherals, Kaylee helped me reach an untapped market: the girls at school desperate for uppers to study for the SATs or to get as emaciated as possible before their senior prom.

I WROTE THIS FOR ATTENTION

"This is just the start," she said. "If we're gonna do this, we do it big."

MY ELANTRA RUMBLED south toward San Ysidro, the last stop before Mexico. The border town always brought back the image of Cory and the Fourth of July, the way his chapped lips curled without warmth and the confusion clouding his bloodshot eyes as we found him slumped in the encampment near the bridge at the border.

Kaylee was beside me, gluing on the last acrylic to her fingernails while her toes sat in separators hanging out the window air drying. When she finished applying her nails, she tickled them lightly against the back of my head. It snapped me out of my trance, her eyes—always glinting with mischief and defiance. She loved the idea of us crossing the border, the thrill of dancing so close to the edge.

We were partners in crime, literally. Just the two of us. After Owen tried to play us and pocket more of his share, we booted him from our ring.

"Trust No Bitch" wasn't just ink for a tramp stamp; it was our mantra. Trust no one. We lived by it. Not even each other. Maybe that was part of what made us work. There was something romantic about our bond being this constantly swinging pendulum, the way we would break up and get back together, yet always landing back on each other. We knew what it was to hustle, to fuck up, and to survive.

"You look guilty," she said. "Stop looking so nervous."

"I'm not," I lied.

Nearing the border checkpoint, a row of stern-faced agents came into view. My jaw tightened until it felt like the hinges might snap. Beside me, Kaylee kicked her feet on the dashboard and blew on her toenails.

The agent took one heart-eyed look at Kaylee, as she looked up in her Hello-Kitty sunglasses, and waved us right through.

"See?" Kaylee said, flashing me her teeth.

The pharmacy wasn't far. It was in a small white building surrounded by two dilapidated office spaces. Kaylee played the role of an innocent tourist, chatting up the pharmacist in broken Spanglish while I hung back, scanning the shelves, quietly admiring her genius.

"¡Hola!" she chirped. "¡Uh . . . Buenos días!"

The pharmacist, a middle-aged woman with dead eyes, barely glanced up from her phone.

"Soy turista. De, uh . . . Canadá, um, muy nerviosa, Do you— tienes . . . Xanax? Y . . . Adderall?"

No words were exchanged. The pharmacist just handed over a bunch of boxed medication and exchanged pesos, and that was that.

"¡Gracias!" Kaylee called out before linking my arms with hers.

As soon as we slammed the doors to my Elantra shut, Kaylee let out a triumphant squeal, flipping her hair off her shoulders before yanking me into a kiss—our way of celebrating our first (and ultimately only) international drug deal. Sure, I wasn't Ryan from *The O.C.*, racing off to rescue my girl from a roofied bender in Tijuana. Maybe not as heroic, but at least I was a half-assed outlaw, smuggling contraband with the girl who made my heart race—and that had to count for something.

"Come on, baby, we've got girls to feed," Kaylee cackled before slapping the dashboard.

I WROTE THIS FOR ATTENTION

For Kaylee, drug dealing was another form of foreplay in our relationship. For me, it was stability. A safety net around me if everything else fell apart. The intrusive thoughts—the ones insisting that things falling apart with my dad were only the beginning, that eventually everything and everyone would be ripped away—were getting louder, more incessant. They weren't the occasional whisper anymore; they were blaring sirens, always at night, and always uninvited. The only thing that silenced them was hustling. If I was too busy dealing, or working at the retirement center—I could shove my fears aside and quiet my mind. I chased that quiet with everything I had.

The trouble with running from your fears is sometimes you ignore the ones you really, really shouldn't.

Kaylee was many things: cunning, bold, and scrappy. She was a natural leader. But she was also heedless. Maybe it was because she didn't fear juvie, she didn't fear the system, or maybe she was just cooked as fuck. Either way, Kaylee stopped following the safety precautions we'd agreed to abide by: never *ever* put anything in writing. She'd sit there in Spanish class, spacing out and writing out her ledger. *Brianna Mckenzie owes 30; need 65 from Tori/ASB bitch. 15 more Addy for Krystal w/ a scar; Lukas deal w/ Carly.*

One day, in a different classroom entirely, the school transport assistant pulled up on her golf cart looking for me. Celeste had the kind of Crocodile Dundee leathery skin that you get from spending nearly three decades baking under the Southern California sun, chauffeuring kids like me around the school grounds.

"Lukas, the principal wants to see you," Celeste said in a put-on stern voice.

Deep down, we were homies. We both knew the act was just

for show, she didn't believe in the version I was selling, either. I understood she had a role to play, just like I did.

"For sure," I said in a nervous voice that was not put-on. I could feel in my bones that shit was about to go sideways.

In the mornings, the marine layer would drape our campus in a briny film of fog. However, that afternoon the fog had lifted, revealing the ocean below, as picturesque as the murals my classmates had painted on the grounds. Celeste slammed the brakes of the golf cart and tilted up her Oakleys, widening her raccoon-tanned eyes before throwing me a lifeline.

"You have ten seconds to delete anything incriminating off your phone. They're onto you," she told me in her deep rasp.

I nodded back at her, consumed by what I've always referred to as "little earthquakes"—that pulsating spreading sensation where your body can feel your anxiety before your brain is able to process it. With too much to delete and not enough time, I had Celeste whip a U-turn back to the bell tower so I could come up with a plan. It wasn't a perfect one, but with my nerves twitching like tectonic plates, all I could think to do was jam my Samsung Sidekick between my ass cheeks. The result was neither discreet nor secure, but the second it was in place, Celeste hightailed us out of there.

When we pulled up to the office, two cops were already there, waiting. "Do you have any idea why you're here today?" the officer asked as I sat down.

"No, sir," I said, trying to sound as bamboozled and clueless as I could.

"We found some notes of your girlfriend Kaylee's that say otherwise."

My earthquakes were now a magnitude 8.2.

"I'm not sure what you're talking about, sir."

"There's another Lukas with a *k* who goes to this school?" the cop said as he dropped Kaylee's notebook on the desk in front of me.

"I guess so." I shrugged.

"Then you wouldn't mind us checking your pockets?"

"Shouldn't I have a lawyer present?"

The officer looked at his partner and smirked before sighing and looking back at me.

"Don't make this harder on yourself. Get up."

I didn't even make it fully out of my seat before my phone fell straight from my ass to the floor. Without thinking, I started stomping on it until the Sidekick's screen became an opaque web of cracks and scuffs.

The cop shot me a look that telegraphed what a complete dumbass he thought I was, then proceeded to pat me down. When he found the car keys I'd also stashed in my sock, I almost confessed right there and then. Because much like my neighbors who I'd mocked for being stupid enough to just leave drugs in their car, I'd done the same exact thing, my entire supply of drugs sitting pretty in the console of my Hyundai—practically gift wrapped for my downfall.

"Want to save us both the trouble and just let me know what I'll find in your car?"

"Some empty Gatorade bottles, maybe a couple of dirty socks, my mom's P!NK CD," I said.

While the cop searched my car, Ms. Harper used the opportunity to reprimand me, telling me I was wasting my potential and ruining my life with the path I was heading down. As she kept going on and on, all I could think about was the promise I'd made to myself while Sean had gotten arrested by the FBI. I'd sworn to myself that I'd never let reckless choices and dumb love take me down the same path—and now, here I was, relapsing.

"Care to explain how these got in your car?" the cop said once he was back and had my drugs in his possession.

I just bowed my head. I was fucked.

"That's what I thought." The cop cleared his throat. "You have the right to remain silent. Anything you say can and will be used against you in a court of law . . ." he recited, as his partner placed me in the cuffs and escorted me out of the room.

"Oh, and Lukas?" Principal Stevens called out to me.

"Yes, sir?"

"You don't go to this school anymore," he said as the cops herded me out the door.

11.

The Last Bite

For reasons I'll never quite understand, San Diego spared me one last time. While Kaylee had to serve three months, my sentencing was laughably light: logging community service hours by picking up trash on the beach, finishing my high school credits by filling out a workbook about as dense as a gossip column, and attending a set number of AA meetings where, at the very least, I'd hear some solid stories.

Being forced to sit with my emotions—the ones I'd spent years dodging through every vice I could find—was anything but healing. It was like going through withdrawal: stripped of my coping mechanisms I was now wide awake to the uncomfortable, unruly feelings that radiated through me. With no other choice, I submitted to them, hoping I'd resurface intact. Yet somehow, in the midst of it all, the advice in AA, being shared by wise souls like Dakota, an old beekeeper, in one of the meetings I attended regularly, started to resonate.

"There I was, covered in honey from head to toe, about to open the door to the apiary, and then I thought to myself, *Dakota? What are you doing? How did we get here?*" she laughed, shaking her head into the horizon. "This was not my plan, this is not what *he* hoped for me when I was born. And then it hit me like a ton of bricks, falling down on my shed. I *accepted*. I accepted the fact that I was an addict, and the more I tried pushing against it, the more it stuck to me like honey."

I looked up to Dakota—she may have been double my age, and she may have had the eccentricity of a nutty beekeeper, but there was something about her I could relate to. Our struggles weren't identical, and our ways of coping were worlds apart, but at the core, we were both driven by unhealed wounds. We both had difficulty with accepting things as they were, always fighting with ourselves in one way or another.

While I had no intention of staying sober, I couldn't help but absorb the lessons from the people in the AA groups.

"You know," Samantha, another regular attendee, started to say in her gentle voice, "the bees don't fight the honey. You just catch more flies—"

"No cross talk!" another member shouted out.

Dakota smiled and nodded. "That's true, wait for your share. But thank you, Samantha," Dakota whispered loudly. "Who's next to share?" Her eyes landed on me.

"Hey, I'm Lukas," I said, my voice wobbling a little. "I'm an alcoholic."

"Hi, Lukas," the group replied in that singsong chorus.

Usually, my shares were genuine, just like everyone else's. But sometimes that seven-year-old kid writing in his diary about being an *American Idol* contestant with a rampant case of SARS would come bursting out.

While the program cautions against the singular pleasure of sharing war stories, I noticed that everyone in the group couldn't help but relive their wildest escapades. I remember hearing things like, "It was the biggest Ponzi scheme in American history, and there I was stacking prostitutes like Lincoln Logs." Or a personal favorite: "I didn't just punch him in the face . . . I went full Tyson and bit his ear off."

So when my four minutes began I was unsure where to start. "I started selling Adderall and other stuff to kids in my class. I justified it 'cause they were desperate to break fourteen hundred on the SATs, and wanted to look extra snatched for their prom night. I thought I was helping, and of course I dabbled in the supply, and I figured, well, it's not heroin, right?"

A few people nodded, some gave me that soft, knowing look, while some raised their brows, as if to say, *Not exactly, but okay.*

Still, I couldn't shake the fact that selling Adderall to high school girls who wanted to get above a 1400 on the SATs wasn't going to cut it. So, I did what I knew best. I lied.

"The thing is," I continued, "that hustle didn't really fulfill me. I needed something bigger—I fell in with the cartel down in Tijuana, I was running with these . . . I don't wanna name names," I said. I looked around me cautiously. I made it sound like there was a real threat, like there was a hit out on me. "I shouldn't even be talking about it publicly. I've probably said too much. Thank you for listening."

When I looked around the room, I saw Dakota the beekeeper, with her hand over her heart as if she was saying, *I've been there, darling, I've been there with a cartel or two in my heyday.* My eyes danced across my audience; it looked as if the group was hanging on my every word. Retrospectively, that's sort of the whole point of AA: you talk, they listen. Still, walking out of the meeting, I felt like I'd just been christened the best storyteller in the entire world.

After the meeting, I went outside to the courtyard. The cigarette fog was so thick, it was as if they'd managed to hotbox the open air.

"Can I bum a cig?" I asked another attendee.

"Sure thing, El Narco," he responded.

"Excuse me?"

"Very detailed story, you remind me of myself when I was your age."

I'd sat through a few meetings with this guy and knew enough about his past to get the picture. He'd struggled with crack and lived on and off the streets since his teens. Now that he was well into his thirties, his sallow, pockmarked skin could prove it. In another life—if just a couple of breaks had gone his way—he could've been walking a runway in a warehouse somewhere. He had the sort of rugged good looks that made him immediately charming, the kind that would've made your mom just a little *too* friendly with him.

"I'm not sure I follow," I said, taking a drag.

"Those stories you're telling—they're good, you give quite a share. . . . But you're also full of shit," he said.

"I guess. . . ."

"How long have you been clean?"

"Got my thirty days last week."

"That's great, congrats. You ever wanna work through the real shit, gimme a call. I'm Dean."

I wasn't exactly thrilled at the idea of buddying up with this guy, but I didn't have many other options. I was low on people to talk to at the moment: Kaylee and I had finally ended things for good, and everyone else I was still loosely in touch with was out partying, enjoying their senior year.

My days were stuck in this in-between place where nothing really mattered. All I did was watch TV and movies with my mom, who was constantly oscillating between being disappointed in me and relieved I had a reason to stay home with her and out of trouble. So a middle-aged sponsor would have to do.

"Hey, is it still a good time?" I asked when I called him later that evening.

"Always," he said.

I proceeded to give Dean the highlights. I talked about wanting to move to LA so I could chase my dreams of acting and writing. I touched on the dissolution of my relationship with my dad, the worry I had for my older brother, and the ache of losing Tessa. It was as if I were reading out some stilted synopsis of my life—all explanation, no emotion.

"You seem really numb to it all. Sounds like you haven't processed any of it," he said.

"I mean, I've definitely done a lot of grieving and . . ."

"No, jackass, that wasn't a question. What I should've said is you *definitely* haven't processed any of it," Dean said, cracking himself up.

At first, his comment pissed me off. Who the hell was he to tell me I wasn't processing?

"I'm sorry, does crack help you process?"

Dean laughed.

"God, it's like I'm talking to a younger version of myself. You're every bit as insufferable as I was."

Then I was laughing, too. Immediately I felt lighter, and ultimately, like I could finally start being honest.

I admitted how terrified I always was. How I was a scared little bitch who lied to his journal. I told him everything.

"Well, I think you've found yourself a sponsor," Dean said once my rant was over.

"You'd be down for that?"

"Why else do you think I just listened to you yap for hours?" Dean laughed.

Whenever I'm in the presence of an older man, I can't help but go full "pick me"—shape-shifting, tap-dancing, bending over backward to win their approval. It's like a reflex. All I really wanted from these surrogate fathers was for them to validate my entire existence. But Dean? He saw right through the act. He called bullshit on all my artifice from day one.

And the reality was, I had so much shit I had to get off my chest—things I couldn't ignore anymore. I didn't have Kaylee. I didn't have the twins. The new guys I had grown close to at school had all distanced themselves as soon as I was put on probation. Then a few months later, Owen overdosed on an oxy pill laced with fentanyl and died. I saw that the guys were struggling to process it, but it only widened the gulf between us. Grief was something I understood; something I'd been carrying around for a while.

"I don't even know how to talk about it," I mumbled.

"One day at a time," Dean would say.

"Where'd you hear that one?" I asked, shitting on his cliché, though he was right. I needed to take it one day at a time.

When I got back to group, I hovered in the background, letting Double D: Dakota and Dean do most of the talking. He seemed to be a natural at telling the truth, while I was still unsure how to pivot from the stories about my kingpin days to the more emotional shit

I was actually going through. It was easier one-on-one, but with a crowd, I didn't know how to shake the impulse to deflect.

Finally, I got up the courage to say, "Hi, my name is Lukas, and I feel really tired of running from myself. Exhausted from trying to be anyone but myself, from constantly chasing some version of me that I don't even know exists."

I watched as the rest of the group stared at me, processing my words and genuinely relating to what I had to say. When my time was up, a middle-aged man in the room went next.

"Thank you for your share, Lukas," he said, his voice steady. "It brought up a lot for me. . . ."

He paused, as if gathering his thoughts, then continued, "Honestly, I've been running from myself, too. And hearing you say that, it hit me harder than I thought it would."

As he spoke, I shot a glance over at Dean, who nodded at me in approval. I wasn't just running from my past; I was searching for something to shape the future.

Up until then, I never really questioned why acting was the one thing I kept coming back to. I assumed it was just because I was starved for attention. Or that acting camp in Lake Arrowhead was the first time I felt like I fit in. As those months stretched on and on, acting seemed like the only thing that gave me a purpose, something to work toward.

With all my extra downtime, I had too much space to think about what the hell I was going to do once I got out of this place. Eventually, I started making a plan and mapped out everything I needed to do so that by next year, I'd officially be in LA and on my way to pursuing my dreams of being an actor.

I was so unequivocal about the choice that I disregarded that my résumé consisted of only a warts commercial, an infomercial, and one disastrous regional theater production. Instead, I resolved to educate myself. I spent my time putting away the dating shows and studying old movies I hadn't seen before, like *Network*, trying to mimic the actors' intensity, or the rapid-fire rhythm of speaking like in *His Girl Friday*. It wasn't formal training, but it made the time pass with a feeling that I was achieving something.

And then, almost without realizing it, a year had passed.

I was back in that church, except this time I was standing in front of everyone, being handed my one-year chip and celebrating the end of my probation.

"Can't lie, I never pictured this day happening when I agreed to be your sponsor," Dean said.

"What the fuck?" I asked.

"I'm just fucking with you, dude. You think I'd take on a hopeless cause?"

Other than Brody and Bunny, I'd never had a genuine friend in my entire life. I'd wanted one so badly, whether it be my brothers or the kids at my middle school who had rejected me. Dean, Buddy, Brody, and I had gravitated toward each other because we were outsiders and needed one another. Dean had a full life outside of the program, and a whole other universe of loved ones that I didn't even know about. And still, he opted to let me in. To make me his friend.

The twins had done the same. They never left. I did. When my dad pulled away from me, I pulled away from them. And while my twelve-step work had helped me see there was a long line of people I owed amends to, Brody and Bunny were the two I still couldn't bring myself to face.

I spent a lot of time thinking about what I wanted to say to the twins. *I'm sorry for taking you for granted* didn't feel like enough. *I missed you so much you're the only people who have truly ever un-*

derstood me, and I threw it all away felt like too much. Finally, I stopped overthinking and dialed their number.

"Well, it only took you a year," Brody stated when he picked up the phone.

"I'm sorry—"

"For which thing? Telling everyone that we looked like formula babies?" Brody asked.

I nervously laughed. "Oh, that was—"

"Or that our mother wasn't able to breastfeed, and that's why we were lopsided," Brody retorted.

"Maybe I took the preemie thing too far—"

"It's really hard to breastfeed in an incubator!" Bunny shrieked in the background.

"I don't know the logistics! I was a fucking dick, but I really miss you guys. Truce?" I asked, fearful of the idea of another rejection.

"Fine. . . . It's not like we *didn't* miss you either," Brody said.

"Thank you. Guys, you have no idea how shit things have been," I said.

"Karma . . . Ugh. How can we help?" Bunny asked.

"Honestly . . . my curfew finally got lifted, and I need a night with my twins again."

An hour later, Brody and Bunny picked me up to go to a party at some house about twenty minutes south. When we got there, everyone was hanging out back by the cliff-front infinity pool, playing beer pong and dancing to Jessie J's "Price Tag." Now that I was able to drink again, I beelined to the bar, throwing out the sobriety that I had worked toward for a year. I headed to the kitchen and slapped the bag of Franzia wine, which felt like smacking the ass of freedom and guzzling the acidic taste of confidence.

I scanned the crowd and couldn't find a single familiar face. It wasn't new; we'd crashed parties like this before, but this time it felt more obvious. Though we all looked like we were ripped out of the same Sunglass Hut catalog—these kids' glazed-over eyes and disaffected smiles made it clear we were from entirely different worlds.

I guided Brody and Bunny over to a table where there was a big group playing "Never Have I Ever."

"Never have I ever . . . cut myself . . ." one girl started. The girl next to her gave her a knowing look.

"Somewhere you could see it!" she added, laughing nervously to herself and gulping back a shot.

"Downer!" A guy to her left snickered.

"Okay, my turn. Never have I ever . . . been double-teamed." The friend giggled, while a surprising number of her friends' fingers lowered, sipping their drink.

The game continued circling around and around the table, as the revelations got more detailed but far less plausible. Eventually, they moved onto the outer circle, and Brody was up next.

"Never have I ever . . . had a finger up my ass," Brody blurted out in his usual flippant, shit-stirring manner. He erupted into laughter, his lithe limbs jiggling with each laugh. My focus was elsewhere—on the way the guys stiffened; they all seemed to have just placed their finger not in a hole but instead on what exactly it was they didn't like about Brody.

"The *fuck?* You gay, dude?" the bro asked while rising from his seat.

"Are you, dude?" Brody responded without hesitation, puffing up his bird-boned chest as he spoke.

"Nah, I'm not a faggot, brother," the bro said, taking another step forward to reveal his brawny, red-blooded frame.

"You sure? 'Cause you're wearing a pink tank top. You *seem* like a faggot," Brody said.

"You're the faggot," the bro said as all the blood rushed to his face.

"Indeed, I am. But takes one to know one," Brody said so triumphantly that, for a moment, I thought he might've won the faggot-off.

That was until the bro lunged forward, grabbing Brody by the neck, and trapping him in a headlock. In his grasp, Brody looked like a folded origami crane. Though Brody tried wriggling his way out—kicking his feet and barking like a rabid dog—he only enraged the guy even more. He began squeezing Brody's neck tighter while wrestling him to the ground without letting go of his chokehold.

Then, before I knew it, I was on top of the tank-topped bro, pushing him off Brody. I punched him in the nose again and again, just like I saw in the movies. Or maybe it just felt that way in the moment. All I truly remember is that soon enough, his buddies were beating the living shit out of me. Wailing me in the ribs and knocking me in the face until I fell flat onto a puddle of my blood. My vision began to blur, surrendering to a concussion.

Before it went completely black, I felt a hand cover my mouth, with its fingers stretching out to seal my nose. In those final moments of consciousness, something old, something buried deep within me, kicked in, an instinct, raw and animal: I bit him.

I felt my teeth sink into the tender flesh of his palm as I heard the bro gasp and pull back.

"He fucking bit me!" the guy shrieked, his hand now bleeding heavily.

"You stupid fuck," said one of his friends before kicking my face so hard that I finally lost consciousness.

It was, to put it mildly, not a great night. There were a few seconds, though, between that first punch and lights out, where I actually enjoyed myself. It reminded me of those first weeks of probation, when every emotion I'd ever repressed came storming up to the surface. In the throes of the fight, I had an outlet for those feelings—and for that brief, brutal moment, I felt free.

I thought my sole motivation for jumping in was to defend Brody. Because at the time, I also thought I was totally, 100 percent straight. I'd been so happy for Brody that night he came out in the limo bus, but subconsciously, that was probably part of the reason I drifted from the twins in the first place. I wasn't ready to look at my own sexuality: My reaction was mixed-up with the confusion I experienced that night in the tent with the girl and that counselor at camp. The part of me that was curious and how much I hated myself for it. I wasn't ready to grapple with any of it.

Hearing the word *faggot* hurled at my best friend with such rage snapped something inside of me. I wasn't just fighting for Brody. I was fighting for that little boy in the tent, the one too scared to face what he already knew.

"His eyes are dilated. Hey man . . . can you hear me?" an unfamiliar voice called out.

When I first opened my eyes, all I could see was the iPhone flashlight that was beaming in front of my face, blinding me.

"You're awake. Phew. That's great. Can you follow this light with your eyes for me?" said the guy while he glided the iPhone torch in front of my face.

"Good. Can you tell me what your name is?" he asked.

"Yeah. It's, uh, Barkley," I stammered out.

"This is so fucked," Brody choked out between heaving tears.

"I'm fucking with you, I know I'm Lukas. Where the fuck am I?" I asked.

With the iPhone no longer in my face, everything slowly came into view. The guy who'd been tending to me was actually a greasy-faced teenage kid in a BMX motorsports jersey.

I'd been deposited in the back seat of what I assumed was this stranger's pickup truck, and Brody and Bunny were squeezed into the middle seat beside me.

"Oh, thank God you're awake, man. We were so worried about you," said the jersey guy.

"Sorry, who are you?" I asked.

"Jason. I'm a nurse," he said.

"Aren't you still in high school?" I asked.

"I'm going to nursing school in the fall. You're asking good questions, that's a good sign," Jason said.

I tried to pull myself upright, but my body gave out all over again. The rest of the car ride unspooled in disjointed flashes: the sting of something cold against my face, the neon green of a Monster Energy can as Jason pressed it to my swollen skin, the blur of his voice, my own confusion over who he was, and why he was touching me.

It wasn't until I was lying in a hospital bed, the sterile scent of antiseptic thick in the air, that reality finally snapped back into focus.

Growing up, I was never afraid of doctors like other kids were. I always associated them with a sense of pride. At the hospital, my dad was important, respected even. It felt good to witness him in his element. As I got older, hospitals just made me feel shitty and I could only dwell on the fact I'd never meet that version of my dad again.

But this time, when I woke up, all I felt was gratitude. There was my mom, stroking my hand—the only parent I ever needed.

"You really had me pay for three rounds of braces just for you to get your teeth all jacked up?" were the first words out of her mouth.

"I'm sorry," I mumbled through my painfully dry lips.

"I'm just so happy you're alive. We'll figure out your teeth later," she said.

"They're that bad?"

"The nose, too."

"*What?*"

"Shh. You just rest."

When the doctor came in with my chart, I learned that my mom was actually underplaying how fucked up my face was. My orbitals were broken, as was my nose. My jaw was fractured; my teeth chipped beyond repair.

"I'm such a piece of shit," I said to my mom when the doctor left.

"Honey, you're not a piece of shit, you're an idiot. I always said Brody was going to get his ass kicked one day. He's got a big mouth on a little body. Now look at you." She sighed. "You were defending him. You did the right thing."

I didn't have the heart to tell her that I wasn't just referring to the fight, I was talking about my entire existence. I'd spent the past year working so hard to get myself to a place where I could leave San Diego and all the mistakes I thought I'd left behind. However, the second I had the opportunity to return to the life I swore I was done with, there I was, ten toes down. You dumb fuck, Dean texted later that afternoon.

I know. I am such a dumb bitch. I feel so bad, I wrote back.

I WROTE THIS FOR ATTENTION

One day at a time, remember? Everyone relapses, it's part of recovery.

Are you saying I'm not special?

That's exactly what I'm saying, you little rat.

My stint in the hospital lasted only a few days, but the doctors informed me that I'd have to lay low for the next few months and focus on recuperating. And even though I'd spent the past year chained to my house, chomping at the bit to get to LA, I was grateful to have that extra time with my mom.

Growing up, it was rare for just the two of us to have the place to ourselves. Between my brothers, their friends, and all the neighborhood kids, it was like living in a fog of Axe Body Spray and pubescent volatility. By the time it was my eighteenth birthday, it was just me. The lingering scent of stale cologne and sweat had finally faded, replaced by something unfamiliar: stillness, and now, I was the last to leave the coop.

My oldest brother, Jesse, had been gone for years, building a life with his childhood sweetheart. Travis, though still physically within the county lines, felt like he lived in a completely different country. He'd distanced himself from the chaos of our family and found his own apartment, a girlfriend, and a job delivering both weed and pizzas. Meanwhile, Sean was home, but he was running out of time, with just a few months left before he was due in prison.

And even though Cory was just a few streets away, holed up in his trailer, we hardly ever saw him. So when I pulled up to the house after a shift at the retirement home and found him standing by the curb, I had to do a double take. He'd cut off his stringy black hair in favor of a buzz cut so short that his scalp gleamed under the streetlight. It wasn't just the hair—it was something deeper. He looked smaller.

"Luke, come here, man," he slurred, one hand reaching out while the other took another gulp from his energy drink. "I love you, bro." He looked anxiously toward the house and started pacing. "Mom's flipping out . . . I need to get the hell out of California. I'm so happy I caught you, bro."

"What the hell are you talking about? Why do you look like a middle school PE teacher?"

Cory slid a hand over his smooth head where his dyed, jet-black hair once hung in fried strands.

"I can't escape the system, man. I just . . . I keep fucking it up. I only had three beers—barely over the limit. They took me in. Another DUI on my record."

Anytime Cory got arrested, it was always just three beers.

"Anyway," he continued, "there's too many opportunities to do drugs in San Diego. It's fucking impossible to be sober here."

Impossible was another one of Cory's most used words in his personal *Merriam-Webster*. It was always "impossible" to get a job, "impossible" to make an appointment. Every task was "impossible," though I'd seen time and time again throughout my childhood that if Cory was sober, anything, in fact, was possible for him.

"This town's a fucking heroin hub. The only way to escape it is to leave. I don't know what else to do, man." His voice cracked for just a second before he pushed it back down with an inhale of his cigarette.

"I'm out of moves . . . I got a buddy who's a recruiter, he can get me stationed right away, but it's in the middle-of-fucking-nowhere Missouri."

I nodded, taking him in. It was clear he was scared shitless, and as much as I was going to miss him, I was hoping that it wasn't going to be "impossible" for him to thrive in Missouri.

"I get it."

"I love you," he said.

"I love you, too. Just please don't become a fucking bro-y jarhead," I said as a taxi pulled up in front of our house.

"And watch out for any privates named Ryan."

"What?"

"Nothing."

"Don't get too used to me being gone," Cory said, slinging the duffel over his shoulder and pulling me in tight.

He was doing what he'd always done: slinking out, not making a scene, but still leaving behind turmoil in his wake. Like all the times before it, all I could do was watch as he left.

Later that night, I laid with my mom in bed, trying to comfort her with reality TV and back scratches as she wept.

"Oh God, they'll ship him overseas in a heartbeat. He doesn't even believe in war; he's not a fighter, and then what? He'll come back in a box, that's what!" she cried. To her, Missouri might as well have been an active war zone.

Listening to her only made my guilt feel more potent. *Would leaving make me a traitor, or just another person trying to survive?* I wondered to myself. For a moment I thought about using the opportunity to come clean to her—to let her know that I, too, was gearing up to ship off.

"Mom, can I ask you something?" I said, trying to summon the courage.

"Yeah"—she sniffled—"but it has to be quick, I need to see the end of this season," she said, her hands still in my hair, only half focused on the TV.

"Do you ever wish you didn't have kids?"

"Yes," she said, petting our dog instead. "I should have just had dogs."

"Wow, thanks." I nudged her, and finally she laughed a little.

"I'm kidding, some are harder than others. Cory and you aren't exactly a walk in the park, but I love you guys so much."

"Do you ever wish you'd had an abortion?"

"My God, why would you ask me something so awful?"

"I don't know, sorry."

"I have had one."

"What? When?"

"When I was seventeen, when I was twenty-two, then one other time when I was—"

"Wait, what?!"

"Yes, it was the eighties! And the nineties... but I always knew I wanted some semblance of a family; I wanted to have the family I saw on TV, like *Ozzie and Harriet*, the mom had a pretty dress on, the husband would come home after work, and the kids were well-behaved and groomed." She took a while staring off. "It was all fake."

Her voice was different than I'd ever heard it before. It sounded small and wounded, not loud and unrestrained. I knew my mom loved her kids more than anything in this world. It wasn't that I questioned her love for me. I just couldn't wrap my head around how she could still keep loving us so unconditionally through all the pain we'd caused her.

"Aren't you tired of having to love us?"

"You have no idea, do you? You're mine. All of you. I'm not going anywhere."

12.

Leaving Las Laughlin

In my family, outbursts are our comfort zone. Silence is not. On the road trip my mother had planned for the two of us to accompany Sean as he self-surrendered at a federal penitentiary in Tucson, Arizona, the best we could do was small talk. Just run-of-the-mill comments on the traffic patterns, weather changes, and radio stations.

"I wish Trav could have gotten the day off work; they always make him work too much," Mom muttered to herself.

"Are you guys hot? It's boiling out today. This damn air-conditioning doesn't work for shit," she said again to nobody in particular as she fiddled with the AC.

Then, silence again.

Still, the silence was only an illusion. We all knew one another well enough to know exactly what we were all thinking. Those loud, daunting thoughts rattling in all of our heads were bumping up against one another, whether we wanted them to or not.

For a moment, my mom opened her mouth as if to say something, anything to fill the heavy space. Instead, she closed it, the words not coming, feeling the weight of whatever it was beneath the surface pressing harder than before.

When we finally pulled off the highway, a cluster of palm trees draped in fluorescent Christmas lights announced our first stop: Laughlin, a small casino resort enclave at the southern tip of Nevada. If Reno is the poor man's Vegas, then Laughlin is a degenerate's Disneyland.

We'd gone hours off-course just to stretch the trip a little longer. None of us said it out loud, but it was clear: we weren't in a rush to get to the ending. My mom booked us an evening at Silver Sands, and from the moment we hit the cracked asphalt of the parking lot, the atmosphere in the car shifted. My toes unclenched, Sean went back to his rambling, and my mom was electrified.

Before we could even check into our room, we lost my mom to the slots. With a Coors Light in one hand, and the other on a lever, she looked hopeful. There was so much in her life she couldn't control: from her partner to her exes to her sons. For whatever reason, when she was playing the slots, she had the power. Like that $50,000 jackpot she'd won so long ago was still within her reach, as long as she kept on playing the game.

"Why don't we give your mom some alone time?" Sean said.

"Sure," I said.

Walking outside in the desert heat, it felt as if I'd been bitch-slapped by the sun. Silver Sands, like every casino I'd grown up in, was wrapped in layers of heavily tinted, double-paned glass doors. The cacophonous ringing of the *Game of Thrones*, Cleopatra, and Da Vinci Diamonds slot machines made the ambience more disorienting. I think that's another reason my mom was so drawn to the slots, on that day and all the others before it. Between the adrenaline and overstimulation, there wasn't any room left to worry about the real shit.

One of the casino's main selling points was its location on the Colorado River. To attract families as well as gamblers—or, more realistically, the families of gamblers—they'd built a small, man-made beach on the river's edge. There you could hit the bar for burgers and watered-down tiki drinks, or, if they were feeling particularly adventurous, brave the grimy slides that slid down into the piss-tinged shallow end.

When Sean appeared in a pair of shorts adorned with a fire-breathing dragon crawling up his leg, he officially became the tackiest looking vacationer in a resort with nothing but gaudy dressers.

"Pretty cool, right?" Sean asked, entirely genuine. I looked down at his shorts that hung down so low they met his socks. There was no skin, just shorts and socks.

"Yup. So sick," I said, sounding more twatish than I intended.

"Let's grab some piña coladas?" he asked.

"Let's do it." I smiled. I was eighteen but inherited Travis's ID. Meaning I stole it from his wallet when he turned twenty-one. Sorry, Travis.

"I got it," I said as he lifted his wallet out. "This is on me."

With our drinks secured, we grabbed a pair of neon inner tubes and made our way toward the lazy river. Floating there, I felt all the unease of the car ride dissipate. In its place a wave of nostalgia crept in. Sean had annoyed the living shit out of me when he first came into my life when I was nine years old. His presence meant less time with my mom. However, over time there were things that I grew to love about him. He always supported me, especially with anything creative. In fact, he championed it. He was there for me when it counted: bailing me out of any trouble I got into, or whistling louder than anyone else while watching me from the bleachers as I walked down the podium and finally graduated from high school a month prior.

"Those girls over there are totally checking you out," Sean said while pointing at a pair of twentysomethings.

"Maybe they're checking *you* out," I said, going with the bit.

"Oh, yeah, with this gut," he said, slapping his stomach.

Looking at Sean laughing at himself, I started considering what he must've been feeling. I'd always known that my parents weren't these perfect, infallible human beings, Sean included. It's a lot easier to accept the mistakes your parents have made than to try to empathize with their own shame they've brought upon themselves.

"Not to be a buzzkill right now, but aren't you scared . . . ?" I finally asked.

"Of course I am," he replied, his smile fading just a little. "But I'll be fine. Don't worry about me. You just take care of your mom, okay? Hold it down while I'm gone."

I nodded.

"You hear me? Don't worry. Before you know it, I'll be back."

Although I'd convinced myself I was just worried about my mom being left by herself, Sean going away was taking its toll on me, too. By now, I'd gotten used to people vanishing from my life. With each departure, I became even more convinced I'd never quite belong anywhere. That as soon as I did start to delude myself into trying to fit back in, the universe would find some new and spectacular way to pull the rug out from under me.

"I didn't think I'd ever fuck with you as much as I do," I said. "I'm sorry for talking shit about you behind your back. Even though you're going to prison, it turns out you're not, like, *one of the bad guys*."

"Thank you? I think." Sean laughed. "You weren't exactly the 'ideal stepson,' either. But . . . I wouldn't have it any other way, little buddy."

Sean and I laid out on the tubes for another hour or so, before deciding it was time to pull my mom away from the slots for dinner. I filled my plate up with all the weird assortment of shit the buffet had to offer: chicken alfredo pasta, something that looked like crab, and beef Wellington. Being back among the deep-fried and poorly defrosted food of my childhood really helped with the fantasy my mom was trying to create for the three of us. That we were just a normal family on a normal road trip getaway.

We left early the following morning, since we were still five hours away from the barren desert town where the prison was located. I tried to fall back asleep, so my mom kept the radio off for the first half of the ride. Her anxious humming and tapping on the steering wheel kept me awake. Eventually she just started talking outright. She was too uncomfortable with the silence; we all were.

My mom turned to Sean, taking him in for a moment. "You look like a sunburned yeti."

"Thank you, sweetheart. How'd you do last night?" Sean smiled.

"I lost $300. Those damn slots didn't pay, but wasn't that hotel great? Did you have fun?" my mom asked for the sixth time this morning.

"Yeah," I replied.

"Anyone else feel sick from the buffet?" Sean asked, chewing on a Pepto Bismol tablet.

"No, because most people don't eat half the buffet." My mom grimaced as he chewed the meds.

"Oh! Before I forget," my mom said, reaching into her knockoff Longchamp and handing Sean an envelope.

"How much did you put in there?" Sean asked.

"I told you—eight hundred dollars," my mom said.

"But the limit's a thousand a month?"

"I'm not gonna max out your commissary money every month just so you can buy all the ice cream and Reese's Pieces you want," she said, now snapping.

"Do you think they have Reese's Pieces?" he asked, trying in his best effort to make light of the situation.

The closer we got to Tucson, the more relentless the heat became, with the temperature pushing 106 degrees Fahrenheit by the time we arrived at its perimeter. Everything around us looked sunburned. The adobe-red dunes, yellowing cacti, even the wild boars that were barely visible beneath the ashy haze. I wondered if Sean would be able to see all of this from his cell window. Did prisons have views?

As we inched closer to the base, we were greeted by a large sign that read: "You have escaped if you have passed this." For a moment, I wasn't sure if it was some kind of fucked-up attempt at irony. Then I realized why one would have a prison in the heart of the Arizona desert. Even if someone made it beyond the sign, there was nowhere to go—only the vast, unforgiving wasteland stretching endlessly in every direction.

My mom took one look at the sign, and without saying anything, grabbed another crumpled hundred-dollar bill from her bag.

"Here," she said quietly, offering it to Sean.

The prison complex was set on 640 acres and divided into several different units organized by security levels. The grounds were paved with the same shade of red dirt as the dunes surrounding it. It reminded me of the dreary, utilitarian slabs of concrete I'd gone to middle school in, only here they were adorned with barbed wire and chain-link fences.

Sean headed inside the detention center, where he had to officially surrender before saying his final goodbyes. We sat inside the waiting room behind the plexiglass barriers, and when he came back about five minutes later, he'd changed into a thin, starched pair of gray sweatpants and a matching shirt. My mom started crying as soon as she saw him in the uniform. Sean remained oddly mellow about the whole thing—as if after almost two years of going on about how he'd "never heard of any other broker being sent to prison for wire fraud," he'd finally accepted his fate and was at peace with it.

"Why is this happening?" my mom kept asking, now fully sobbing.

"I don't know, I didn't do anything," Sean whispered.

"They don't send people to prison who haven't done anything, dumbass," my mom snapped.

"I really didn't—"

My mom put a hand up to him to stop talking as she worked through her tears.

"Hey, on the bright side. I have all this time to work out. The next time you see me, I promise I'll be less fat," Sean joked, but my mom's crying just got louder and louder, and the security started to take notice.

A guard took a step closer, his hand resting on the radio at his side, ready to intervene if things escalated further.

"I think we might need to leave now," I said, turning to her.

My mom was too worked up to respond. She just hugged Sean one more time.

"I love you," my mom whispered into Sean's ear, a confession that she didn't like to admit.

"I love you, too. I'll be fine," Sean reassured her.

After they parted, Sean kept his head down as if he were trying not to have his last mental image of my mom be such a painful one. Right as I was carrying my mom through the door, out of the corner of my eye I saw Sean's head pick back up, and his gaze met mine. We shared a look that felt heavier than words, and then instinctively, I flipped him the bird. Our silent code for saying *I love you*. And when I saw him raise his middle finger in the air right back at me, I realized this was what unconditional love really felt like. This man had been at times reckless with his life and his career, and had hurt my mom in the process, but despite everything, I still loved him.

"It's going to be okay, Mom. I promise," I kept repeating to her all the way to the car.

"I don't know if it will," she cried.

"You always tell me how tough I am. Well, you're the strongest bitch I know—"

"Don't say *bitch*," she said through her tears.

"Sorry. But, really, you are the strongest person I know. You're going to get through this; we're going to get through this," I continued over and over through her crying.

Once we were back in the car, I lost it entirely. Never one to be outdone, I wept so forcefully that I managed to drown out the Evanescence CD my mom had put on.

Wake me up inside. I can't wake up, Amy Lee screamed through our stereo system.

With each *wake me up*, my adrenaline spiked further, until I felt so keyed up that all the secret plans I'd been keeping from her kept threatening to spill out. I'd avoided burdening her for so long, only now realizing how much I'd been burdening myself.

Three hours into our drive, while we were passing through the thick of Yuma County's mountain range, the CD started back over again from the top. Before we even got to the chorus of the song, I snapped, slamming the music off and word vomiting all over the car.

"We really need to talk," I said.

"What's up?" she said between taking deep breaths to steady her nervous system.

I managed a weak smile, not able to produce the words.

She sighed, glancing at me before fixing her eyes back on the road. "Come on," she said, curt, wiping the dried tears from her eyes, "I really don't have time for a game of charades, not today. Just say it, whatever it is."

"I'm moving to LA," I finally blurted out.

For a moment, she didn't say anything. Her hands stilled, and her expression flickered between surprise and something unreadable. Then she carefully swallowed a flood of emotions, something she always seemed to be able to do.

"I'm going to be an actor," I murmured.

Then, finally, she nodded.

"Is this what you really want?" she asked.

"Yes."

"Then you should. That's exactly what you should do," she said, then turned the CD back on.

The final leg of our drive passed by in relative silence. This time, the quiet took on the ease of our new shared understanding.

13.

The Shitty Committee

"The Lizard King came inside me."

The handwriting Sharpied onto the door on the Jim Morrison room of the Alta Cienega Motel was neater than it had any right to be. I couldn't afford the room itself, so I booked the one adjacent. The place was filthy. The carpet was striped, but it was so stained that the lines looked like a polygraph test made of shit. And yet, living there felt like the most thrilling, glamorous thing I'd ever done. I was in LA. I was eighteen years old, and I was on my way to becoming an actor.

My money from the warts commercial was finally accessible now that I was an adult. The cash gave me a smooth start in my transition to LA. It paid for the motel and let me focus on different acting classes. I quickly enrolled in one closest to me—a daily gauntlet run by a woman who treated the theater like it was her religion. She delighted in reminding me that being hot shit in Seattle didn't mean that I was hot shit here. I kept correcting her—I was from San Diego—but she didn't seem to care; no one in LA seemed to give a shit about anything other than themselves.

Outside of class, I went from cattle call auditions to stalking agents across town desperate to land a meeting. Despite cranky teachers and uninterested agents, I was in awe and in love with my new city—the palm tree–lined streets, the majestic jagged hills, the towering neon billboard posters. I was a clueless little shit, but delusion makes for a good sidekick when you're just getting started.

The headshots I handed out came with a fabricated résumé. An inspired work of fiction. I created credits of shows with names like *Two of a Kind* on ABC, about twins who were separated at birth. I claimed I'd studied theater at some university in some program that felt niche enough to not be questioned. And after enough lies and enough laps around LA trying to get people to like me, I landed at an agency. It no longer exists, but at the time, they anointed themselves "the Best Acting Agency in the Valley."

I was just getting started, but I hustled my way into a few small roles—one-liners, maybe two if the universe was feeling generous. Just enough to keep those Valley agents convinced I had something worth betting on. Even if, more often than not, my line would vanish in the edit, erased so completely it was as if I'd never been there in the first place.

I carried on. I stood on the studio lots, soaking it in like it might seep into my oversize pores—wondering if the casting couch would've been easier than all this waiting and hoping. I ran through Stars Hollow and the *Friends* set, marveling at a world I'd seen only through a screen. I held on to the hope that one day, my line would make the cut, my place on the lot would feel permanent, and I would feel like I belonged.

Most nights, I'd run past the stairwell crew of the Alta Cienega

Motel. I usually gave them a wave or a smile but never overstayed my welcome. They were always there, gathered on the cracked steps, the royalty of the motel holding court.

"Yo, actor boy!" one of them called out as I was heading to my room.

It was Yvonne, her voice raspy from years of chain-smoking only yellow American Spirits, which she claimed were "healthier." She worked out of her hotel room, though she never bothered to elaborate on what she did exactly.

"Come here. Don't be shy." She waved her cigarette like a wand, beckoning me over.

"You want to hang out with us for once?" Yaya chimed in, a younger girl with a goth vibe, her long-sleeve shirt ripped at the wrists for her thumbs to poke through, and a tall can of Mickey's clutched in her hand.

I hesitated for a moment, mulling it over. Since moving to LA, I'd been a full-blown hermit, laser-focused and never giving myself permission to slow down. Relaxing felt like a trap—like if I let my guard down for even a second, the old Lukas from San Diego might claw his way back in. And I couldn't afford that.

"Nah, I've got—" I gestured vaguely at the backpack slung over my shoulder. "Stuff to do."

Yvonne smirked. "Let me guess. Another one of those plays? What was it last time, something about a glass circus?"

"Menagerie," I corrected.

Instead of joining them, I retreated to my dim motel room. I dropped onto the creaky bed and spread out my script for *This Is Our Youth*, by Kenneth Lonergan, a play about aimless teenagers stumbling their way through life. It felt fitting—art imitating life, or maybe the other way around.

I'd sit in front of the mirror, reciting monologues over and over, determined to nail them without glancing at the page.

Afterward, I'd do my vocal drills until the other motel guests would start screaming and slapping the walls, begging me to stop. If the price of my dreams was a few pissed-off residents of the Alta Cienega, so be it. I was determined to break free from my San Diego mumble, to make my voice something worth listening to. And as my "red leather, yellow leather" drills got faster, and more precise, my conviction got stronger.

I FIRST HEARD of Leigh Kilton-Smith from an agent, one who told me I was too green but that there was a teacher for me who'd be a perfect match. He was right. Every week, Leigh showed up decked out in some bright suit, her wild curls spilling over her shoulder pads. We felt like two long-lost twins, each given half a medallion at birth, and now we were finally fitting the pieces together after a lifetime apart. Working with Leigh felt less like "class" and more like collaboration. It felt like teaming up with a pro who wasn't afraid to call it as she saw it. She had no time for sugarcoating, but her critiques didn't tear you down like in other classes. Instead, they propelled you forward.

One day after class, I stopped her on her way out of the studio.

"Leigh, can I talk to you for a second?"

She paused for a moment before she continued loading her infant squirrels into their crates in the back of her car. She prefaced that the baby squirrels had to accompany us in class in order to keep up with their feeding schedule. It was not just actors she was keeping alive.

"Give me a second, let me make sure that Buddy and Thug are tucked in. . . ."

"I think I might be shit," I said over the sound of the squirrels clawing anxiously around their crate.

"Ah, the shitty committee fucking with you again?"

The shitty committee was the name she'd given the voices in our heads that remind us what a worthless piece of shit we were.

"So it would seem, but I need you to really tell me the truth, rip me to shreds, what is the worst thing about my acting?" I begged her.

"First of all, stop asking people to rip you to shreds. It's not necessary. It's gonna lead to abusive relationships that you're gonna mistake for love."

Leigh took a big breath and narrowed in on me.

"You know my biggest criticism right now of where you are in your career," she started, her voice swaying with that Southern drawl that somehow made every word sound like an invitation. "I see the plan."

"What?"

"Did I stutter? I said I see your plan. I see that you've done the work and now a day later you're stuck in your preparation, and you haven't done the necessary work to let your plan go."

When she locked eyes with me, she forced me to let go of every false version of myself I'd been holding on to.

"You're relying on your plan, and that's when your work runs the chance of being dull and uninteresting. You're many things, Lukas, but uninteresting ain't one of them," she said.

Before Leigh, every casting director always had the same note about me: "We just don't know what to do with him."

My agents were just as baffled, telling me things like, "You need to figure yourself out and present them with who you are. Are you a jock? A goth? Nerdy? And, for the love of God, get your hair figured out. It's so overprocessed. Just a natural fair color so your eyes pop." Leigh saw past the confusion, the labels, and all the feedback that had me second guessing everything about myself.

"Did you hear me?" Leigh asked.

"Yes."

For a moment, I thought I might cry. I hadn't expected her to say it so simply, and even though I knew she was right, I didn't know how to fully accept it.

"But if I don't know what's going to happen—"

BAM!

Something was suddenly flying toward my head, a squirrel? No . . . though it was definitely something. Instead of ducking, I reached out with my hand and caught the foreign object in the air.

It was a tissue box that she'd thrown at me from the trunk of her car.

"What the actual fuck?"

"Bet you didn't see that coming, did you?"

I did not.

"And yet you caught it. You didn't have to think about it. You didn't have to reference any notes on how to catch a tissue box being thrown at your head by your crazy acting teacher. You simply caught it, instinct kicked in, and you were in a state of trust."

"And shock," I interrupted.

"Trust! Trust in yourself. It's what's missing from your characters, and from you, Lukas. The art suffers and runs the risk of looking and feeling and smelling and being like everyone else."

"Trust. That's it?" I shouted louder than I anticipated.

"Don't yell. Oh, that reminds me, you use volume in place of honest emotion. Stop doing that also. But yes, that's the big advice. Trust."

"I barely *trust myself*. I haven't been to drama school; I have a practically empty résumé—"

"You're yelling at me again." She cut me off. "You have to stop paying so much attention to what you haven't done or you're going to be doing that for the rest of your life. Pay attention to what you *can* do. You can audition, learn, fall in love, get your heart broken, audition again, fall in love, get your heart broken again—and at every stage of the game, if you are honest and create from wherever you are, then your work will be, too."

This peroxided Miyagi was making sense.

"I can only say all this because I'm also deeply and profoundly afraid every moment of every day. I am a fuckup, I'm a fraud, but I either trust my life experiences and *my* path or I become the world's oldest hooker."

It was then that I knew Leigh wasn't just my teacher, she was my mirror. We were both overprocessed blonds with big mouths and even bigger dreams. We were a disaster pairing that somehow worked perfectly.

Hollywood traffics in homogeneity. It favors the type of malleable actor they can slot into place. Leigh had no interest in having me blend in with the fold. Her words struck me in a way that felt if I didn't listen to her, I would truly be fucked and that no one else could offer what was mine to give: my life, my mistakes, my vocal fry.

"Lukas?"

"Yes?"

"For the love of God, start having more fun with all of this, please."

"Thanks." I smiled.

"Now get the fuck out of my driveway, I gotta go feed these squirrels."

I drove down the 101 freeway, away from Leigh's, playing our conversation back on repeat. *Trust.* I thought of Leigh's voice, her Southern twang echoing in my head. *Trust.* I turned on some Lana Del Rey, and opened the windows.

THINGS DIDN'T SHIFT overnight. The rejection kept coming, as merciless and unforgiving as a series of bad one-night stands. I didn't care. I knew how brutal this game was going to be—my father had prepared me for rejection my whole life.

He and I had barely talked since the day he sat me down in that Orange County bar and told me about his *new* life. I still hadn't met his wife or their twin daughters, and, honestly, I wasn't sure I ever would.

And though I'd made peace with the disintegration of our relationship, it still left thorns all over my body that I hadn't been able to fully pluck off. His rejection would come to me like a ringing in my ears: It was like tinnitus, this persistent ringing voice inaudible to anyone but me, whispering that I was never good enough to keep around.

Sometimes, when an audition didn't go my way, that whisper would be amplified into a roar. It would remind me that I wasn't good enough—not for Hollywood, not for anyone, and definitely not for myself. And just when the noise threatened to fully consume me, Leigh's words drowned them right out: *If they don't want what you're selling, hop onto the next chair. There's a whole line of people waiting to buy that chair.*

A few months and many more rejections later, a casting director saw something in what I had to offer. When I was done with an audition, she took the lollipop out of her mouth and said, "You got a good voice." She booked me the next day to play the crush of Sally Draper, who was played by Kiernan Shipka on *Mad Men*.

The fitting for the show took place at Western Costume, a dimly lit warehouse in the Valley that smelled like a laundromat. As they pulled out several vintage outfits, I stood there in front of the mirror that seemed to reflect not only me, but myself in 1960, or whenever *Mad Men* took place. An era when people dressed with a level of class and sophistication I'd only ever seen in old films.

The night before, I had completely lost my voice. I couldn't speak. It could have been fear, a bacterial infection, or cosmic retribution for listening through the door while the guy before me auditioned for the part and stealing all the notes they gave him. When the costume designers took my measurements and asked me for my input, I did my best to power through with impish smiles and polite nods.

"Step over there for me, just behind the tape. Gotta grab a few shots."

We cycled through fit after fit, each one sketching out a different version of the character they were trying to build.

The moment I put on the last outfit—a pair of shorts, and no shirt—the wardrobe lady's eyes went wide as she did a double take. She had finally caught sight of what I'd been slyly keeping under wraps: a massive tattoo running along my ribs and a black Mockingjay perched on my calf. (Yes, from *The Hunger Games*. I really connected to the books when they came out!)

"Let me, uh—just get a couple shots for approvals, thank you."

While she snapped the photos and tried to act like everything was fine, I looked down and stared at my feet. At my dumb fucking tattoo. I could tell the odds were no longer in my favor.

I headed downtown toward LA Center Studios, where we were filming. The security guard barely glanced at me before shaking his head.

Word of my definitely-not-from-the-sixties tats had made the rounds. A few minutes later, my phone was buzzing with a call from the "Best Talent Agency in the Valley."

"They're letting you go. Oh man, I can't believe you're losing out on something like *Mad Men* over a tattoo!" *Click.*

I was told later that it would have taken too much time to cover up my tattoos in the makeup chair and the plan had been to start with the shirtless scene at top of the day. According to Kiernan Shipka, who, as fate would have it, became one of my closest friends, I was referred to as the "tattoo boy" on set. I may not have made it to set, but my legacy lived on for the rest of the season.

I pulled a U-turn to head north on the 101, devastated. That night, I lay in bed crying, convinced that all my efforts to outgrow the San Diego version of myself had been pointless. Some things time couldn't erase—especially the ones etched into my skin on a drunken night.

EVENTUALLY, I'D MANAGED to love LA again. Not in the way you love something safe, something steady. LA was a fickle mistress, tempting me with the discount lap dance of success, only to slap my hand away when I started believing she actually liked me.

Still, I kept coming back, constantly edged by her. All tease, no release.

Then one day, LA finally showed me she loved me back. I walked into my next audition messy, and unpolished. I didn't try to play the part, I just *was* the part. I wanted to show them who my character was before they had a chance to tell me who he should be. I infused him with everything Leigh told me to keep: my grit, my monotone speech, the parts of me that felt real. After the read, I saw the casting director's lips curl into a smile.

"You've got great instincts."

When they asked me to come in the next day for a callback with the showrunner, however, I had to turn it down. The timing clashed with my day job, working at a café, and no one was available to cover for me. I remember hesitating for a second, wondering if I should just risk calling out, but I couldn't afford to lose the job. Instead, I asked if there was another time to audition, fully expecting that to be the end of it.

Apparently, that je ne sais quoi of not giving a fuck—or at least the appearance of it—was exactly what got me the role. I was the only kid who didn't go to callbacks, and it somehow worked in my favor.

T@gged was a web series that would eventually go on to Hulu, but I didn't know that when I booked the gig. I also didn't know it would be the first time I would feel like I actually belonged to something, to a group, to a *family* of sorts.

We were filming in the middle of the New Mexico desert. There, we were just kids, playing make-believe, finding our way through this industry. None of us were precious about it. We were just living in the moment, figuring it out as we went along.

My role was a character named Brandon Darrow, a high school

bully who lived to wreak havoc. It was a real, breathing part, one that felt like it was made for me. Brandon's impulsiveness and loud emotions reflected parts of myself I hadn't fully examined.

Working on T@gged every day for three months gave us all the stability to feel at ease with one another. Even if we were living in a run-down hotel tucked beneath the freeway that had walls pockmarked with bullet holes.

"Lukas!" my castmate Claudia called out to me. She'd quickly become one of my closest friends on set. It was one of her first shows, too, but she had made a living since she was a fetus doing vlogs. With delicate features that made her look like a Polish princess and a charisma that pulled people in, Claudia had a way of making an impression. Everyone fell in love with her, wanted to be her best friend, or wanted to be her after the first five seconds of meeting her.

"What's up?"

"Can you help me run my lines? I feel like you really nail the scenes where you're being a dick," she whispered.

"Years of practice," I said, flashing a smile.

"No, seriously." She laughed, holding her script out to me. "Can you help? It sounds insane when I do it."

She pointed to a section of dialogue where my character rips into hers. I skimmed the lines, then turned back to her.

"Okay, what if you do the opposite of what the stage directions ask? Like instead of yelling it, just say this line casually. It might even come off bitchier," I said.

"Wait, yes, you're so right," Claudia said, pulling me into a hug. "You're the best."

Hannah, our director, rolled in later with sunglasses pushed up into her hair.

"All right, I'll be quick because every second I'm talking and we're not shooting, we're wasting more of our budget. No overtime today, please. We're shooting the hallway scene first with Brandon's fight with Hailey. Then, Claudia, your scene before lunch, and we'll end with you waiting at home for Rowan to come over," she said, shooting me a quick smile.

By the last scene of the day, we were racing against the clock, too crunched for time to head back to base camp to change. Instead, the wardrobe department came to set for a costume change. I was in the middle of swapping my shirt for the next scene when I felt Hannah's eyes on me. *Fuck, am I going to get let go again?*

She glanced at me for a moment, then at my chest down to my ribs, where my tattoo commemorating Tessa stood out in full force. She studied it for a beat, before tapping her script thoughtfully.

"You know," she said, "I think Brandon would absolutely have a tattoo in high school. Would you feel comfortable wearing no shirt?"

It was then that I started to actually *trust*. I trusted that I wasn't just going to end up back in San Diego, stuck in the same old loop, going nowhere fast. I trusted that while my path wasn't going to be clean or pretty, it was leading me forward not backward. Maybe not at my preferred speed, but nevertheless moving.

What Leigh said lingered with me: the kid who had faked an escape letter to break out of boot camp, who hustled his way into becoming the world's worst drug dealer, who shape-shifted his way through North County—he was still there. That scrappy, defiant kid was starting to grow up, but his spirit hadn't changed.

It was that same boldness that I had to hold on to, the same reckless determination that carried me through auditions and made sure every time I fell, I got back up.

I truly believe that if I'd been softer, more obedient, more willing to play it safe, I wouldn't have started working. The impulsiveness that once got me into trouble had also been my saving grace. The younger self I once saw as a walking disaster was really just a kid doing whatever it took to survive. The same fire that once burned me could now be the thing that fueled me.

I just had to trust that it wouldn't consume me first.

14.

The D in Apartment 23

The allure of living in the Alta Cienega wore off quicker than I'd imagined. New Mexico had given me the perspective to see that the motel wasn't some bohemian launchpad for my dreams. It was just a shithole. The complimentary pastry basket left by the front desk each morning had begun to look like what it really was: a box of doughnuts that the staff had been picking at all night. The shit-stained zigzag carpet was exactly what it looked like: a carpet full of shit.

I began to search Craigslist, errantly at first, and then more and more desperately. I found a two-bedroom, one that if I split with someone would only cost me a thousand a month, which, in LA, was a steal. So, I pounced on it like a cat on a hot tin roof.

The search for potential prospects to be my roommate was an . . . experience. First up was a twink who informed me that one of his kinks was to be ignored, and he preferred to be treated like a ghost. (Despite fully understanding and relating to this, I knew it wasn't a match.) Another prospect was an older lady with a parrot.

At first, I thought it was cool that the bird could talk. Then I realized it wasn't just her pet—it was her partner. That parrot could do more with that beak than just mimic, if you know what I mean. . . .

It became clear that I wasn't just looking for someone to split the rent and not murder me, I was looking for someone who could make the place feel like *home*.

So I called Travis. At the time, he was learning to become a mechanic, and I figured he'd be the perfect candidate since he could also fix anything that went wrong with the place. In reality, Travis was the key to helping me be a little less homesick.

"I found a place," I said, not wasting time. "It's small, but it's got character. I need you to do this for me."

"What? Why? I hate LA," Travis mumbled, half asleep.

"What could you possibly be doing in San Diego? Look, I'll pay more on my share, just don't leave me alone. What if I get murdered, or taken, please, please, please I need my big brother," I pleaded.

There was a long silence.

"Jesus Christ," he groaned. "Fuck it. I just broke up with Megan, so consider it good timing."

"I always thought she sucked. Thank you. Good night. Oh, also I get the bigger bedroom for paying more. Love you. You're the best."

My first apartment in LA was on the same street as my day job at Real, Raw, Live, which, contrary to the name, was not a porn studio but just an overpriced organic café. It was right in the heart of Franklin Village. At the time, that part of town didn't feel like LA; it felt ripped from the mid-gentrification days of Williamsburg, right after all the liberal arts students descended upon it and opened up vintage pop-up shops that served distressed denim and turmeric lattes.

Meanwhile, Travis would drive fifty miles each day to attend classes at an automotive school in Rancho Cucamonga. And even though I would tease him relentlessly, asking him about his UTI (which actually stood for Universal Technical Institute), I was so grateful he made the effort just so I wouldn't feel alone.

Our days started in separate worlds, but every evening we'd reconvene and find our way back to the living room. I'd grab the remote, throw on *Rock of Love* reruns, and he'd settle in beside me. Travis wasn't a superfan, but he never flinched. He just drank his Mountain Dew, smoked his pot, and sat beside me.

"You've been quieter than usual," he said.

"Just trying to figure some stuff out." I shrugged.

"I get it." He nodded. My brother, always a man of few words.

After a few minutes, I broke the silence again.

"Doesn't it trip you out that Dad lives like two miles away, but we don't know where? We've never met his kids, or his wife, or seen his place. If we wanted to, we could just . . . walk there right now."

Travis started tapping his hand against his mouth, the tic he inherited from our dad that always made me want to scream. And, just like Dad, he dodged the question.

"Nobody walks in LA."

There was a pause. He didn't say anything else, just stared at the TV like he was processing what I said. Finally, he exhaled. "I think it's easier to just not know, y'know?"

Travis pushed himself up with a groan. "I'm going to pass out. Night." He shuffled off, muttering something about traffic as he disappeared into his room.

Even with Travis there, and my few friends from *T@gged*, I still felt lonely in my new city. I tried to avoid slipping back into my old habits—abandoning my work to get drunk or high, or falling in love with anyone or anything, anytime I faced something too big and heavy to name.

The hollow feeling was relentless, coaxing me to fill it with something.

THE FIRST THING I noticed about him was his contradictions. He was in nurse scrubs but a pack of cigarettes were peeking out of his shirt pocket. Purposeful and reckless. Responsible yet self-destructive.

"Do you have a light?"

I stepped closer to the table he was sitting at outside of Real, Raw, Live as he fumbled in his pockets, still dazed.

"How old are you?"

"Twenty," I lied. I was nineteen, but twenty sounded so much hotter. I've always hated an odd number.

He smiled at me, exposing his big green eyes.

"I'm thirty, as of last night. Don't recommend it. Hangovers suck when you're my age," he said.

"Thirty is the new twenty."

"Thank you. I needed that," he said. "I'm Anthony. Are you free? Do you want to go on a walk?" he asked, already up from his seat.

I nodded, realizing I was definitely about to skip my acting class—a rare move from me, but for some reason, I felt like I had to, like I was about to step into something I couldn't quite explain.

We chatted as we walked up the foothills of the canyon, passing all the sprawling homes with their terra-cotta roofs, boxwood hedges, and sprawling bougainvillea. Then he stopped walking and looked over at me with a contorted smile.

"What?"

"You have horrible posture." Anthony laughed.

"What are you, a chiropractor?"

He let out another laugh, "I wish, I work in the ICU."

"I . . . C . . . U . . . are a judgmental little hunchback," I teased.

"Oh, okay, touché," he said, straightening up his posture. "Well, I started going to this new hot yoga place down the street, you should come."

"Yeah, maybe." I shrugged.

"Maybe? Give me your phone. I'm putting my number in," he said, reaching out his hand before I gave it to him.

We kept walking, until he suddenly stopped in his tracks to cross his legs like he was tucking his dick back.

"Dude, you good?" I asked, watching him wobble.

"All I've had the past twelve hours is cold brew and Jameson."

"And cigarettes," I added.

"Yes, and that. I gotta . . ." He pointed toward the bottom of the hill.

"Oh no." I laughed.

"Don't laugh," he cut me off.

We were moving fast now, rushing downhill as I struggled to keep up. He darted around corners, glancing back as I was holding in laughter, while his hands gripped his stomach. Until finally we reached the bottom of the hill and turned the corner to my new brick building. I looked up at the familiar structure. He looked at me, a confused expression crossing his face.

"Guess this is where I leave you. Sorry—"

"No worries. I'll text you," I said.

"Sounds good." He moved toward the front door, and I followed. He glanced back. "Are you stalking me?"

"What? This is my building."

His eyebrows lifted. "Wait? You live here?"

"Yeah? I just moved in."

He ran up the stairs while I lingered out front, scrolling my phone, replaying the way he looked at me, his eyes too kind.

Come to 23, he texted.

When he opened the door, I was hit with a sense of déjà vu. It wasn't just that his apartment had an almost identical layout to mine, but it also somehow felt like my father's house. Empty but not quiet. Stripped to the essentials—a mattress and a record player. Nothing else.

Before I could say anything, Anthony put on a record and passed me a smoke. From then on, we hung out every night. Anthony had gone to boarding school in New England before going on to an Ivy League college. Everything about him felt like an education: from his music—a mix of the greats like Joni Mitchell and Neil Young, to books—ensuring I read everything by Cormac McCarthy. I'd try to impress him with something obscure that would belie my "barely graduated from high school" level of education, sharing Ingmar Bergman movies or "philosophical" podcasts. When he would compliment my taste, it reinforced my self-worth. But no matter how many arthouse films I watched or niche cultural references I memorized, his taste always seemed to outclass mine.

I also couldn't ignore that Anthony was a decade older than me. The dynamic seeped into everything we did together. At some point, he got me to go to yoga, where my core got stronger, my posture improved, and I learned how to breathe.

During savasana, his hand would occasionally brush mine. That's kind of gay, I'd think. But as time went by, I'd let the thought linger—curiously—longer and longer with each errant pass of a pinkie.

Anthony had a sense of humor that was infectious. Sometimes when he caught a good joke, he held on to it like a dog with a bone, repeating it over and over until it became part of our language. My horrible echolalia only made it worse—I'd unconsciously echo his catchphrases and jokes back to him like a broken record, which only encouraged him more.

By day, I'd fall into my usual routine of making juices and coffees, or going to auditions. I was starting to feel stimulated and hopeful, better than any SSRIs ever made me feel. I found myself excited to get out of bed in the mornings. I had a real friend. The kind I'd been searching for since I moved to LA a couple of years ago. Someone I could talk to for hours on end. Until one night, I must have been talking too much—because mid-sentence, he suddenly interrupted me—

"All right, so I'm going to kiss you now."

"For sure. Wait, what?"

I began nervously laughing.

"Why are you laughing?"

I couldn't help it. I've always had a tendency to laugh when I'm nervous or when I'm masking my fear. This feeling was a mix of both. I took a deep breath, and I finally stopped laughing. I leaned forward and let him kiss me.

It was brief, but as soon as our lips parted, a wave of panic hit me. I pulled away abruptly, my lips stinging from his beard. I was paralyzed by a fear—no, worse, a knowing—that the kiss had ignited something irreversible deep inside of me. I was turned on but also unnerved: *Was I such a good liar that I'd even managed to deceive myself?*

Impulsivity was my second nature—if I wanted something, I went for it. This time, in the aftermath of that kiss, something was different. I ran back to my apartment and locked the door as if it would block out what had just happened.

I FELL IN love before Anthony did. I'm certain of it. Even though he was my secret—something I hadn't shared with my closest friends—I wondered if I was his, too. I pictured him with his patients and doctors, and I wondered if he talked about me.

One evening, as we sat on the fire escape, I handed him a gift—a War on Drugs record I had picked up at Amoeba. He turned it over in his hands, tracing the cover, then looked at me with a softness I hadn't seen before.

"Thank you," he said casually, "this is really thoughtful, you just get it. You can't teach taste."

He put his hand on mine. "I think you underestimate yourself, you're really amazing."

I held his gaze for a moment. Then: "Are you fucking around with other people, or is this something?"

"What?" He laughed.

"I just don't know what we're doing here," I said.

He grew quiet for a moment as the thoughts in my head grew loud enough to drown out "Red Eyes" still playing on the vinyl.

"I love you, Lukas," he said simply. "You know what this is."

So, surprise! That's how I wound up with my first boyfriend. I imagine if you read the chapter where I listened to Britney Spears in the bathtub every day as a child and guessed I liked men, then you clocked it even earlier than I did. Congrats!

"So, surprise . . . I have my first boyfriend," was also something along the lines of what I told Brody when I rang him.

"I knew it!" Brody cackled on the phone. "How the fuck do I live in SF, and been a colossal faggot since I came out of the womb, but I still can't catch a dick?"

How I never knew is still a mystery, but somewhere along the way I guess I had convinced myself. After all, I had girlfriends, I loved Kaylee, I loved the woman I watched in the Skinemax porn . . . Yet here I was in my first real relationship with a man.

Despite the deep affection I had for Anthony, there was an undeniable allure in the secrecy of it all. The hushed phone calls, the sneaking around, the thrill of having something that was just for me. I had always gotten off on the power of knowing I was breaking rules and getting away with it, just this time, I wasn't sure exactly what would happen if I got caught. But Anthony didn't see the excitement in walking on the edge. He wasn't wired for secrets.

"I'm serious," he said as we lay next to each other. "It's going on too long; I know it's hard for you, but I want to meet your family, your friends."

"Why?"

"Because they're important to you," he said. "And you're important to me."

I guess that was all the convincing I needed, because the next night I waited for Travis to come home, pacing around the apartment, feeling the weight of what I was about to say. I had rehearsed it in my head a dozen times, but now, sitting in the silence of the space we shared, I started to second-guess everything.

When I heard the familiar jingle of his keys and the distant drone of Joe Rogan's podcast crackling from his phone speaker, I froze. This was it.

Time to stop being a little bitch.

"'Sup," Travis nodded.

"Hey," I answered meekly.

He plopped on the couch after a long day of classes and went straight for his pipe, immediately exhaling a cloud of smoke as he turned on *Rick and Morty*.

"Want some?" he asked, passing it over without missing a beat.

I shook my head. "Nah, I'm good. Thanks."

The cartoon blared in the background, Travis was stoned and in good spirits, but my stomach still felt like it was in the upside down.

"Do you know why I've been staying out all night?" I finally asked.

He didn't even flinch. His eyes stayed on me for a moment before he exhaled and leaned back.

"I know," he said casually, like it was the most obvious thing in the world.

"You know what?" I asked.

He laughed, shaking his head as if I'd missed something glaringly obvious.

"You're not sly at all, Lukas. I've known since you were two."

I just stared at him, caught off guard by how little surprise there was in his tone. There was no lead-up, no suspense, no disbelief, nothing.

"Wait—what?" I managed to sputter out.

He just shrugged, taking another hit from the bong. "C'mon. It's not exactly a secret. It's in your eyes."

"What? Do I have gay eyes or something?" I asked.
"What? No," Travis said.
"How . . . how did you know?"
"A brother's intuition."

I blinked, hearing him and Brody say it so matter-of-factly—like it was something *they* had always known. Something I was only now catching up to.

As if on cue, my phone vibrated in my hand with a text from Kaylee.

hey kooky.

A flurry of frenetic texts followed:

Bitch, you like pussy, don't play yourself . . .

ur bi . . .

Sorry, I'm drunk, Brody told Bunny and her ass told me

I told Bunny I wouldn't say shit. Oops.

Remember bitch, you weren't gey when you were eating this pussy. I know you miss this ass. Don't lie to yo self ;)

I laughed, shaking my head. Kaylee was cooked as ever, but maybe she was sort of onto something. The things that attracted me to her and Anthony had nothing to do with gender but everything to do with how they made me feel.

With Kaylee, I took on the role of the protector. I was the one who kept things grounded whenever she spiraled. With Anthony, it was the opposite. He cared for me, cushioning me from all the jagged edges of LA. He felt like the human embodiment of what I'd always been looking for when I ran aimlessly around Long Beach.

I wondered how I would tell the rest of my family. I hadn't seen Sean or Cory in person for years. Sean's three-year prison sentence had been cut short; he was now in a halfway house where we could only exchange letters and brief phone calls. I thought of writing him something, but I didn't even know where to begin. I looked up at the postcard photos littered on my fridge, all practically the same: him surrounded by his new friends with face tattoos and orange jumpsuits. He had a look of pride in his eyes from the weight he'd lost since he'd been locked up. I wondered if that version of him was still the same person I remembered.

Cory kept in touch in his own way—sporadic images from Missouri, his head shaved close and his body in the best shape it had ever been. He seemed to be finding himself there, or holding on to the remnants of who he once was, trying to stay sturdy in a world that had continuously tried to break him.

Cory and Sean might have been unreachable, but Nana was still my constant. Now that I was living in LA, we'd have our weekly date at the food court in Century City mall, sharing fries, talking shit about my dad's new wife, and talking through all my auditions.

When I told her, she just dipped a fry in ketchup, looked up at me with a little smile, and said, "I always figured you liked both."

I blinked, surprised by how casually she said it.

"Why the hell did no one tell me?"

She dipped another fry. "Eat. You're too skinny."

I looked at her blankly.

"Oh sweetheart, I think you told me when you were four. You said, 'I'm a little gay, too, you know? Not in the happy way.'"

"I said that?"

"Yes, you were such a funny little kid. Plus, you always wanted to be the girl character in whatever game you were playing. What was it called?"

"*The Sims*," I muttered sheepishly.

"Yeah, that's it." She started making herself crack up. "You were always playing that stupid game! You didn't sleep for nights on end. We had to take the computer out of the house."

She looked at me with so much warmth. "I don't care what you are. I just want you to be happy."

On the way back to my apartment, I gave Anthony the play-by-play over the phone.

"It went perfect . . . it's all been fine. I mean, everyone's been cool, but—" I paused, trying to collect my thoughts.

I could hear Anthony's steady breathing on the other end of the line, the soft shuffle of a hospital break room.

"You're still freaking out about your mom, aren't you?"

"Yeah," I muttered quietly.

I knew my mom loved her kids more than anything in the world, but for some reason, she was the one I was the most afraid to tell. Between Jesse, Cory, Travis, and all my bullshit—how many more surprises could one woman take?

"You're spiraling, and thinking of all the worst-case scenarios, like you did with your brother and your grandma. And look how that turned out," Anthony said calmly.

"It's just . . . it's really fucking weird being this honest, it doesn't come naturally," I told him. What I really wanted to say was that the weird thrill of having this secret, this thing that was only mine, was less thrilling now that I had to live in it.

"I know. But you're doing great, I'm proud of you. Everything else is just noise, your mom is going to be relieved; I'd be pissed if one of our kids didn't turn out gay or at least pan," Anthony said, shifting on the other end. "I gotta head back. We just got a new patient. I love you. I'll see you later."

I spent more weeks putting off telling my mom. Which meant dodging her calls, ignoring her messages, and carrying the weight of it everywhere I went. It gnawed at me until I couldn't take it anymore.

Then one afternoon, as I sat in a waiting room to read for a movie, it all caught up with me. This wasn't a typical audition, one where I could rely on my preparation. There was no character to embody. No script to disappear into. We were just asked to bring one thing: ourselves.

And at that time, that was my hardest role to play.

A casting director stepped into the waiting room and read my name off a clipboard. She smiled politely before she brought me into a room, where some of the producers were waiting to meet me.

They weren't just looking for someone to read lines—they wanted to really see us, the people behind the performances. Just a conversation.

I entered the room and exchanged pleasantries, and then the casting director pressed Record.

"Lukas, tell me about yourself."

I froze for a moment. "Uh, well, I'm from San Diego, I'm one of four boys, I—"

"Awesome," she interrupted. "What's one thing people might be surprised to know about you?"

Instead of offering up one of the lighthearted and casual fun facts she was expecting like "I can do a back handspring" or "I have a Fabergé egg collection I've been keeping since I was five years old," I launched right into the next most viable option: "I've been having a relationship with a man for the past six months and hiding it from my mom."

Silence. The only sound was my own breath, shaky and uneven, before I felt the first tear slip down. Then the crescendoing sounds of my sobs until one of the casting associates mumbled, "Oh, wow, thank you so much for . . . sharing with us."

There were only two things I knew for certain at that moment: That I was *not* getting the part, and that I needed to call my mom.

On the second ring, she picked up the phone.

"Lulu, I've been trying to get ahold of you." Her voice came through, warm but with a touch of concern. Oh, and there I went. Crying again. "What's wrong?"

"Mom . . . I . . ."

"What is it? You're scaring me, spit it out—"

"I'm in love with a man."

There was silence on the other end of the line. I could feel her trying to process it.

"What?" she asked as though she hadn't quite understood what I said.

"I . . . I don't know what this means, if I am . . ." I continued, the words now tumbling out faster, "bi, gay . . . I don't know, but I've been with a guy for six months, and . . . he's my boyfriend."

There was another pause. I could almost feel her mind working. I wondered if she was trying to reconcile the words with the image she had of me, of who I was supposed to be.

"What about Kaylee? Your girlfriends? Were they . . ." she asked, her voice cracking with confusion.

"I don't know; I loved her, but I love him, too."

There was another pause before she skirted right over the coming-out portion of the call and straight to "You're dating someone and I don't know them? I'm driving up tonight."

"You still love me?" I asked.

Though my mom always assured me her love was unconditional, deep down a part of me had been terrified that her love wasn't as limitless as I had imagined. That it was somehow contingent on me being the son that I envisioned a mom would want. I wanted to be the kind of son she could proudly show off to her friends and family. I feared that this version of myself, the one I had just confessed to her, would somehow tarnish that.

"What the hell are you talking about? Are you insane? Of course I love you. You're my baby. You are my son, I love you more than this world. I'm just pissed you hid it from me for so long."

We made a plan for my mom to meet Anthony that night. When she came through the doors of Sunset Thai, I pulled her into a tight hug, and we slid into the mismatched, colorful chairs under a canopy of paper lanterns and fairy lights.

My mom was kind at first, but not her usual overtly warm self. There was a guardedness to her, a quiet skepticism in her tone. She sipped her Coors Light slowly, her eyes locked on Anthony, studying his every move like a hawk sizing up potential prey. Anthony kept repeating the same joke—*I want to spring roll into this new year with your approval*—attempting to break the ice.

"That's not funny," my mom snapped.

"Mom, be nice."

"I am, that just wasn't funny." She shrugged.

Under the table I reached for her hand, giving it a small squeeze. She pulled away.

"I'll be right back," I said before heading to the bathroom.

The evening wasn't unfolding as I had hoped. The bathroom mirror stared back at me, reflecting a person who was holding on to a version of family that wasn't real. I had dreamed of a world where my family and Anthony's could come together, where we'd all be this big unit, laughing over dinner, sharing the kind of moments that were so far and few between in my childhood.

Let it go, I told myself.

When I came back to the table, I was surprised to find them actually laughing—genuinely laughing—at his dumb dad jokes.

I sat back down, my foot jittering uncontrollably against the table leg. I tried to steady myself, but the restless energy wouldn't go away. Then, without a word, my mom placed a gentle hand on my knee, holding it steady.

Maybe the person who had the biggest problem with all of this was me.

OVER THE COURSE of my two years with Anthony, my mom's caution gave way to something warmer—she didn't just accept Anthony, she loved him. And so did I. But I didn't just love him—I *clung* to him—because in a world of uncertainty, he was the one thing I knew for sure.

I spent those years trying to be everything he needed, bending, shrinking, sacrificing parts of myself just to keep living in the sense of security he had built around me. So when he unceremoniously, completely casually mentioned that he was moving out of the building, all I could ask him was "Why?"

He shrugged in that way he always did, like it wasn't a big deal.

"I just listened to this podcast on a run last night, that French lady, Esther Perel, the one that you showed me and it taught me that maybe I can't do monogamy or maybe it's just our relationship has run its course," he said, like that explained *anything*. Like moving across the country and turning our relationship into a memory was just a Sunday decision.

"First of all, she's Belgain. Second of all, you went on a run and listened to *one* podcast, and now you realized that you no longer love me?" I said slowly and carefully, trying to piece it together myself.

"Well, on paper like that it sounds bad, but yeah, kinda." He shrugged.

I hadn't expected this much physical pain. The drawn-out panic sat in my stomach, stretching into every nerve. My throat burned like the onset of strep. Was heartache always this tangible, or was this just the shape mine took?

After he left, I realized I'd been living at his whims for so long I had no idea how to exist without him pulling the strings. His absence wasn't just physical; it was everywhere, suffocating me. Every time I passed his now-vacant apartment, it felt like walking past a brutal crime scene, except I was both the victim and the suspect. The ghost of him lingered in the hallway, in the stairwell, in the space between where we used to be and where I was now.

When I tried to get back into my routine, I moved through my days like I was underwater, everything felt blurred around the edges. I cried during class, and Leigh would just hug me and tell me that it would pass. It didn't feel like it ever would. My focus was completely scattered. I needed to hate him. I needed to get even.

So, I did what any twenty-one-year-old with $2,000 in their

bank account and a bunch of important auditions that could potentially change the trajectory of his life would do—I abandoned them all and went on my own *Eat, Pray, Love* adventure across Europe. And, naturally, went into debt by doing so.

THE TRIP TURNED out to be more like Cry, Pray, Eat Shit.

In Rome, I discovered the unique shame of drunk crying into a water bottle of wine in the Colosseum, while tourists took selfies nearby. I wondered if the gladiators ever had heartbreak this bad. While they fought lions and cool shit like that, I was just fighting my own bruised ego.

I ate shit in Portugal in my hostel when an Irish man told me to stop chomping my chips—or, as he called them, "crisps"—so loudly in the middle of the night. When I carried on with my bingeing, he jumped off the top bunk and promptly punched me in my chest.

In Paris, the city of love, I convinced myself that I was embarking on some unconventional romance. One night began in a haze of wine in Montmartre at the Hotel Particulier, which overlooked the whole city. There I met a couple, Pierre and Astrid, who seemed to embody everything I wasn't. They were chic, effortlessly nonchalant, and not impulsively expressive. Pierre had a jawline like a prison yard shiv, while Astrid looked like Jennifer Connelly's character in *Requiem for a Dream*, before the drugs wrecked her. They were perfect.

"So what are you doing here?" Astrid asked, half curious, half amused. Her accent made the words sound less like she was asking and more that she was telling me.

"I—uh, got my heart ripped out and now I just want to find myself. I don't know, I read *Eat, Pray, Love*, and that helped that lady, she's a lesbian now, and a best-selling author," I said, trying not to slur, but the strong flush in my cheeks betrayed me.

Pierre smirked, his cigarette hanging languidly between two fingers. Astrid leaned forward, her hand lingering on mine.

"Let's forget all that and have a night, yes?" Pierre said, raising his shot glass. "Salut."

We took turns riding on the back of Pierre's moped, weaving through the narrow streets of Montmartre. We made our way to one lookout, where the lights of the Eiffel Tower flickered in the distance. We sat with Astrid between us, her hands on each of our crotches. We were definitely about to Eiffel Tower her.

Later that night, we stumbled back to their loft, perched above a bar where the music bled through the floorboards. The loft was a tangled mess of mismatched furniture, wine bottles, and the scent of tobacco. We played music, and I kept talking, filling every pause with anything to keep the feeling of closeness alive.

"I mean . . . This is what life is all about, connecting, sharing, sharing everything . . . nights, wisdom, bodily fluids, whatever?"

Astrid raised an eyebrow. "What are you saying? Is this flirting?"

I was convinced we were in love, and maybe the path back to myself was through twice the love, twice the affection. But instead, it turned out to be the worst threesome of my life when mid-hookup Pierre started laughing.

"You're still talking? Pfft, Americans . . . talking, talking. J'ai essayé, Astrid," he said before peeling himself out of the bed.

They left the room, blabbering in rapid-fire French. I lay in their bed, naked beneath the duvet, trying to shield myself from the cold but mostly from my thoughts.

From Anthony.

His name echoed in my mind. The bigger the nights got, the more obvious the hole felt in the cold light of day.

I left their loft, wobbling my way through the streets, my steps unsteady from the night's excess. As I wandered, I pulled out my phone and called Anthony.

"Hello?" I could hear the sounds of lighthearted laughter, glasses clinking, and some Kings of Leon headass indie cover band blasting in the background. Clearly, he was living his best life.

"I'll be right there!" I shouted ahead, at no one, pretending I, too, was at my own, raucous party. "Oh, sorry, hello?"

"Hello?"

"What is it?" I asked.

"Huh? You called me?" Anthony said.

"Whatever."

"What's up?"

"You know what?"

"What?"

"Fuck you!"

"What?"

"You're like a fucking robot, you know that? How could you move on so quickly!" I cried out, losing my cool.

"Really?" he said in the most robotic way possible.

"Yeah, *re-al-ly*! Did you just have a glitch?"

"All right, Lukas, you have a good night."

"Wait. Answer me, you owe me a fucking real answer. Why did you—"

"I was suffocating, okay?! You suffocated me."

Suffocating.

"I hate you."

"No, you don't. You know that we relied on each other way too much; it was unhealthy. You're so young. And look! Now you're seeing the world! You're branching out—"

"Oh, fuck you." I cut him off, my blood boiling. "Don't try to spin this like you did some act of charity, like you saved me."

"It's true. You'll see. . . ."

"Oh. You want me to thank you?"

Anthony took a deep breath; I could hear guilt in his voice this time, "Look, I gotta go. I know I broke your heart, and I know this hurts so bad, but I promise one day, you'll see that this was the right thing—"

"You're fake."

There was a pause. Then, the line went dead.

Maybe he was right. Maybe one day I *would* see it.

What I could see clearly in that moment was that the anger I'd been trying to fight, fuck, or feast out of my system wasn't for him—it was for myself. I'd sworn off *stupid love* after Kaylee, vowing never to chase the highs that never lasted and the lows that only ever got lower. Yet here I was, fresh out of my first *adult* relationship, feeling dumber about love than ever.

I didn't need to hate him. I didn't need to replace him. I needed to figure out who I was again.

15.

The 14 Percent

LA had done its fair share of fucking me, but I did my fair share of fucking it back—and I'm not talking about the people . . . or am I? The heartache from my breakup had slowly faded into the background, and I was finally able to put my focus where it belonged: my work.

I started to feel like myself again, settling into the right shade of blond and realigning all my chakras with different reiki healers who promised me the world. (Shut up, it made me feel better.) I still believed the next job might finally prove I wasn't a fluke.

Three seasons of *T@gged* had come and gone, and I was determined that my next project would free me of the endless grind of cafés and catering jobs. As I stacked up bit parts on various shows, I saw firsthand what it really took to carry a lead role in a production that big.

On one high-profile set, I witnessed a talented but green performer buckle under the weight of their leading role. I made a mental note: If I wanted to be the kind of actor who had longevity, I didn't want to blow my load too soon. As much as I craved that kind of opportunity, I didn't want to jump in before I was ready—not that anyone was lining up to offer it to me!

I decided I wanted to try to be intentional with my career. I couldn't do that in my relationships, but I could do that in my work.

I kept myself busy. More auditions, more rehearsals, more anything that kept me from sitting still for too long. If I was moving, I wasn't thinking. And in all that running around I stumbled upon an indie that stuck to me like salt water taffy on a Nantucket whore in the middle of a heat wave. *Another Happy Day* had premiered at Sundance Film Festival more than five years prior, and starred Ellen Burstyn and Ellen Barkin. It centered on a family gripped by the eldest son's addiction. In it, I saw my own frustration and my own unwavering devotion to my sibling—I saw myself and Cory.

I discovered it was written and directed by Sam Levinson. The film was semi-autobiographical, drawing from Levinson's own addiction and struggles with his family. His ability to translate his pain into art was the kind of work that I wanted to be a part of.

So I did what any deeply moved, slightly unhinged actor would do: I tracked down his email and sent him a message, telling him exactly how much his film meant to me.

Meanwhile, checking casting breakdowns had become part of my daily routine. Most days, nothing. And then, one day, there it was. *Levinson's name*, and his next project, *Assassination Nation* had just begun its preproduction. Seeing Sam's name on the list felt like hope. Which lately felt like a suspicious thing for me to have.

I WROTE THIS FOR ATTENTION

I devoured the script. It was abrasive and polarizing, something I knew that was taking a swing, for better or for worse. And I knew that I wanted in.

"There's this script called *Assassination Nation*—" I said to the Best Agent in the Valley as I paced around my apartment, phone in hand.

"Oh, yeah. It's going to be splashy. But they already cast all the leads. We tried to get you an appointment—"

"Okay, I figured. There are so many other roles in the script, though. Not leads but still tons of parts," I pressed.

"They'll probably cast those locally," he said while clacking away on his keyboard, sounding more than distracted. "I gotta run into a staff meeting, but I'll dig into it, okay? Chat later!"

Before I could respond, the line went dead.

I had a suspicion I was going to need to think out of the box on this one.

A quick Google search told me *Assassination Nation* was filming in Louisiana. From there, I went full Nancy Drew, typing *Louisiana Talent Agencies* into the search bar, and started calling them at random.

Most hung up, saying they didn't accept unsolicited submissions.

Then, I called one agency, Open Sky Talent. A woman answered the phone, her voice dripping with a sweet yet commanding Southern drawl.

"Hello?" she said.

"Hi, my name is Lukas. I just recently finished acting school and got your contact information from one of your actors I met there," I said, thinking on my feet.

"Oh?" she replied. "Who?"

"Stanley," I lied, holding my breath.

"I don't think I remember Stanley . . . Sheila? Reina?" she called out to her underlings. "Y'all know if we represent anyone named Stanley?"

I cut her off before she could probe further, just as my agent had taught me. "Anyway," I hurried on, "I have homes in both LA and New Orleans, so I'm looking for Southern representation to work as a local in both cities, and I heard there's a movie called *Assassination Nation* about to start filming, and I'd love the chance to audition."

Her voice was stern but curious. "Yes, there are auditions for that happening this week . . . Stanley who? I'm racking my brain here."

"Look, I'm not going to lie to you," I started. ". . . I don't remember his last name. If this audition doesn't work out, you can drop me. Just please give me a chance. Represent me. If I don't book it, I promise I won't bother you again."

I could almost hear her mulling it over on the other end of the line. After what felt like forever, she finally said, "Can you come to my office tomorrow?"

The moment she agreed, I scrambled to book a flight. Luckily, I had Southwest points saved from filming *T@gged* in New Mexico, so the ticket was free, which was important, since my bank account was depleted from my Euro trip.

The next day, I was at the New Orleans airport, waiting at the baggage claim. I typed her address into my maps . . . only to see the blue dot appear over a hundred miles away.

"Fuck!" I blurted out.

Her office was in Baton Rouge. I had just assumed all of Louisiana was *basically* New Orleans. I stood there, watching the bags circle the carousel like they might somehow provide a solution. They didn't.

If Vanessa Carlton would walk one thousand miles, I could figure out a way to go one hundred. I eventually found the next bus headed north.

The bus doors hissed shut behind me, sealing me in for the three-hour ride to Baton Rouge. I slumped into the back row of the Greyhound—stale air, everything sticky, my shirt stuck to the pleather seats. I closed my eyes. By the time I arrived that afternoon, I dragged myself through the heat until I found the stately Tudor that housed the agency. I was greeted at the door by who I assumed were Sheila and Reina, two younger women with their hair pulled back into neat buns. They wore pencil skirts and carried themselves like *Mad Men* actors who actually made it to the taping.

The assistant led me into the waiting room, which was filled with porcelain angel figurines and crosses. Sunlight streamed through the windows, casting a glow over a garden of pecan trees outside.

When Trish, the owner, appeared, she entered the room deliberately and poised. It was clear she came from old money. Her demeanor was warm yet steely—a mix of Southern hospitality and no-nonsense straight to business.

"Have you prepared a scene?" she asked.

"Uh, yes," I lied, though panic immediately set in. Thankfully, I had a fallback: *Donnie Darko*, the movie I'd memorized by heart since I was a kid. I launched into the monologue where Donnie debates his belief in God with his therapist, weighing the pros and cons.

When I finished, Trish studied me for a moment before asking, "Why would you pick that piece?"

"I wanted to play someone different than me. Someone who was questioning his faith," I said feeling slightly bad for lying, though it wasn't entirely untrue. I didn't *not* believe in God—I just didn't know if I believed in religion. I didn't feel bad enough to resist lifting up my shirt to show her the cross I had tattooed on my ribs in Tessa's honor. (I don't think I understood the contradiction of being Jewish with a cross on me, but I digress!)

She studied me for a moment, lips pressed together, then nodded.

"The last round of auditions for *Assassination Nation* is in two days, in New Orleans," she said.

I couldn't hide the grin spreading across my face. "Oh my God. Thank you, thank you, thank you."

On the bus back to New Orleans, I realized that I had no clue where I was going to stay. I googled hostels and landed on one that looked so haunted, I couldn't resist—Madame Isabelle's House, right in the heart of the French Quarter. Creepy. Cheap. *Perfect*.

I booked a bed in one of its seven-person mixed dorms, which had the lingering presence of voodoo witchcraft seeped into its musty corners. From the windows, you could hear the streets pulsing with music.

As I unpacked, the door creaked open. It was one of my bunkmates, a twentysomething in an Alabama State T-shirt that clung to his linebacker shoulders. At first we just nodded at each other—the kind of nod that strangers exchange when placed in unfamiliar settings. Then he stepped forward, extending a firm handshake.

"I'm Duke," he said, with an air of gentility.

"I always thought that was a dog's name," I said.

"So, what brings you to NOLA?" he asked ignoring my comment.

"Work," I said, keeping it brief.

Clearly, Duke and I were not of like minds.

"Ha! Good luck getting anything done here. This is *the* best place in the world to party. Hands down. First time?" he asked with a grin.

"Yep."

So, Duke and I had more in common than I thought.

"First round's on me?" he asked.

I wasn't sure if this was a curse or a blessing that we found each other. But when in Rome! Or when in New Orleans! I figured why the hell not. For the next two days, Duke became my drinking partner and unofficial tour guide. The first night, we wandered aimlessly through the French Quarter on a ghost tour, drinking from a canteen of whiskey. From there, we went to Rick's strip club, where a stripper with braces gave me a lap dance and, mid-grind, whispered her transcendental meditation practice into my ear. She swore me to secrecy and then told me her mantra. And no, I will *not* be violating her trust and sharing it.

The second night also marked the start of Mardi Gras—of course, the universe wasn't done taunting me. We tore through the streets, crashing parades, dancing with strangers, while Duke shouted at people to flash him. Beads rained down on me, hitting me in the face so often I started to worry I'd go blind before my big meeting the next day. Hell with it, the city was alive, and so was I.

The next morning, my phone alarm jolted me awake—its shrill beeping sliced through the haze of a sleepless night. I had tried—really tried—to wake up early and get my shit together, but my body had other plans. I stumbled out of bed, straight into the sweltering heat of the city, head pounding like one of the drum lines that had stormed the streets the night before.

I kept walking, the heat of New Orleans clinging to me like a second skin, while I tried to burn off all my nerves and the Hurricanes I'd downed the night before. I spotted a bench and sat down for just a second—but before I knew it, my eyelids had drooped, and I'd passed out right there, out in the open.

When I woke up two hours later, I grabbed my phone and saw the time—twenty minutes until the time of my appointment. Panic surged through me as I bolted back into the heat, dodging slow-moving tourists, drunken day partiers, and treacherous, uneven sidewalks. Mid-sprint, I caught a glimpse of myself in the side mirror of a parked car and found my face was now the color of a lobster. Who would ever cast me while I was this shade of maroon?

By the time I reached the office, I was panicked, convinced my audition was doomed before it even began.

Then I saw it—a line stretching out the door. Relief flooded through me.

I had time.

I grabbed the sides from the counter, skimmed the pages, and tried to pull myself together. Luckily, the scene took place at a party, so if anyone asked why I looked like such a hungover harlot, I could just say that I'd been doing my research, that I was method.

The day dragged on, a revolving door of actors coming and going, their faces all blurring together. When they called my name, I jumped up and took in a deep inhale.

The moment I stepped in, I felt their eyes on me—half amused, half judging.

Sam sat at a table across from me, carrying the weight of someone who had truly lived too many lives. His Juul dangled from his mouth, and he may or may not have had two different shoes on.

Beside him sat a girl who appeared to be his assistant. She had a nest of blond hair piled high atop her egg-shaped head, but her alabaster face was warm and inviting, despite the fact that it looked like she hadn't slept for two weeks.

"Oh my God, why do you look like that? Why are you so . . . red?" the assistant asked.

"I, um, fell asleep on a bench outside," I said. I felt my face get even redder.

"In New Orleans?" Sam and the girl blinked at me, confused.

"Does the city really matter?" I asked.

"That's true, I guess any bench is not a great idea," the girl said.

"Well, I'm Sam, and this is Phoebe. Do you have any questions about the script or the character of Mason?" he asked.

"Nope," I said.

We started reading. At first, I was just saying the words, feeling my way through the rhythm of the scene. Then I looked up, and I saw their faces. They were paying attention to me; it was finally my moment. Finally, people were watching, so I decided . . . I was here, and I was gonna give them a show. I let the pages fall on the floor and got on top of the chair as if I were standing on one at a party:

"Everybody tell your crew to get to Greenwald's party. Rally your crew and get your ass out there," I spat out even messier than intended. I saw Sam's eyes flicker, and felt the assistant, Phoebe, lean forward.

"Everyone but Lily is invited, you want to know why?" I locked into Phoebe's eyes, her mouth agape. She was reading with me, and I had thrown her a bit of a curveball—none of this was in the script. Sam nudged her.

"Oh . . ." Phoebe said, looking down at the script and fumbling to find her place. "What the fuck are you even talking about, Mason?"

"Lily Colson jerked off Greenwald's dog. That's right, I walked into his crib, and Lily was on her knees tugging on his RED ROCKET!"

"Damn," Sam whispered, a small smile pulling at his lips. That flicker of approval was all I needed. The improvised lines spilled out of me, one after another, until I eventually stopped. They looked pleased, but I wasn't totally sure.

I left the room and walked the interminable twenty feet down the hall, past the rows and rows of actors still waiting to get in front of Sam. I remember trying to avoid their eyes, hoping that whatever I had just done would be enough, hoping that I would be able to say that some of my craziness had finally paid off.

Right before I left the doors of the building, I felt a tap on my shoulder:

"You! Wait!"

I turned around to find that assistant, somehow breathless from the twenty feet she'd traversed. She looked a little wild-eyed.

"Is there something wrong?" I asked, terrified that I may have offended her with my bestiality-based improv.

"No, there's something right." She grinned. "We really liked what you did in there. Actually, don't tell them I'm telling you this, but . . ."

She looked around at all the actors' expectant faces, then pulled me over to the side.

"So, here's the situation. We already cast the role," she told me, low and rushed.

"Wait, really? Seriously, Mason?"

"Mason is over, Mason is done. Forget about Mason. How would you feel about reading for Eric, though?" she asked. I looked at her, unsure of how to respond. This was bad . . . or good? I couldn't really tell yet.

"Um . . ." I hedged, but then Phoebe grabbed my shoulder, spun me around, and pushed me back toward the audition room.

"Sam really liked what you just did, so we wanna see if you could read for this other part—Eric. Does that sound good?"

I nodded, dumbstruck. She held out some pages she had with her.

"Do you want to look at these for a second?"

I shook my head. And then finally found my voice.

"No, no. I don't need a second. I got it."

She smiled and led me back into the room where Sam was still puffing on his Juul.

"That was really funny, man. You wanna give Eric a shot?" he said.

I assume I said yes, because the next thing I knew, he was saying: "Congratulations, Eric. I'll see you at the table read."

The second I stepped out of the building, I grabbed my phone and immediately called my mom.

"What?! Tell me! Tell me!"

I couldn't hold back my excitement, "I GOT THE PART IN THE ROOM, MOM!!!"

There was a half-second pause before my mom screamed like a giddy twelve-year-old girl into the phone, "You did!? Oh my God, of course you did. I knew you would. I love you!"

ASSASSINATION NATION TURNED out to be an incredible experience. My role was small, but the lessons I learned and the doors it opened were anything but. For anyone who comes up to me and asks, "How do you break through? How do you make it in this industry?"—this is how: sheer dumb luck, delusional confidence, and having a lot of balls.

If I hadn't lied to that agent, faked my way to Louisiana, and thrown myself into the unknown, I believe my path would have been much different. That chance encounter with the director and producers ultimately led to them calling me in for *Euphoria*, and that's really when more opportunities started to come my way. I was crazy. I still probably am. I did what Leigh had always pushed me to do—I bet on myself. I listened to that gut feeling, cliché as it may be, and it paid off.

Beyond the work, *Assassination Nation* gave me something even more meaningful: my people. Phoebe, Maude, Charlie, Kelvin, and Danny weren't just my castmates—they became my found family.

Being on set is a job, but there's also so much free time, and in those free hours there was nothing but time to form intimate relationships. Especially since we were only shooting nights and everyone we knew back home was asleep, we couldn't ignore each other on set and be glued to our phones. We were forced to get close fast.

"Remember when you guys all thought I was the chubby casting director and then found out I was just the chubby assistant?" Phoebe said once we were back in Los Angeles, all piled into a diner booth at 3:00 a.m.

"The *hot* thick assistant," I corrected her.

"Who's to say we didn't think you were just the gorgeous lead actress," Maude jumped in.

"Who's to say!" Kelvin, Danny, and I would all echo in unison.

Eventually, I even managed to integrate Brody into the mix. He'd drive up to LA on the weekends and was welcomed with open arms. But soon, most of our time with Brody moved to FaceTime—he'd checked himself into a rehab center in Arizona. Even from afar, though, he was still part of the crew.

A YEAR LATER, when I got the call to read for roles in Sam's next project, *Euphoria*, I auditioned for every single character, right down to Rue's mom. (Just kidding, but you know I would've if given the chance.)

When I finally got the call that I got a part in the show, I was over the moon: working with Sam again, on an HBO show, was already a dream come true. Finding out my now closest friends, Phoebe and Maude, were both on board, that was the cherry on top.

I'd like to think Sam brought me on the show because of my abilities, but honestly, I suspect it had more to do with how punchable my face is. The character I ultimately landed, Tyler, starts the season by hooking up with Maddy in a pool in the middle of a party—only to have her boyfriend, Nate, beat the living shit out of him a few episodes later. (See, getting jumped *does* have its benefits!)

On the day of the scene, I spent five hours in bloodied, broken facial prosthetics, getting absolutely annihilated by Jacob Elordi. I lay there take after take, writhing around on the floor, screaming my voice raw.

By the time we neared the end of the day, exhaustion had started to creep in, but I kept pushing—trying to prove to everyone, mostly myself, that I belonged there. Then Sam pulled me aside, looked me in the eyes, and said, "I just want you to know that you are clearly meant to do this. You were born to be here, doing this. I got everything we need; it's amazing, seriously. Now I just want you to let it go. We have it—you have it—and I'm so proud of you. Now just fuck it all, but I want you to do this last take for you."

Sam returned to his monitor, and I stood there, overwhelmed by a feeling I hadn't allowed myself to believe in for a long time. I was here. I belonged.

The momentary relief Sam provided me still hasn't stopped me from constantly looking for Daddy behind every monitor. I'm not sure I'll ever be able to stop feeling the gnawing, pathological hunger to prove my worth to every director, producer, or writer I work with. But if nothing else, that brief exchange reminded me that I bring something uniquely "me" to the table—even if it's the PTSD of the younger San Diego kid who got jumped—and that was enough for that moment.

AFTER *EUPHORIA*, THE industry's doors creaked open just a smidge—like they weren't ready to unlock completely but they did want a glimpse of me beyond the peephole. In auditions, the blank stares turned into soft squints, as if they were trying to place me. I became "that one guy"—not famous, but slightly familiar.

"Where do I know you from?" they'd ask.

Suddenly, people wanted to actually get to know me—inviting me in for general meetings and asking where I came from, and what rock I'd been hiding under. I always found it hard to just *be* in a general. I'd try to be whoever I thought they wanted me to be. I might not have had lines but I was still acting—trying to embody a version of me I thought they'd like. If I thought they wanted the brooding, mysterious guy, I'd show up to the meeting all quiet and intense, but not *too* intense, so I didn't come off like a dick or too difficult to work with. Or if I thought they wanted the wild, fun guy, I'd be cracking jokes and flirting my way through it—but not *too* funny and flirty, just enough to be magnetic but not so much that I looked like I wasn't taking any of it seriously.

It was a constant balancing act. Always calibrating. Always methodical.

Old habits.

Then, in one general meeting, one kind producer asked me, "What would twelve-year-old Lukas think of you right now? Would he be proud?"

"I think . . ." I trailed off, reaching to answer honestly.

Tears started to form in the corners of my eyes.

"Fuck, I'm so . . . this is so actory of me," I said, trying to brush it off.

"Well, I hate to put a label on it, but you are." She laughed.

I realized that even though my dreams had finally started to come true, nothing changed. I wasn't and am still not a big Hollywood star. I had wanted so badly to just be a working actor—a career so difficult that only 14 percent of SAG-AFTRA members work enough to qualify for health insurance—and I had done it. Yet instead of contentment, I was met with a persistent state of wanting more, more, more.

At the same time, I was watching my colleagues' careers blossom on shows, magazine covers, and all over social media. It was like the internet consisted solely of articles detailing all the amazing, life-changing jobs they were getting. I read each announcement or accolade of theirs as a declaration of "I'm special, I'm good," while I'd sit and think, *I wasn't offered that, I suck.* Even for things I didn't go out for, things that I was utterly wrong for. I could never have played the sister on *Mr. Robot*, and yet somehow I still felt rejected. What an asshole.

Driving down Sunset had a way of making my resentment feel like a spectator sport. There they were, the friends I genuinely loved yet found myself hating more and more with each "For Your Consideration" billboard or "sultry yet artistic" building-size product advertisement I passed with their faces plastered on it. (Hollywood isn't exactly known for its subtlety, but even the most uninspired exec would deem them looking down on me a *bit* too on the nose.)

Sometimes I'd feel the impulse to hold my breath like I'd done as a kid passing a cemetery, to keep the bitterness from settling in. Other times it came up in the back of my throat, sharp and acidic, the kind that comes from comparison. It was a reminder of the same dark truth: that one day you can be the flavor everyone craves, the next you're an aftertaste, forgotten as soon as something sweeter comes along.

I pulled onto Mulholland and let Lana's poetry book play

through the speaker. (If you haven't noticed, Lana really hits for me when I feel like I don't know where I belong.) I reminded myself that I couldn't let my envy define me. I had to hold on to something real. But as I stared out over the neon-drenched city, I couldn't shake the feeling that maybe it already had.

16.

Don't Put Me in a (Four-by-Four) Box

Going viral is a lot like having an orgy. On the surface, they both seem like a good time. If it's this much fun with two people, I'll probably see God with a whole group, right? One would think. If it's not clear by now, I love receiving positive feedback from friends and family, so wouldn't it be even sweeter for the whole world to see how fun and cool and, most important, worthy of affection I am?

What initially seems like a good way to get a little more love in your life can suddenly turn into you, sitting flaccid, watching other people having the time of their lives. (Trust me on this.) You spiral, thinking of all the ways you don't fit in, all the ways you should have done something differently, all the ways you hate your body, and the fact that people are seeing you naked.

Back in 2020, I didn't know that yet. Not as I was staring into a spit-shined marble floor, the weight of my phone in my hands strangely heavy, burdensome even. Behind me, the open veranda opened out onto Wailea Beach, where the moonlight was sparkling across the water's rippled surface. I was in a hotel lobby with some of history's greatest comedic talents, watching a video of a director roasting my apartment. But how did I get there?

It was 2020. (I know: The less said about this time, the better. We all know what happened. We get it.) All things considered, I'd gotten off easy. I was incredibly fortunate not to have lost anyone I loved. The only problem was that work had come to a standstill, and my career momentum had as well.

This is it, I kept thinking to myself. *You aren't cut out for it, anyway. You would have cracked.* At least I could blame my inability to level up on the pandemic.

During the pandemic, I was erratic and living like it really was the end of the world—drifting from one wild impulse to the next. I spent all my time on the apps—from Raya to WriteAPrisoner.com—connecting with strangers over our feelings of isolation. A few weeks in, I even threw caution and shelter-in-place protocols aside to fly out to Denver to meet up with one of my matches.

It was a surreal moment: boarding the plane and finding myself one of two passengers. The emptiness should have felt eerie, but I ignored it. I had no idea what the future held, and I definitely wasn't ready to face it. Denial was easier. Still, I couldn't bring myself to tell anyone the truth. My friends kept calling, and on FaceTime I pretended to be in sunny San Diego, plastering on a smile while trying to not flash the camera in the direction of the snow-capped Rocky Mountains unmistakably behind me.

They didn't buy it, of course. The world felt like it was unraveling, and rather than hold on, I let myself free fall—whether out of defiance, or a simple unwillingness to accept that life as I knew it had changed. So when I was invited to an underground rave with first responders in LA, I didn't think twice. If they thought it was safe, who was I to say otherwise?

Obviously, I was an idiot, and obviously, most of the party ended up with COVID. I spent the next two weeks lying horizontally in bed, sweating through my sheets, chastising myself for letting TikTok convince me that things weren't as bad as the news had let on. When my symptoms subsided, I settled into the same sourdough and *Tiger King* hole as the rest of the world.

At first, it was kind of nice—fermenting in my own misery, pretending this was just a weird little vacation and that the world as we knew it wasn't ending. But then four months passed. Four months of doing nothing. Just me, my tragic loaves of sourdough bread, and the slow, creeping realization that I had no skills, no backup plan, and no prospects.

So when my agent's name appeared on my phone, I practically dove across the bed to answer it.

"Hello?" I blurted, way too fast.

"Whoa. Hi. You still remember how to act?" he asked.

"What? Yes! Why?"

"I have an audition that just came in for you, it's for a new comedy on Fox, and it's one of the first things they're going to shoot under these new COVID protocols."

"Oh thank God," I exhaled. "I'm starting to lose it. Please send it, send it, send it."

The script didn't necessarily excite me, but that didn't matter. I needed to work. I needed to do something before my apartment, and whatever was left of my grip on reality disappeared entirely. Naturally, everything took place over Zoom, which was an entirely new process.

And, as with every entirely new process, people were fucking up. A lot. For starters, actors had to record the auditions themselves. Zoom was always crashing or having technical issues. We had to find decent lighting, pray our internet held up, and perfect the subtle art of not looking like we were obviously reading our lines off the screen.

To make it worse, everyone but the actor had their cameras off. Performing a scene for a computer full of little black boxes was about as pointless as waiting for the rain in a drought. And it required you to have to really flex your acting muscles, and after months of watching nothing but mind-rotting reality TV, mine had atrophied.

Still, I did my best to prepare, running my lines, adjusting the frame, and convincing myself that this would go smoothly—that I still *had it*.

I took a deep breath, psyched myself up, and pressed Join Meeting.

The screen flickered. A brief pause.

Then, just my own reflection staring back at me, waiting.

Several boxes of strangers started to pop up, and we exchanged pleasantries about these unprecedented times. They asked if I had any questions. I did not. They told me who I was going to be reading with, we exchanged a smile, and the screens disappeared into disembodied names in Helvetica.

And then I hit Record.

Silence. As was the etiquette at the time, the anonymous boxes all put themselves on mute while I made sure my hair looked just the right amount of disheveled. Then I took a breath to begin my first line of dialogue, only to hear my laptop speakers crackle.

You might have seen the rest.

Before I could get out a line, a British voice straight out of *Pride and Prejudice* spoke: "These poor people live in these tiny apartments..."

What's going on? I thought. In the video, you can see me do a quick scan of the screen before realizing that the director wasn't muted. "Like, I'm looking at his background, and he's got his TV and his bed and his . . ."

Unsure what exactly to do, I acted on instinct.

"Yeah, you're unmuted . . ."

More silence, so I just kept going.

"I know, it's a shitty apartment. That's why you should give me this job so I can get a better one!"

Truthfully, I didn't think it was a shitty apartment. I was actually pretty proud of it. It wasn't big, but it had charm. It had a cozy kitchen nook where I'd drink coffee in the mornings. I had stumbled across the studio two years prior, while going for a walk in the foothills of Beachwood Canyon after my breakup with Anthony, and after Travis decided LA was definitely not for him.

The director then told me he was *so* sorry, I turned to the script, hoping that would be that and we could just move on. The director apologized again.

"Listen, I'm living in a four-by-four box—it's fine. Just give me the job, and we'll be fine!" I responded.

There was some more awkward back-and-forth before I finally did the scene, and only then was that truly that.

Afterward, I went about my day, but that comment kept playing in my head—maybe the dual color paint job was a little much, and maybe the TV didn't need to be that close to my bed. I reconsidered my multicolor paint job and started wondering if the sectional, bed, and television I'd crammed into the same room was perhaps not arranged in the right way. Had I fucked up the feng shui?

As an impulsive person who has put my foot in my mouth

plenty of times, I understood that he genuinely wasn't trying to be malicious. He assumed it was muted. He didn't think I would ever hear, and I doubt he intended to be cruel; he probably genuinely felt sorry for me and was just shooting the shit with his wife or friends who were with him. That didn't keep his words from quietly winding around my body like an invisible straitjacket.

I paced the apartment, back and forth. *Did that encounter affect my chances of landing the role? Or would they feel so embarrassed that they'll just give it to me? Then again, the director might feel so deeply ashamed that he knows there's no way he could show up on set every day. Who knows? Only time will—*

"Yeah, they didn't go with you."

My agent broke the news a week later.

"But I've got this HBO thing I think you'll love, and they're looking to move fast!"

Any lingering hang-ups I had about losing the role and getting dragged for my apartment vanished the moment I finished reading *The White Lotus* pilot. I immediately fell in love. It took a scalpel to class and privilege, exposing rich people's entitlement in a way that was as darkly funny as it was painfully honest. I wanted in. There was nothing I wouldn't do to be a part of it.

The audition process unfolded in a whirlwind of self-tapes and phone calls and emails. At first, my agent pushed to have me audition for one of the lead roles, but casting felt I skewed a bit too old. (Would it have killed them to lie?) The show was quickly turning out to be a stacked cast, surely there had to be another role that I was right for.

I combed the script for any other parts that would make sense.

"Wait, what about this surfer hotel staffer, Dillon?" I asked my agent. "Are they going to cast locally? Because I could play that shit in my sleep. I'm blond, from San Diego, and I know exactly what it's like to do ketamine with my boss!"

The casting director agreed that it was a potential fit, so I immediately sent off another flurry of self-tapes. This time, I imbued the character with the traits of people I'd grown up with—Owen, Brody, and all the other carefree, sensitive, and sometimes stupid kids from San Diego.

Within a few days, I found out I'd been pinned. That's industry speak for "You have to wait with baited breath because it's between you and one other person, and if we go with the other person, it's definitely personal."

A day later, my agent gave me a ring.

"Pack your bags. You're going to Hawaii."

I let out a breath I hadn't realized I'd been holding, my chest tight with the kind of bottom-of-my-stomach anxiety that makes me feel both completely alive and completely ready to die. Getting to work again—in Hawaii, no less—felt like a dream. Which is probably why I was so sure I'd ruin it somehow.

For the first time in a while, I really did feel like one lucky motherfucker.

THE FOUR SEASONS in Maui was undoubtedly the most beautiful place I'd ever been to. From the window of the hotel room, where I spent my two-week pre-shoot quarantine, I watched the sky's vibrant oranges and reds fade into the ocean.

"Nana, it's incredible here," I said, sinking down onto the edge of the hotel bed. The phone, balanced on a pillow near the nightstand, showed just enough of my face as I tugged open my suitcase.

Her voice crackled through FaceTime. "Oh, I'm so happy for

you, sweetheart. You deserve this. Enjoy every second of it. Be kind to yourself."

"I will. It's so beautiful," I said, reversing the camera for her to see. "I wish you were here with me."

It was actually so nice that I started to feel a little guilty, like I'd escaped the pandemic while the rest of my loved ones back home were figuring out what the hell they were going to do to get by. There I was idling away the days watching *Below Deck* (important research) and ordering lava cake in a jar from room service. *Did I deserve to be here while the world is falling apart?*

Ironically, that was the crux of *The White Lotus*'s message: once you're in a privileged position and not consumed by day-to-day survival, your worries become existential.

Still, I couldn't help but feel disconnected when most of my conversations were with a screen. Even when it was with Sean, who had finally finished his sentencing and whose voice I hadn't heard in years, and who couldn't help himself from telling me about all the Marvel movies he missed while he was locked away. And when I finally got through to Cory, I saw someone who had managed to find a little peace. His black hair was straightened again, just like I remembered it. He was gearing up to start training as a blackjack dealer in casinos—my mother's son to the core.

When I wasn't catching up with my family, I had nothing else to do but spiral deeper into anxiety about the production. Unchecked nerves are a death sentence for any performer, and my coping mechanism has always been the same: dive in the water (remember, I'm a bitch who loves a bath). But in this case, it was impossible to do that. The two weeks of quarantine felt like a flight on too many edibles (near death but also disorientingly exhilarating). I didn't do much except rummage through my insecurities, vices, toxic traits, and paranoia. Imagining myself getting fired in increasingly creative ways—like sneaking off for a hookup at a Hawaiian luau and accidentally shutting down production.

I'd imagined my (few) scenes a million times, playing out what I might say to people, how I'd get everyone to like me, what labored efforts I'd make to prove that I was worthy of being there.

The first day we were allowed to leave our rooms, I walked to breakfast, stomach tingling with excitement and nerves. The moment of truth was here. I headed into the dining room, ready to make all my first impressions—and collided right into Jennifer Coolidge.

"I lost my damn phone. I'm always doing that. Of course the first day, I lose it immediately," she said, offering a self-deprecating roll of the eyes.

Even with a face mask on she was unmistakable. She was draped in the blue satin bathrobe from the hotel room and was peering into a bush while a hotel staffer reached their arm into it.

All I could think was *Holyshitholyshitholyshitholyshit*. Somehow, I got it together long enough to muster a reply. "God, me too. I do that all the time."

I was full of shit, my phone was superglued to my hand. But I really didn't know what else to say.

"Oh good, I'm glad I'm not the only one. I'm Jennifer," she said.

"Nice to meet you! I'm Lukas."

"Oh, it's nice to meet you. You have incredible hair."

It didn't cure my impostor syndrome, but it put me at ease to know how lovely Jennifer was. Her warmth was an omen of good things to come.

The circumstances of the production were so unique, so specific, that it created an amplified feeling of community. It was like

Lord of the Flies, if Piggy never lost his glasses and had access to room service and infinity pools.

Sydney Sweeney was my one person there I knew from back home, and though she was another of my *Euphoria* costars whose star had been rising faster than mine, it was clear she hadn't grown jaded or any less in awe of the opportunity before us. Sydney's groundedness had always buoyed her, and on the shoot, it kept me afloat as well.

After wrapping for the day, we'd all eat dinner, then grab a few drinks, and spend hours by the bay—taking in its thick ocean air—talking about everything and nothing. It felt like being at a summer camp, but the actors were actually talented and no one was getting molested.

Talk always circled back to the lives we'd chosen—this delusional career path that felt more like a shared trauma.

The parallels caught me off guard. Each of us had an arsenal of tales: glimpses of success, the ups and downs of relevancy, early roles that shaped us into who we'd become, and the sting of rejection and countless casting horror stories. Auditioning is the most fucked-up thing you can do to an artist. You're handed a few pieces of paper usually the night before and at 9 a.m. the next morning expected to sell your soul—with charisma. Prepandemic, it meant filing into a holding pen with your competition, all of whom look like rough drafts of you. Some are hotter, taller, or more experienced. Actually, maybe you're a rough draft of them.

Now, we all missed that room. As stressful as it was, at least you didn't have to worry about all the technical problems of virtual meetings.

So sitting with my castmates, it only felt natural for me to show them the audition video. I expected a few laughs and secondhand embarrassment. Which came. What I didn't expect was how much it actually hit home for everyone.

"I can't believe you have a documented moment of how terrible actors can be treated," Molly Shannon said.

Seeing what I thought of as a funny little video had actually affected her gave me pause. Was it possible that I might be sitting on something that wasn't just funny but, kind of, important?

"I've been wanting to post it, but I feel like I would, like, get canceled?"

"Why would you get canceled?" somebody asked.

I didn't really have an answer for that.

"Or blacklisted? I don't know. I don't want to take someone down, or ruin some guy's life, I guess?"

They pointed out that there was nothing identifying him or suggesting who he was, and I would certainly never name him. I'd kept the video private out of fear of something bad happening, but now I wondered if maybe those fears were unfounded.

We stayed up talking all night, yet I was gripped with the feeling that I was peering over the edge of a cliff and trying to decide if I had the balls to jump.

I tried to sleep it off, but when I woke up, I found myself still completely consumed by whether I should post the video.

Outside, the once-soothing sound of the waves gently crashing on the shore started to feel like they were egging me on, so I rolled over and grabbed my phone from the bedside table. *Maybe I should write a draft of something to post, just to see how it feels. I'll just cosplay for a second, get everything out of my system*, I thought to myself.

I started typing out a heartfelt message full of phrases like "shed light." Then I stopped myself, deleting it all. It didn't feel right. It felt too earnest, too cheap, too insincere. So I let instinct guide me.

> psa if youre a shit talking director make sure to mute ur shit on zoom mtgings

It was a bit too strong, and definitely overused the word *shit*, but *fuck it*, I told myself.
Tweet. Copy. Paste. Post.

I sat up in bed, listening to the waves growing louder and more violent. *You're such a fucking idiot*, they seemed to call out to me. *You shouldn't have done that. What the fuck?*

I tossed the phone away, hoping the distance would silence the noise in my head. When it landed at the foot of the bed, I found myself crawling to the edge, looking at it from above. No part of me could force myself to look away.

For a good five minutes or so, I stayed there—naked, with the covers bunched beneath me, and my head peering over the mattress—waiting for the worst to come. But my phone remained silent.

Maybe this is going to be okay. People will get a good laugh out of it and this will just be a fun reminder to try to make this process for actors a bit easier, I kept repeating to myself before finally falling asleep.

"WHERE HAVE YOU BEEN?" Phoebe screamed at me over the phone when I finally woke up, a few hours later.

"What do you mean?" I asked, wiping my eyes.

"Lukas. Where. Have. You. Been?"

"What do you mean? I've been asleep."

"How can you be asleep at a time like this?"

"WHAT ARE YOU TALKING ABOUT?"

"LUKAS, YOU JUST DROPPED THE MOST INSANE VIRAL VIDEO AND WENT TO SLEEP?"

"WHAT?"

I switched her over to speaker as I pulled up Twitter. And that's when the proverbial bats got loose. (There were also real bats near the bay of the hotel.)

"I need to call you back," I said to Phoebe, barely able to speak.

My phone was practically a vibrator, perpetually buzzing with notification after notification. Every second brought another text, call, and email. For the first few minutes, I was hit with a rush of excitement. It felt like some primal itch that had been there my whole life had finally been scratched. Every ping was a microdose of approval.

The praise was coming from everywhere—Seth MacFarlane, the Jonas Brothers, people I never expected to know I existed. Strangers around the world congratulated me on how composed, strong, and brave I was. In my heart of hearts, did I believe these things were true? Well, no, but—

Then, an all-consuming dread started to set in: I'd spent my whole life begging to be seen, and now they'd seen me, and I wanted to hide.

I was petrified that they were going to uncover "the truth." What "the truth" was, I didn't exactly know, but at the very least, I knew that if they kept scrolling they'd find my tweet about how every cat I've ever met had tried to hook up with me.

When I was released back on set, the other actors were all supportive and happy to see me. Some were even proud. I avoided the producers like the plague—which was exhausting, considering we were in an actual plague.

The familiar lights and sounds should've felt like routine. But they didn't. Every muffled conversation felt like it was about me.

"What?" I asked, when I saw a PA showing another assistant something on their phone.

"We were just putting in lunch orders . . ." he answered, clearly confused by how unwell I sounded.

All I could imagine was the discussion they'd have after work about what a liability I was and how they couldn't have this kind of mess hanging over them. I just knew they were going to fire me and find someone else to get his ass eaten on camera.

That night, I shut myself in my room. I figured that if I just hid, this could all go away. I wanted it to disappear. I stared at myself in the mirror, doing that cliché "splash water on your face" after something really traumatic happens. It didn't help, it just broke my AirPods.

I got messages from other producers and directors; apparently all British people sound alike? Because they all seemed to have some daughter, niece, or great-aunt who was convinced it was them on the other side of that Zoom. They'd ask me to confirm that it wasn't them and that they didn't deserve to be canceled. I answered some of their requests, confirming who it *wasn't*. However, it only set off a chain reaction from strangers, demanding that I say who it was.

I called Phoebe back in a panic.

"WHAT DID I DO? WHAT HAVE I DONE? WHAT AM I GOING TO DO?"

"What do you mean? This is amazing," she said, laughing. "Joe Jonas just gave you his full-throated support."

"Wait, really? Hot."

"Yeah! You need to listen to me. This is a good thing. You're like fully viral."

"What if I don't want to be viral, though?"

"Why the fuck would you post it then?"

"I don't know!"

"Why would you not want to be viral? Especially for something so funny."

"Well . . . what if they turn on me?"

"Why would 'they' do that? They love you, and they hate him. It's a no-lose situation."

"Exactly. I don't like that. This is all getting way too out of hand. I just posted it to be funny, and now people are like . . . freaking out. What if they find out who it is? I didn't even care that much, I don't want to ruin someone's life—"

"Relax. Relax. You didn't name him. And you didn't do anything wrong. You posted a funny audition tape."

"I don't want to be known as the viral-audition-tape guy for the rest of my career."

"Lukas. People don't have the attention span to care about anything for longer than, like, a day. Enjoy your moment in the sun, and also enjoy the literal sunshine in Hawaii."

For a moment, her words reassured me. But when she hung up, I forgot everything. All night, doomsday scenarios kept running through my head, like what if a nude of me in an unflattering position suddenly surfaced online? *This must be what real famous people feel like*, I thought to myself. So I went to the most trustworthy famous person available to me, Jennifer Coolidge.

"Coolidge, what the fuck did I do?" I asked, cornering her at the breakfast bar.

Then she stepped away from the pressed-celery juice, drew a deep breath, and gave me the best advice I've ever gotten. Words I've lived by ever since.

"Who cares?!" she said, looking at me with a cheeky, conspiratorial grin. *Who cares?!* I repeated it over and over in my head, like she'd just handed me the meaning of life. And in that moment, God, I believed it. Because really in that moment, who cared?

The next day, tired and bleary-eyed, I went down to the beach to try to calm my nerves. I told myself I wasn't going to check my phone. That I'd give myself over to the universe, or whatever that meant. The moment I sat my ass in a beach chair, my phone rang. An unknown number.

I ignored it.

Then it rang again. The same number.

And again.

And again—

"Yes? Hello? What do you want—" I said, flustered.

"Lukas, this is COVID compliance. You tested positive. Please self-quarantine for the next fourteen days, and do not come into contact with anyone."

Fuck. I'd gone viral. Again.

17.

Big-Penis Disorder

For a place devoted to mental health, the facility had a funny way of making me feel completely insane. My therapist's office was too quiet, too beige, too *calm*. It had that stagnant quality that made my skin itch. I needed something to do with my hands. I reached into my pocket.

"Do you mind if I hit my vape?" I asked, already bringing it to my mouth.

"I'm sorry. We don't allow any kind of smoking," my therapist said, her lips pursed.

"I just need a hit. You can punish me or whatever, but I . . ."

She smiled a bit. "Okay, just this once. You know that stuff gives you popcorn lung."

"Then call me Orville Redenbacher because I'm not giving this shit up."

I made myself laugh through my tears. I slid down the plush chair I'd been sitting in for the past God-knows-how-long, and leaned my head back.

"Sorry," I said, my voice rough like sandpaper. "It's just . . . it's been a really shit two months. Honestly, I can't believe I'm even here right now."

The therapist gave me a nod and a soft smile.

"That's a great place to begin. Intake can be a bit tedious, but let's start there, with how you found yourself here."

I pressed my palms to my temple like I was attempting to keep everything from flooding out all at once.

THANKSGIVING AT MY mom's was supposed to be a reset—a chance to clear my head and get back on track. Instead, my sense of self was at an all-time low. After *The White Lotus*, I spent a year bouncing between New York and London, shooting different projects. In the middle of the momentum of my career building again, I'd fallen into a relationship—fast and hard, the kind that felt all-consuming and moved at warp speed. But by the time I got back home to LA, it had completely unraveled, and I was left completely sideways.

The breakup came at the perfect time: the holidays. The time of year when you're expected to celebrate life. Meanwhile, I was actively trying not to want to end mine. I was back home in San Diego, feeling more disconnected from myself and my loved ones than ever before.

Travis, Cory, and Sean were home, too, and in honor of our first night back under the same roof we decided to watch a movie as a family—something we hadn't done together since I was little. It was the kind of moment I'd been chasing for years, ever since I was a teenager, ever since Tessa had lived with us.

I was twenty-seven now, and the need for us to feel like a real unit hadn't faded. However, movie night didn't feel quite as wholesome as I'd imagined. Instead of focusing on the TV, my eyes kept drifting to the worn brown rug we'd had since I was kid, which was beside the matching brown sofa, adorned with the same wooden brown trinkets. *What was it about the color brown my mom loved so much?* I wondered.

As the film played on the screen, I felt tears start to slip down my face. Silent at first, until they weren't. The quiet crying grew into sobs, and the sobs unraveled into something that teetered on the edge of a death rattle.

"Come on," Mom said, her voice gentle but still firm. I took a big gulp from my glass of wine to help block the noises coming out of me.

"Why are you drinking? You know it ages you and you have your father's deep crow's-feet," my mom said.

"I don't care, I'm allowed. My heart hurts," I slurred. I'd been drunk for so long that slurring was now just a part of my speech pattern.

"You've got to get ahold of yourself," my mom said, shaking her head.

I wanted to pull it together—I really did. I was sick of my shit, too. I could feel how selfish I was acting. Everyone was so excited to be back together for the first time in years, and there I was, sloshing red wine over the turd-toned rug, taking my turn at ruining a holiday.

Cory stood abruptly, his bony frame now layered with the lean muscle he'd built in the army, yet his patience worn thinner than ever.

"I'm going to have a smoke," he said, looking over at me. "You need one? Or anything . . . to stop crying?"

I shook my head, not looking up. Cory lit his cigarette halfway out the glass door before slipping outside. Meanwhile, Sean was back to his pre-prison size, happily working through a bag of Buncha Crunch; the globs of chocolate rattling around his mouth made my teeth hurt. All I wanted was for *anyone* to pull me close, to tell me it was okay to feel all this, and that I wasn't crazy. I buried my face in my hands, muffling the heaving as best I could.

"Really, this is the worst thing that's happened to you? A breakup over someone you constantly complained about?!" my mom snapped.

Suddenly, I was overwhelmed by the familiar storm of anxiety, anger, and alienation that had defined my childhood. I'd spent my life trying to bury it, numbing myself with one distraction after another. Maybe it was rage, maybe it was a one-man show, or maybe by that point the only way I could express emotion was to perform it. Whatever it was that made me do it, when I looked down my fist had gone through the door. At first, the glass splintered: a web of jagged cracks emerging around the hole where my hand still stood. Then, with a final shattering crack, the glass gave way, exploding over me like a jagged downpour.

"What the fuck?!" Cory called out from outside, stepping around the glass as he stubbed out his cigarette.

"Oh my God, WHAT DID YOU DO?! THE FRENCH DOORS?! Seriously?" my mom cried out.

For a moment, I felt like I had splintered, too. And the parts of me that remained were free of all the weight I'd been carrying. The only thing I could feel was the cool wind on my knuckles and the strange feeling of release. I noticed the blood trickling down my wrists, streaking across my forearms, and the panic returned.

I was back to myself, terrified by the horrifying truth of who I was becoming.

My voice broke as I whispered, "I'm sorry. Why did I just do that? That was so fucking stupid. I'm sorry. What the fuck is wrong with me?"

Travis was the first to move. Without a word, he grabbed a towel and wrapped it around my hand.

"It's deep. You're going to need stitches," he said, his voice soft but on the verge of breaking into tears.

"I'm sorry, I'm sorry, I'm sorry. I'll buy a new one I promise," I kept repeating to my crying mother as Travis ushered me out the door.

In the car, Travis's tears fell. I turned my face toward the window, unable to meet his eyes. The sight of him unraveling—the one who always held everything together—was too much to bear. And knowing I was the reason only made matters worse.

"You need to get help," Travis said, his voice cracking as we pulled up to the hospital. "Please. I hate seeing you in so much pain."

In the emergency room I watched Travis chew on his fingers like it was the only thing tethering him to this world. I wished I had something to anchor me. I thought back to when I was a kid, how my emotions felt like those little earthquakes. These massive meltdowns that I couldn't explain, where the tears would come too fast and too hot. As a teenager, I learned that getting high and making impulsive decisions helped keep those episodes at bay. But sitting there as an adult, watching my blood seep through the gauze, it became blatantly obvious that avoiding my feelings for years didn't teach me shit about how to actually feel them.

"I can't begin to tell you how sorry I am," I said after we got the green light to go home.

"You've said that. But what are you going to do?" Travis asked.

"I don't know yet."

"Whatever you need from me, I'll do it. You're loved. I know you think you're not, but that's the furthest thing from the truth," he said.

"I love you," I said, pulling him into a big hug, something that was hard for Travis, who was always allergic to physical displays of emotion.

"I promise I will get my shit together, but I need you to do something for me first. . . . Can you drop me off at Moonlight?"

My brother nodded, though I could see the hesitation in his eyes. I knew he wanted to tell me to just come home, but instead, he kept quiet and gave me what I needed.

The lookout of Moonlight beach had changed since I was a kid. The shack bar where Brody and Bunny and I used to take Coricidin and smoke out of apples had been replaced by a sleek outdoor café with built-in tables and showers. It was polished and modern—but it felt hollow now, like something essential had been scrubbed away along with the grime. The lookout itself remained intact—a weathered relic, unchanged by the town's progress.

The lot was deserted, except for Brody and Bunny's car.

"You look like shit," Bunny said. The mix of several ayahuasca trips and a philosophy degree gave her a hyperconfidence that made her almost unrecognizable as the self-conscious girl she'd been in high school.

"Good to see you, too."

Bunny slid off the hood of the car and tugged me into a hug. Her long curls smelled like weed and salt. Brody leaned off the car, eyes flicking to my bandaged hand.

"Nice." Brody smirked.

"What the hell happened?" Bunny asked.

"Got into a brawl with a window."

"Window fucked you up, brother," Brody said. He looked exactly the same as he did the day I met him the first week of middle school: perpetually wet and still shaking like a leaf. I climbed onto the hood of their car, settling beside them as we stared out at the waves.

For a while, none of us said anything. The crash of the tide filled the silence between us.

"I feel like I'm losing my mind," I said. "Like everything's falling apart . . . and I don't know why I'm constantly oscillating from feeling like I'm too much or that I'm never enough."

"You're just . . . really . . . off right now, and you need to adjust. It takes time. It happens to the best of us," Brody said.

"Yeah, but not like this," I said, shaking my head. "I need to adjust immediately. I'm going to ruin my life, all over someone I don't think I even want."

"You just have to get back to yourself, the version of you who doesn't call us crying all the time. I loved him! Where's he?" Bunny said, softening.

I choked out a small laugh, surprising both myself and the twins. It had been so long since I'd even been able to force the muscles in my face to form a smile.

"Yeah, this can be like . . . your year of rest and relaxation, but not like the book. . . . It's nice taking time off of life to just work on yourself," Brody said.

"I think you've had enough time, Brody," Bunny cut in, her eyes locking on him.

Brody rolled his eyes and flipped Bunny off. Despite his revolving door of rehabs over the past four years, he was far from fixed. But even in his most chaotic moments, Brody still had a way of owning his identity and knowing exactly who he was. Something I had never managed to figure out.

"I think you're scared of people sticking around," Bunny said. "And when they prove you right and leave, it makes you feel better about yourself, at least for a little while. It's comfortable. Maybe now it's time to get uncomfortable and let people stay."

I nodded.

"Go break this pattern. It's been there since we were kids," Bunny added softly.

THE THERAPIST STARED at me for a moment, her pen frozen midair, unsure of which part of my journey that led me to this room to dive into first.

"Well," she said after a moment, "I think it's brave that you took your friends' and family's advice and came straight here," she said.

"Not exactly," I replied. "First, I had to screw things up a little more. Go on a rampage in Miami. Really hit my rock bottom. Then, when I couldn't stand myself anymore and couldn't drown out their voices in my head during the plane ride back because the TVs were broken, I caved. I signed up, and now, voilà, I'm here." I gestured vaguely around the office.

She nodded but didn't say anything. She just watched me with that typical therapist prolonged eye contact that made me want to crawl out of my skin.

"Would you say this is a pattern? Do you find yourself going to extremes in an attempt to find clarity?" she asked.

"Yeah. I think so, especially when I was a kid. Trying to find myself or whatever."

"I see—"

"I want to save both of us time and trouble. I really, really just want my mind to click back into place. I just need everything to settle—like it did before everything fell apart. Before everyone gave me that concerned look, like they're either worried about me or they've finally realized that they never actually fucked with me."

I could hear her scribble something on a notepad. Was she talking shit about me? I wondered if all the therapists got together at the end of the day and laughed about who had the most unhinged patient.

"I can understand that," she said, nodding. "Do you find yourself worrying about people liking you?"

"Yeah. I think that's everybody to some extent."

"And when it comes to your relationships with others, would you say you tend to be a people pleaser, or do you have strong boundaries?"

"You have really good skin, you know that?" I asked, trying to flirt my way out of the question at hand. She tilted her head, the compliment sliding right past her.

"I appreciate the sentiment, but this is about you. I want you to try to dig deeper. . . . Did you feel like anyone noticed when you were struggling, or was it just overlooked?"

"Um, yeah, sometimes. I've always felt like they could have more, y'know? I wanted people to see me—really see me."

"Was there something you wished someone had noticed?" she asked, her voice careful.

It was the kind of question that sneaks up on you, the one that makes you feel like you might break open without any warning.

"Just, um, I mean . . . I guess one thing that comes to mind is . . . I was molested at camp," I said, my fingers fidgeting with the frayed fabric on the arm of the chair.

"I'm so sorry," she said.

"No, please, don't do that. It's really fine."

"It's not," she said.

"Yeah, no, I know it's not." I scoffed. "But, yeah, I think it would have been nice if people were like mind readers and could have noticed I was a little off after that, and that maybe that was the start of my 'lashing out.'"

A long uncomfortable pause filled the room.

"Hasn't everyone been molested?" I continued, the words coming out like a rehearsed bit.

"Is that a familiar type of protection for you? Humor?"

"Probably that and . . . I lie. I lied as a kid, to my journal, to friends, family. Why?" I asked.

"There's nothing wrong with it. I was just noticing. Humor is an excellent self-defense mechanism. It sounds like you've been carrying around a lot. It also sounds like there's something else you're running from—"

I could feel the tears starting to form, and I patted my eyes to try and tuck them away.

"It's okay. If the tears could talk, what would they say?" she asked, handing me a tissue box.

As I sat there, wanting to escape this game of twenty-one questions, I pinched the bridge of my nose and tried to make sense of the past month. The breakdowns. The sleepless nights. The dissociation. The erratic mood swings. The frantic, desperate efforts to outrun the looming abandonment that *he* left behind.

Then Phoebe's texts resurfaced in my mind. The words she sent right before I entered the facility:

You tried running from it, and you're still miserable. This isn't about him. It's about something deeper, something you need to face. Also, I can't handle you talking about HIM for one more minute. I love you but you seriously need to stfu.

Him.
I'm not going to name him, we're just going to call him the Ex.

THE EX LOOKED like if you gave an AI art generator the prompt: "*The Hills Have Eyes* character with an Equinox membership" and it spit out a Roman ideal of man. A statue—a weathered and worn one, but with the same disposition, one who often had blueberries and protein powder stuck in his teeth.

I fell in love with this beautiful, blueberry-filled statue. In the beginning, he was kind and would tell me how he was impressed by the way I think. Every dumb thing I said was suddenly poetic and accidentally insightful, and, for the first time in a long time, I felt *special*.

Like every good LA love story, ours had begun on Raya. I will reiterate he was very hot. And initially, I only thought I was in for a fun night or two. However, I ended up doing what I do best: falling into a deeply unhealthy and codependent relationship, convincing myself that I had found "the one" after three days of knowing a complete stranger.

Three days turned into a week, and we were inseparable, convinced we were undoubtedly soulmates. So, without having met any of each other's friends or family, we decided to make things official. Exactly like our parents taught us to.

The thing I loved most—and what originally attracted me to the Ex—was his lack of pretense. On our first date, I'd done the whole "I'm not really into the scene" thing. (Even though that's bullshit and everybody is kind of into the scene.) And when he told me that he was also vehemently against the LA circuit, it felt genuine. Refreshing, even. He lived in Malibu, right off the Pacific Coast Highway. It felt like an escape from the rat race of Hollywood. It was a life I didn't know how badly I'd been craving until I was living it.

The Ex spent all his time surfing and doing yoga with his neighbors, which consisted of a motley crew of Real Housewives of Malibu types. And soon enough, I was spending all my time surfing at the beach and getting CoolSculpting with Cheryl and Rhonda down the street.

Two months after we started dating, the fairy tale was interrupted. I was sent off to London for six months to shoot a season of the Netflix series *You*. I was thrilled about the opportunity, but I wasn't quite ready to leave behind what felt like the beginning of something perfect.

We decided that once I'd found my footing after a couple of months, he would fly over and visit me, and we could dive headfirst into a romantic European fantasy for a few months.

Before I jetted off, Phoebe's birthday conveniently lined up with my going-away party. So we decided to celebrate at Tom-Tom, the bar from one of our favorite reality shows, *Vanderpump Rules*. Beyond blacking out with the cast, the real aim of the party was to finally introduce my friends to this mystery man who I had completely gone AWOL for.

It didn't take long to notice my friends weren't totally in love with him. He had a habit of getting really weird when he was drunk. One moment, he'd be launching into a slurred, unprompted TED Talk, mansplaining the mechanics of biohacking; the next, he'd be inches from your face, declaring how intermittent fasting makes for a very powerful, tantric experience. Nevertheless, I was certain if my friends met him in the light of day, they'd love him!

The next morning, I flew off to London and told myself it was my time to fully immerse myself in this experience. If we were meant to be, the way I thought we were, it would all fall into place. I tried to settle in, convincing myself that distance would be a test, not a threat.

Not even a full week later, he told me that he was boarding a flight to London. That night, I rushed back from the set, imagining I'd sweep him off his feet and take him to a romantic dinner in Piccadilly Circus or Notting Hill. But when I showed up at my apartment, I opened the door to find him partying with three strangers—people he apparently grew up with, or so he claimed.

To be fair, he had never said he was *not* part of the London scene.

He leaned in to kiss me, tongue locked and loaded, but the second it touched mine, something inside me glitched. It felt like my entire DNA had been reprogrammed in an instant. His breath didn't smell, but his touch was riddled with halitosis. I felt like the person I was with five days before had been traded in for a shittier, downgraded version. This couldn't have been the person I had been with back in LA, the easygoing, earthy Malibu himbo who I couldn't go three seconds without texting. Had he always been this sloppy? Had there always been a film of creatine left over on his teeth? Had he always seemed like someone who'd just been roofied, struggling to form a complete sentence? From then on, even the sound of his breathing pissed me off.

Maybe it was just one of those nights where everything felt off. I reminded myself that he came across the world for *me*. Surely that meant there was some genuine care and love buried under all the mess?

But in a matter of days, the crumbling mess of my relationship began to overshadow everything else. Even the excitement of filming *You* in London. The tension was palpable. He started leaving for different European countries to meet up with friends, and I found myself encouraging him to leave. A part of me genuinely wanted him to go, and a part of me was preparing for the inevitable.

Instead of feeling accomplished, I felt empty, isolated, disconnected not just from my surroundings but from my very self, both on set and in my own skin.

There was something rotting deep inside me—something more serious and sinister than my poor gut health. It was like a darkness that I could feel coming over me whenever the possibility of being abandoned seemed like it was lurking in the unknown just around the corner. Each time it approached, it was like flinching before a slap, even when I didn't know when I'd be hit.

The truth was, I was just as ready to leave him as he was to leave me. We were caught in a cycle—one we both perpetuated—using each other as a distraction from the discomfort festering inside us. Deep down, I knew neither of us wanted to face it, so we just kept going, not out of love, but out of fear of what might happen if we stopped.

I WROTE THIS FOR ATTENTION

"THAT'S A LOT for us to unpack. Let's take a moment to sit with this, and we'll pick up where we left off tomorrow," the therapist said.

After my session, I made my way to group therapy, which was held in a half-empty room that hummed with discomfort. Group didn't have the heart that I'd experienced in AA. For one, we had a skills leader, Erika, who guided us through impersonal, almost mechanical exercises designed to help us regulate our emotions and reconnect with ourselves.

In theory, techniques like holding ice cubes to ground yourself or listening to music with "opposite emotions" had their merits, I guess, though they seemed too basic. More like emotional busywork than actual healing—like ticking off boxes on some scavenger hunt, all crammed together into this bizarre, albatross-shaped box, following step-by-step instructions to put us back together again.

"I want to shake things up a bit today," Erika said. "I know that the skills group can feel tedious at times, so I thought we'd try something different. Today, I want us to have an open conversation about higher powers."

I felt a small spark of hope.

"And just to clarify," she added quickly, "this doesn't have to be anything religious. But I'm curious. Do any of you have a sense of who or what your higher power is?"

Ava, a girl from Pensacola, raised her hand. She was a big talker, her neck was weighted down with puka shells, and her skin marked with a permanent farmer's tan.

"So, I'm like *such* a big believer in energies, and I feel like my higher power is energy. I legit can tell what everyone's aura is."

"That's great—" our group leader started before Ava cut her off.

"I would love to give everyone a free reading of their aura color," she said, practically vibrating with enthusiasm.

She went around the room, assigning everyone an aura color and general vibe. When she got to me, she froze, almost fearful.

"You have a really dark aura," she said. "Whoa, I, like, sorry, I can't even look at you."

I just nodded, like, *Sounds about right.*

Another girl, a younger one, who looked oddly like Kaylee, raised her hand and said, "My boyfriend is my higher power."

Again I nodded, like, *Sounds about right.*

THE NEXT DAY in my one-on-one session, my therapist was waiting for me with a candle burning on the table between us; a séance for my unresolved issues.

"Welcome back, how have the last few days been going?"

"Yeah, pretty great," I lied.

"How is the DBT therapy and groups going?"

"Also good," I lied again.

"Last time we met, we started talking about your ex. How long were you seeing each other?"

"Um, like six months total? It felt more like six years because of how intense the whole thing was."

She nodded sympathetically. "Have you ever heard of the concept of 'favorite person'?"

"You mean how I want to be everyone's favorite person?" I asked.

"Not exactly. In psychology, a favorite person is someone—usually a romantic partner—we form an intense attachment to. We rely heavily on them for validation, a sense of security . . ."

"So basically a support animal, but in human form?"

She sighed but smiled. "It's not . . . the worst analogy I've heard."

I exhaled through my nose, my eyes landing on the pearl headband she always wore. It tilted slightly whenever she was leaning in for me to go further.

"You know, humor as well as lying can be brilliant tools when you're a kid. They can make life more interesting or help you avoid your feelings, or shield you from pain. I'd love for you and I to integrate some more honesty in our sessions."

"Right now?"

"Sure. Tell me exactly what you are thinking or feeling, without telling me what I want to hear."

"Okay I . . ." I said, inhaling sharply. "I really . . . hate your headband. There's something about the pearls on it that reminds me of a girl at cotillion who really wants to be a princess."

"Excellent," she said, trying to force herself to be proud instead of offended.

"I just feel like . . . and I know we just met . . . but you're not a real headband wearer. This feels like a new thing for you, that you're trying on. You're obviously very smart, and I know a headband doesn't have anything to do with intelligence but that's the first thing that came up for me . . . sorry."

"No, don't be sorry. You might be right. Let's keep it honest. Tell me, how is this week going? How was dialectical group—"

"DBT is so gay, like enough with *all* the worksheets, I just want to talk about my problems and have someone give me a straightforward answer," I blurted out. "It just seems like I'm going in circles a lot here, and I just want to know if I'm actually crazy. Seems like if it's taking this much time to try and figure it out, I'm probably not."

"I understand," she said.

"And maybe my friends, my family, and I were all overreacting by having me come here, maybe I need to get back to my life, maybe, like, too much self-help just leads to self-obsession. Should anyone *really* be talking about themselves this much?" I continued.

As much as I loved talking about myself, this was different. I didn't want to keep unraveling every thought or life decision for this long. The truth was, I just wanted a prescription, something to dull the edge and make these unbearable feelings disappear. I wanted to fast-forward to the part where everything felt normal again.

"First of all, there's no such thing as crazy. That would imply something is wrong with you. What we're trying to figure out is the source of why you are experiencing these emotions the way you do, and if that experience is preventing you from living a happy, healthy, emotionally regulated life."

"Okay..."

"What set off your outburst? What do you think . . . made you punch your hand through a window?" she asked.

I drummed my fingers on the armchair. Closed my eyes. This wasn't like boot camp, where there was a right answer to unlock. I was an adult; I could leave of my own accord. I'd chosen to be here.

"I couldn't keep it in anymore," I said.

"What in?" she gently pushed on.

AFTER FINISHING FILMING *You* that summer, I packed my bags and traded in my UK flat for the Ex's Malibu beach house. I hoped we could delete the past six months from our memories, but when we got home, it felt like our relationship was still lost in the gloomy London fog.

The Ex felt like a different person—normal, more himself than he had been during our time overseas. When we were back in the rhythm of our old routine, surrounded by the familiarity of our city, everything else faded into the background. It felt like we'd found our way back to each other. Our days unfolded with simplicity: surfing, reading books as we basked in the sun, going to yoga with Cheryl and Rhonda. We disconnected from the noise of others—no phones, no social media—and in that space, I rediscovered why I cherished my relationship with the Ex.

Soon, the ease of it all began to unravel. The things I'd once found so insightful about him now started to feel like indifference. He'd just sit for hours on end, reveling in the mundanity. He'd memorize questionable facts about whatever microbiomes are and recite them with a twinkle in his eye that, initially, I'd swooned over. Until I realized that twinkle was empty, just like him, just like us.

I tried reintroducing him to my friends, but even in the light of day, they didn't seem to be warming up to him.

"Lukas, I have to be honest, I've never heard him talk about anything other than himself. He's never asked me one question in the several months I've 'known' him."

"He asked if Marvin Gaye was an up-and-coming artist . . ."

"He talks inside my mouth."

We'll call it mixed reviews. On the surface, I was like, *They just don't know him like I do! Why do they care so much?*

Deep down, I knew they were right. Still, I was bullheaded and hasty, always have been, and it was going to take more than earnest pleas from people I love and trust most in life to change my mind.

Summer collapsed into fall, and I continued to pretend I wasn't noticing more and more the things that were wrong with the relationship. I started spending more time with Cheryl and Rhonda while he would hit up Equinox for hours on end.

One day, as I was getting out of the ocean, I felt something strange—a tingling sensation on my penis. Had something stung me in the water? I quickly opened my suit to check, and sure enough, the tip of my penis looked like a raw, red stoplight.

That night, I showed it to the Ex. He looked perplexed and shrugged.

"Could it be a bacterial infection? From the water?"

I was pretty sure that wasn't a thing, but I also didn't want to rule it out as a possibility.

"Let's keep an eye on it," he said.

When I woke up the next day, the burning sensation was even worse.

"I think this might be something serious," I said to him, but he kept insisting that it was likely some kind of bacteria. All day, I went down a Reddit rabbit hole: *Anyone experiencing a penis bacterial infection from swimming in the Malibu beaches today? This week? Ever?*

Unfortunately, evidence was slim. When the Ex got back from the gym, I was waiting on the couch, my anxiety practically radiating off me. I'd been running over everything in my head for hours. When I told him what Reddit said, he cut me off.

"I'm telling you, I know people who have had this happen to them, Lukas!"

He had a tendency to say my name at the end of every sentence. It felt like he was trying a little too hard to make sure I knew he was talking to me, as if I'd somehow forgotten.

"Okay, please just tell me the truth. Is this an STD?"

His mouth dropped. "Oh my God. No. Are you kidding me?"

I almost felt bad for accusing him, but I was running out of explanations for why my penis felt like it was marinated in Tabasco.

I WROTE THIS FOR ATTENTION

That night in bed, I stared at the ceiling, trying to self-soothe and quiet all the warning signs telling me shit was about to hit the fan.

In the morning, we'd gone nuclear: my dick was leaking toxic waste like Chernobyl. I asked him to give me a ride to the walk-in clinic, and he happily agreed. He grabbed his car keys and his protein smoothie, and reassured me it was going to be fine. He was being so casual about it. Maybe there wasn't anything wrong. Maybe he was being truthful and I was just always expecting the worst in people. Maybe I was being paranoid and he was right.

As we sat in his Tesla on the way to the doctor's office, I took a deep breath.

"Listen, I want to give you one last chance to tell me the truth. Did you sleep with someone else? This is your get-out-of-jail-for-free card if you just tell me the truth."

"Lukas, really? Are you really asking that?" He laughed, slightly offended.

"Well, what am I supposed to think? I'm literally leaking slime."

"I don't know! I really don't. What I do know is you are going to feel really silly when they give you some antibiotics and tell you this is all some Malibu bacteria—"

"That's not a fucking thing! That's such a *Glee*-ass lie!"

"What does that mean, Lukas?"

"Stop ending and starting a sentence with my name! People only do that in soap operas!"

"Can we not? You never listen to me, so if it makes you feel better to hear it from a doctor, let's just do it." There it was again, that calmness.

My phone buzzed, and I saw it was my mom calling. I answered and put her on speaker in an effort—because yes, I am close enough with my mother—to get her advice about my penis.

When I explained the bacteria hypothesis, my mom took longer than usual to answer.

"What the hell are you talking about? That's not a thing."

Her response was simple but enough to make my breathing slow. The Ex chimed in.

"Hey, Paulina, Lukas is being neurotic. It is absolutely a thing. There are all these surfers from the pier who have had this happen to them. There's a bunch of sewage that gets dumped into the ocean and causes infections. It's so sad, like, sea life is dying and it's ruining the coral reef."

I held my breath and waited to see how my mom would react.

"I don't know, honey. That may be true, but I don't think it affects your—"

The Ex cut her off again.

"Trust me. It's just a different culture. Come out to Malibu where all the surfers are, and you'll definitely hear about it!"

"I have lived in San Diego my whole life, dear. That *is* my culture."

He didn't have an answer for that.

The conversation dropped off right there, leaving an uncomfortable silence that stretched as we drove down the PCH.

Before I could even take a seat, the nurse led me straight to the back. Ironically, the doctor looked just like one of these Malibu surfers who, according to the Ex, probably suffered from the exact same penile affliction.

"So, what seems to be the problem, buddy?"

"I—I've heard about bacterial infections you can get from the ocean? On your, uh . . . dick?"

He smiled, and shook his head.

"Uh, what?"

He could see the panic in my eyes and put on his best bedside manner.

"Okay, why don't we see what we're dealing with?"

I sheepishly got to my feet and dropped trou. The surfer doc took one look and tried to conceal his laughter.

"Oh yeah, man, that's *definitely* an STD. The ocean's a little more forgiving. We'll get some tests going right now, no worries, bro. But for now, I'm gonna treat you with some antibiotics, cool?"

Turns out it wasn't just one but two: gonorrhea and chlamydia. A double homicide.

A shot in the ass. A round of antibiotics. Then came the confrontation—the arguments, the shouting, and the tears. The STD was the least of my worries. What was a bigger pain in my ass than the shot in my ass was knowing I had handed him the truth on a silver platter—a chance to come clean, no strings attached, no judgment—and he had still lied to my face.

When it was all said and done, I packed my things and loaded my suitcases into Phoebe's trunk. My friends gathered around, embracing me. As they tried to get my mind off it throughout the night, they reminded me, kindly, that they never liked him. I tried to remind myself that, deep down, I probably didn't like him anymore, either.

Here's the most fucked-up part: As furious as I was, I was so afraid of being abandoned, that a few weeks later, my dumb ass let him back in. Not intimately, but emotionally. After weeks of him begging, I gave him one final chance to exist in my life. I allowed him to hit me with all his half-hearted apologies and crocodile tears. And just when I'd accepted that maybe this would be okay, maybe I didn't care that he cheated on me, maybe we were meant to be together and we all make mistakes—

He ghosted me. Full-blown, never spoke to me again. The day I agreed to give him a second chance, he said he was going to a concert with friends and promised to meet me for breakfast burritos the next morning. As it turns out, it wasn't exactly a concert. I later discovered it was a rave, where he fell head over heels with a closeted Mormon on Molly, and moved to Utah the very next day.

And that long-winded story about getting ghosted and STD'd brings us back to the facility in West LA, where a doctor, who, despite the headband, was way smarter than I will ever be, was looking me in my eyes and telling me that this was indeed about more than just a breakup.

"I KNOW IT'S such a basic reason to come to this place, and I need to just get over it, move on, forgive and forget . . ." I said. "It's just that forgiveness feels so performative."

"What's another possibility?" she said. "What if forgiveness wasn't for him? Or for the stuff you told me about your dad? What if it's for you? What if you could see forgiveness as something for your own peace of mind?"

"Can we revisit this? I feel like I can halfway forgive him . . . Maybe I need to stay pissed off for a little while longer."

"Anger's a bridge sometimes," she said. "But you can't stay parked on it forever."

I wanted to make a parallel parking joke so bad, but I stopped myself. The therapist adjusted her glasses and leaned forward slightly.

"Lukas, have you heard of BPD?"

"Big-penis disorder?" I asked. I couldn't help myself.

The therapist stared at me, I stared at her back. Both of us knew it wasn't.

"No, I asked you because you have eight out of nine markers for it."

"Are you sure it's not big-penis disorder?"

"It's borderline personality disorder. I can give you some literature for it," she said.

I immediately felt resistance flood my body.

I'd spent so much time insisting I just wanted to be *seen*. And now, here this therapist was, turning over the corners of my psyche I'd been too scared to touch. It felt like shaking out that old, brown rug my mom had hoarded from house to house, full of dust and secrets.

It wasn't that I disagreed with her.

Outbursts? Clearly. Abandonment issues? Sure. All-or-nothing relationships? Obviously. Distorted identity? Check. Check. Check.

Hearing it laid out made me feel so flattened. So that was it? Not a tortured genius or an enigma. Just someone with a mood disorder and a treatment plan. Maybe I was just . . . vanilla.

It was exactly what I'd been searching for: a fix. A quick and easy solution. But as she sent me home with the pamphlets, the literature, and a couple of prescriptions for mood stabilizing drugs, I realized that maybe there was no quick fix. But if there was even a chance, I'd swallow it whole.

18.

u dont know my alphabet

The Northern Lights look pretty much the same through tears—wobbly, refracted, and blurred. Big enough to swallow a person whole but also, somehow, still delicate. As I stared at the sky, I realized that heartbreak didn't change the shape of things. That heartbreak almost . . . felt good in a place like this.

The trip to Iceland was intended to be a romantic destination, the perfect getaway. Reykjavík was supposed to be our fresh start, a chance to lean into the kind of whirlwind romance people wrote about, the kind that justified how fast I'd disappeared into this next entanglement like I didn't learn a thing from the last time.

The night before, I had planned to go to bed early for a 6:00 a.m. dogsled tour. To be honest, the sled ride was one of the main reasons Iceland had appealed to me in the first place. The thought of gliding across the frozen trek, carried by a pack of panting, breathless dogs, felt like the kind of reckless freedom I hadn't experienced in ages.

From the sled, the Icelandic mountainside looked like Mars:

littered with volcanic rock, a barren landscape, and practically no signs of life.

The dogs barked and leaped, straining against their harnesses, eager to break free. As I loosened the reins, they lunged forward, their frenzy melting into quiet determination. They were just like me.

Now I was pulling at my own reins as the sled sliced through the snow and the arctic air slapped against my face, my tears crystallized on my cheeks. All I could do was ask myself, over and over—*How the fuck did I end up here?*

Well, I didn't have to try that hard to remember. It hadn't lasted very long, so it didn't take up that much RAM in the old hard drive upstairs. A tidy little chunk of memories—pretty succinct, and impossible to forget.

IT'S FUNNY HOW the most insignificant moments can sometimes end up defining everything that comes after.

It started at a party in the hills. (No, not that kind of party—as much of a freak as I am, I have never been to a freak-off.) And, because I was five years younger, true to form at the time, I was admittedly a mess. Okay, maybe I don't remember *everything* of this particular memory, but I do remember him.

I can vaguely recall a five-years-younger me, five-vodka-sodas deep, catching sight of *him* across the room and feeling compelled to strike up a conversation. What exactly? Couldn't tell you. Knowing me, it was probably an overly confident attempt at charm that didn't quite land. At the time, I didn't give the encounter much weight. Life moved on, a string of relationships came and went, and I figured that moment had dissolved into the blur of countless others.

Turns out, our paths would cross again.

After my BPD diagnosis, I thought I'd discovered some profound epiphany about who I was and why I did the things that I did. And in some ways, it did. I could finally see the patterns I'd been blind to before. Every relationship, the same cycle. Too fast, too deep, too reckless. I'd fall in love like my life depended on it, then shatter just as hard when it ended.

Living with borderline personality disorder, simply put, feels like being trapped inside a rage cage. Or splitting. For those who wonder what that means, the best way to describe it is like living out the story of Jekyll and Hyde.

Me, the Lukas I know, the Lukas everyone sees, is real. My thoughts, my feelings, when I'm Lukas, those belong to me. But just like Jekyll has Hyde, I have . . . other Lukas. Maybe Lucas with a *c* didn't die after all. We'll just call him the fucking devil. Because he's a pain in my ass. And when he takes over, it's like a blackout. I can be standing in front of someone I love, someone I cherish, but at that moment, I don't see them. I don't see anything. My body flushes hot, my adrenaline spikes, my hands shake, and venom spills from my mouth before I even know what I'm saying. It's detached from what I truly believe. And when it passes? It leaves behind nothing but shame, regret, and the sinking weight of knowing I'll have to apologize for hurting the ones that I love, yet again.

It's relentless. It's exhausting—for me, my friends, my family, and my romantic partners. I don't envy anyone who loves someone with BPD. The people closest to me are usually the ones caught in the emotional splash zone. And it's not just the rage. It's the desperate hunger to be completely consumed by someone. I'd call it codependence, but that doesn't even feel fair—because I don't think I leave the other person much of a choice. In relationships, my happiness becomes entirely dependent on how much attention I receive from them. I hate admitting that, but it's true. I'm a needy little bitch. But it's not me! It's Lucas with a *c*. My dark passenger.

I struggle daily with the disconnect between the person I am inside and the one the disorder forces out into the world. And the hardest part? Telling people. The disorder is so stigmatized, and the moment someone learns I have BPD, it's like it becomes all they see. Every emotion, every reaction is suddenly under a microscope. My feelings are no longer just feelings—they're symptoms. Even though that's true, I still resent it, the version of me that's not the disease exists within me, too, and he doesn't deserve to be labeled like that! Okay, maybe he does.

I swore I was going to devote at least a year to learning and loving myself. That I wouldn't latch on to my next "favorite person" to fill that spot. However, it turned out the clarity was elusive, and the period of self-care had an expiration date. That, plus a questionable cocktail of meds, I have since realized is the perfect recipe for a meltdown.

I was convinced I had finally mastered the art of being content on my own. I'd moved on from the Ex. But I guess I hadn't fully healed. Not, *fully* fully, because, like a month and a half later, I was engaged. To a new person, not the Ex, to *the Husband*—the one from the party and many years and many life lessons ago.

WHEN I GOT engaged, I was ecstatic to tell my friends and family. All of whom had been on the receiving end of many texts over our few-weeks courtship that consisted of words like "my husband,"

and "I'm in love," and "I'm getting married." So when confronted with the news of the real thing, they mostly just rolled their eyes. *Here we fucking go again.*

Who could blame them? All my relationships started out on this high, this feeling like I was a contestant on *The Bachelor*, which, let's be honest, is, like, the epitome of romance. From there, I'd dive in headfirst into it with them. (Even though, in my gut, I knew it was way too fast.) In my mind, all I could think was *Who gives a shit? It feels good. This is what it feels like to be loved.* And then the ember would inevitably fizzle out, as all embers do. Leaving me, or us, feeling like a smoldering pit of nothing.

But as we know, I always choose to fight fire with fire. So when I was proposed to, my mind went straight to Vegas and the Little White Chapel, there was no other option.

I didn't want any suits. I wanted a goth wedding. I wanted to tie the knot in leather, just like they would have done on *Rock of Love*. Instead, I ended up with a very questionable outfit purchased online a few days prior, which made me look like Siegfried or Roy but without the sexy tigers. (It was a wild animal, guys! What were we expecting! In a way, I was a lot like those tigers—unpredictable, sexy, and about to lash out.)

I was also dealing with a third presence in the relationship: the internet. I'd been trying to find love and live my truth and all that shit, and still people were saying that the relationship was one giant publicity stunt. It also didn't help that I had Kim Kardashian officiating my wedding, and Shania Twain serenading me into holy matrimony.

Another thing that didn't help was it seemed the internet had soured on me. I was no longer the Luigi Mangione of the audition process, but a "queer baiter." An ugly one at that! Seriously, stop comparing me to Shane Dawson and the Bogdanoff twins. We all read the comments, and it's mean! But the queer baiting didn't make any sense. Queer baiting means that there is an implication of queer characters or relationships in a fictional piece of media in order to get LGBTQ+ viewers to tune in, but then they never actually end up depicting those things.

Nevertheless, people started picking apart my identity, tagging me in a post accusing me of stealing roles from queer actors. Until one day I hastily responded with "u don't know my alphabet."

The original poster replied, "then please, enlighten the whole world." (Come on, did you really miss the opportunity to say: "Then please, spell it out for us"? You amateur, if you're going to tweet insults, at least be clever!)

I didn't feel like I had to enlighten the whole world. I wasn't closeted; I just hadn't issued a press release because I didn't expect anyone to care what I did in my own famously tiny boudoir. Yet something about the comment was hard for me to shake off.

So when I found myself getting married less than a year later, the troll in me couldn't help but revel in the spectacle of it all. I'm not saying that my marriage was this conscious reaction to feeling like the subject of a bad first-draft dissertation about LGBTQ+ culture. But maybe, perhaps, there was a part of me attempting to prove something—to claim ownership over a narrative that was mine, and nobody else's to comment on.

A FEW MONTHS later, our nuptials aired on Hulu, on *The Kardashians*, for all the world to share in our lawfully wedded bliss. Except when my friends finally tuned in—the ones who weren't there as I committed myself to this man—they didn't reach out with their well-wishes or to see where I was registered. Instead, they were texting me things like *You didn't seem well*.

They were right. I wasn't well—not at all. I was caught somewhere in and out of hypermanic episodes. And I'm not using those words colloquially. Living with BPD has meant that I've dealt with these highs and lows my whole life—which explains some of the impulsive decisions (which may or may not include me getting married, or may or may not include me agreeing to write this book).

Sometimes the search for the right medications can backfire, worsening the very symptoms they're meant to treat. On the wrong pharmaceuticals, I've found myself spending my savings at Caviar Kaspia or transforming my hair and style to the point where I ended up looking like a yassified Keith Urban.

I'm not sharing this to shirk responsibility for my choice to get married. I happily chose to do that. I just want to explain the moments in the show where I'm kinda gazing into the middle distance and leaving my body on autopilot.

It's not that I wasn't aware on some level—it's just that I couldn't stop myself. I'd buckled in for takeoff and only remembered midair that I hate flying.

A FEW MONTHS after my wedding in ape suits, something clicked. I had an elusive moment of clarity where I truly didn't recognize myself anymore. My sense of identity, agency, and autonomy had vanished. My friends and family had been right all along: somehow I had managed to become even worse.

I decided to stop taking my meds. Cold turkey. As a result, all those overmedicated feelings, the ones I shoved far away, finally surfaced in the bitter Icelandic dusk.

I cried, and I cried, and then it was over.

When I finally looked up after all that hurt and all those tears, the sky had changed. The Northern Lights—the one constant in this strange, icy night—were gone. Had they disappeared, or had I simply stopped seeing them?

It was clear this moment had been set in motion long before the vows, before the breakups, before I even understood what love was supposed to look like.

Maybe it began when I was young, forming ideas of marriage based on my parents and grandparents—each with multiple divorces. I'd learned love by seeing Cory and Tessa, watching their endless cycle of breakups and reconciliations, the disappearing acts followed by tearful reunions. When that's your example, it's hard not to believe that love, that marriages, are doomed to fail. That baggage was still my responsibility, and disregarding it was careless on my part.

In the cold chill of the northernmost pole, it was tempting to pin my behavior on the diagnosis. It made my chaos feel justified, even noble. But the truth was there was a lot I had to confront. There had been so much from my growing up that maybe stopped me from growing up. I wasn't chasing love itself, just the idea of it—or at least my idea of it.

Would I have handled it differently now? Sure. Should I have been logical and been honest from the get-go? Absolutely. Am I a dumb bitch who sometimes burns a few bridges before figuring things out? You're damn right.

In the quiet hours after the storm, I found myself packing my suitcase and getting ready to hop on a flight back to LAX with a dream and a cardigan.

When I started heading out, luggage in hand, I froze in place.

I'd been called selfish my whole life—so fuck it, I was going to be selfish again.

Suddenly there I was on the back of sixteen huskies, with a touch of frostbite. Yet for the first time in what felt like forever, I also had a glimmer of myself back.

I don't view my divorce as a failure. I see it as a necessary rupture. An unlearning. My love of love still hasn't changed and probably never will. I may have four more marriages and four more divorces. It's a chapter in a much bigger story that's still unfolding. Because, if I'm being honest, there are parts of me and this disorder that I won't ever fully cure. Some symptoms are more problematic than others. I will probably always crave love that consumes me. Love that feels like the Northern Lights, big enough to swallow a person whole but still delicate.

CONCLUSION

With a *c* not a *k*

Through the window of my nana's apartment, I could see the sprawling towers of Century City lurking in the distance. Though the area doesn't actually resemble any particular century, nor is it even a city, when I moved to LA, I happily bought into its false promise. Hook, line, and delusional sinker. I signed with my first agent, manager, and contract for one of my first roles in one of those sterile buildings. A few months ago, I signed legal paperwork in one of them—for the marriage that crumbled just the week before. Say what you will about me, but I'm nothing if not committed to a quick turnaround.

I was definitely not the first in my family to end a marriage short. But it was Nana who set the bar for her rotating cast of romantic partners. Ever since I was little, I vowed to be just like her when I grew up. She wasn't just my role model but my biggest supporter. While the rest of my family viewed my childhood interest in acting as just another manifestation of my already too theatrical personality, it was Nana who helped me find headshot photographers on Craigslist. She was always in my corner, even when it came to my dad. Nana was the one who told my dad's new wife that she was no longer welcome in her home until I was welcome in theirs. But now, the woman who championed me through everything was silent.

She was in a coma. The vibrant, larger-than-life woman who had been my fiercest protector, my biggest supporter, was now slipping through my fingers. Those few days leading up to my grandma's final goodbye were the most time my dad and I had spent together in over a decade. And while I knew I should be focused more on being present for my nana—holding her hand and repeating how much I love her and saying anything else I could to wake her up, to keep her tethered to this earth just a little while longer—I couldn't stop fixating on my dad.

Watching him massage his temples, I noticed how much he looked like me, just more visibly Jewish. You look at me, you think WASPy *Karate Kid* villain. Yet tucked inside those blaring contrasts, you can't ignore the fact we're leaves on the same tree. Only his absence had left me with my own personal scars that hadn't faded.

Staring at him, I just kept thinking, *All I want is to see my dad cry like a little bitch.*

My dad put his palm across her forehead to gauge Nana's temperature. When I was little, I wondered what it would be like to be his patient. I'd imagine getting SARS, or any of the other strange illnesses I'd lie about in my journal, and imagine my father feeding me a thermometer. But that was just another offshoot of my real fantasy: that my father would look at me, in all my over-the-topness, and claim each part of me as his own.

As I watched him, I realized he wanted to cry. But he couldn't.

I almost felt bad for him—being a doctor was so much easier for him than being a human.

Across the room, Nana's Husband #3 shuffled his feet and looked over to my dad.

"What should we do with all the Ensure sitting in the fridge?"

My dad turned and frowned.

"What do you mean?"

Husband #3 moved his arms about as if to say, *Isn't it obvious?*

"Once she— Does anybody want it?"

Ensure. That's what that fucking smell was. It was the familiar scent of the SlimFast my dad would chug when we were kids. Chemical and chalky and sweet.

"What do you mean 'Does anybody want it?' What kind of a question is that right now?" my dad asked.

In fairness, it was a stupid question, and his mother was on death's doorstep.

"I just don't think it should go to waste."

"What are you talking to me about this for?"

"I just thought it would be helpful."

"It's not. In what world is asking about the Ensure that will be leftover after my mother dies helpful?"

The third husband stared at him. We all did. It was the first time in a long time I happened to agree with my dad. We all retreated back into our own worlds, and I turned my attention to Nana. Like me, she did a lot of things for attention. From her habit of dramatically clutching her chest like a silent-film star to refusing to go to a gym and instead walking around Nordstrom with tiny ankle weights on for exercise, she always lived her life loudly.

I went back to her and whispered in her ear, saying whatever I could just to steal one final moment. Even though she had been unresponsive for the past few days, I still thought she might open her eyes. Because that's how she had always been, full of surprises. I brushed her now-ivory hair off her face. She seemed immune from whatever us humans have to deal with—weakness, mortality, time. As I held her motionless hand, that illusion was long gone.

Time had won.

While our extended relatives came and went, my brother, dad, stepgrandfather, and I could do nothing but listen to the sound of her heart monitor beeping and the voices in our heads. Mine couldn't stop reminding me of this past year. *When was the last time I called her? Did I selfishly abandon her and everyone else I love while my life spun out?*

I pulled up a voicemail I saved of hers and pressed it to my ear. No one showed love like her. It was like love on steroids. "You better call me back. I want to tell you I miss you so much. I'm so proud of you. I hope you're taking good care of yourself and you're taking your meds and eating. Call me. I love you."

Did I call her back? Tell me I called her back. I scrolled through my call logs. I hadn't. How could I have let myself get so lost this past year that I couldn't call back the one person I loved the most and who loved me the most?

Tears continued to stream down my face onto my shirt. My phone lit up with notifications. Earlier that week, the news had circulated that I was getting a divorce. Now, my phone was blowing up with alerts from tabloid outlets claiming that it was because I'm a cheater. This week was panning out to have it all: death, divorce, and daddy issues.

It had been over seventy-two hours since Travis or I had left the vicinity of Nana's apartment. Travis kept trying to nap while sitting upright, refusing to lay down like a normal person, so his head just lolled from side to side like a decapitated doll. My dad was off in the kitchen, making a plate for himself from the excess deli platters that had accumulated. Whereas I chose my preferred form of self-soothing—the doomscroll.

This guy is so mid. Was this a failed PR stunt?

Is Lukas Gage Nicolas Cage's nepo baby?

Why does anyone care about a random whore z-list actor?

Weird nose.

And finally:

Lukas gives me the ick he will do anything for attention. desperate bitcyh

It's very clear by now that I'm an attention whore, but *desperate*?
As a toddler I did set my room on fire—accidentally, I think. As a child, I bit anyone in kindergarten who wouldn't play with me. As a teen, I fought, stole, and lied. Naturally, I became an actor to guarantee that I'd always be seen and valued. And I don't necessarily mind the criticism: Negative attention comes with a high, too. Like a gambler, sometimes it's not just the wins but the losses that you also crave.
While I love attention, I'm also scared shitless. Because attention doesn't absolve you, it magnifies you. And even though I'm not really anybody, I've come to realize the version of yourself in the spotlight isn't some newer, shinier, infallible one. It's the same

old you—with the same old charms and flaws—but now offered up for the world to dissect.

Right there in my grandmother's apartment, all I wanted was to hide. I wanted to just focus on being a good grandson. I wanted that to feel like it was enough.

I put my phone away but could still feel the phantom notifications in my pants pocket—all those people out there, accusing me of being desperate for attention. I hated it, but I craved it. Even now, I don't know why I'm like this.

Unfortunately, the fact that you've read this book now makes you part of the problem, but that's okay. It's not your fault. I did write this book for attention. And if you're this far in, I got yours. Thanks!

TRAVIS AND I decided to step outside for some fresh air. The moment we got off my grandma's elevator and walked out of the building, the call came.

As soon as my brother and I left her side, she'd said goodbye quietly. Peacefully. After a lifetime's worth of dramatic flourishes, she managed to surprise me one last time.

When we came back, I saw my dad's stoicism finally crumble.

And it was then that I truly saw him—human and broken, just like me. After spending so much of my childhood trying to find all the similarities between us, I could finally see my reflection in my dad's.

I understood that no matter how much I hated my dad as a person, I'll always love him as a human being. And that the only path forward was to be everything he hadn't been for me.

I WROTE THIS FOR ATTENTION

The world is not as dangerous as I'd come to believe. There had been so many moments where my impulse had been to hurt others before they could hurt me. To kill anyone who crossed me, even myself. But now I could make the choice to unlearn the parts of my father that I refused to carry on with me.

I fell into Travis's shoulder, cursing myself for spending the past year doing anything I could to avoid myself—following every whim no matter where it took me; distracted by everything and nothing. And in all that running, I'd managed to outrun the people who had always been there for me. My nana, mom, Cory, Sean—the support system I'd taken for granted. They were okay without me, I told myself. What I hadn't realized was how much I needed them.

I suddenly understood that the only attention that matters to me, the only attention that really matters at all, is the attention of the people I love.

THEORETICALLY, THAT'S WHERE this book should have ended. Because if I had really learned my lesson, the important lesson, the one that you should probably take away from the book, then yeah, that would have been a great final sentence. However, life is messy, and God knows I am, too, and I'm trying this whole being really truthful thing here. . . . That lesson also didn't stick. Not then.

After Nana died, I went back to therapy, got on the right meds, and sought out the tools I needed to live with my BPD. It didn't just pack up and leave after one breakthrough moment. I'm not cured. Now it's just my sidekick instead of my archnemesis.

Then a couple of months later, I found myself scrolling aimlessly online once again. I felt guilty for indulging in the attention of strangers, but not enough to stop me from poring through my Twitter timeline. Passing the accusations and the hate that used to hurt (so good), I kept bracing myself for that old, familiar rush. Yet the more I scrolled, the attention . . . even the nice comments from strangers online, all felt duller. It felt like . . . white noise.

Until one comment cut through: *Lucas Gage is a fucking nazi . . . ?*

Wait a second, that's not right. I've been a chaotic exhibitionist. I've been a sharp-tongued cunt. I've even been a divorcée with IBS.

But a Nazi?

I'm half Jewish. I kept scrolling. The tweets kept coming.

Lukas Gage being a white supremacist was not on my 2023 bingo card.

Like to ban Lukas Gage on Twitter.

Lucas Gage is a despicable skinhead?????

Hold on. I have a full head of hair, the kind that can get away with not showering even for long periods of time when I'm depressed. I know thyself. And this guy is *not* me.

After some more frantic rabbit-holing, I discovered a very interesting coincidence. The name Lukas-with-a-*k*, my name, is actually pretty uncommon. According to a quick Google search, Lucas-with-a-*c* is significantly more common in the United States. Lucas-with-a-*c* actually ranks within the top ten boy names, while Lukas-with-a-*k* is much less frequent and not found in the top one hundred names.

My specialness was now 100 percent backed up by data.

I WROTE THIS FOR ATTENTION

So, out there in the world, on Twitter.com, was another Lucas Gage. But this was @lucasgage, with a *c* NOT a *k*, and also happens to be a far-right, anti-Semitic influencer.

Reading through his tweets, I remembered something that Nana used to say to me when I was younger and acting out. She would sit me down, rub my little shoulders, and say: "Lukey, not all attention is good attention." And suddenly, Nana's lesson hit me over the head in a way that I, a child of the internet, could actually understand. It wasn't just about how people might mistake me for someone I'm not, though that was part of it, it was about what I was seeking and, more important, why.

The craving for validation, recognition, or attention has been a constant undercurrent in my life, pulling me into places that often amplified my pain and disconnection instead of easing them. But the Third Reich? Way too far even for me.

I know that I will always be an attention whore. It's inherent and not something I can erase or deny—it's a part of who I am. What I *can* change is how I pursue it and whether I am receiving attention for the right things.

In an age where everyone can get attention for anything, I want the kind that builds, not breaks; that connects, not isolates.

Because while the need may never go away, I can choose how I let it shape me—and how I want to shape the world in return.

I put down my phone.

Acknowledgments

Writing a book is so much harder than I thought. Thank you, guys, for adding color to my life, for giving me your honest thoughts, and for telling me when I was full of shit: Mom, Travis, Cory, Jesse, Sean, Jen, Pam, Steve, Phoebe, Joanna, Charlie, Maude, Joanne, Cole, Marina, Cassidy, Sylvia, Emily, Bri, Katie, Max, Dylan, Casey, Sophie, Jolie, Emily, Larry, Izzy and Soph, Nic, Ana, Sam, James, Alex, Haley, Hana, Molly, Jennifer, Lena, Pierre, Rick, Lucy, Ruth, Avalon, Phoenix, JJ, Billie, Kelly, Matt, Kiernan, Wendy, Brett, Colleen, Madelyn, Sydney, Liz, Mike, Shawn, Gabe, and everyone else who I'm sure I forgot. I'm really out of brain power after writing this.

About the Author

LUKAS GAGE is an actor, writer, producer, author, and provocateur. He is best known for his role in the first season of the Emmy Award–winning HBO limited series *The White Lotus*. Lukas also starred in Netflix's *You*; *Euphoria* on HBO; Daniel Goldhaber's *How to Blow Up a Pipeline*; and *Down Low*, which he cowrote and stars in. Known for his candid honesty and bold creative choices, Lukas continues to share his experiences with the same boldness that has defined his career.